United States
Department of
Agriculture

Forest Service

Pacific Southwest
Research Station

General Technical
Report

PSW-GTR-237

March 2012

Managing Sierra Nevada Forests

Editor

Malcolm North is a research ecologist, Pacific Southwest Research Station, 1731 Research Park Dr., Davis, CA 95618.

Cover photographs: (top) mixed-conifer forest with an active fire regime, by Marc Meyer; (middle, from left) regeneration in a forest gap, by Malcolm North; chipmunk on a log surrounded by shrub cover, by Brian Oakley; waterfall and pool in Sierra Nevada granite, by Malcolm North; (bottom) prescribed fire at Blodgett Experimental Forest, by Kevin Krasnow.

Managing Sierra Nevada Forests

Malcolm North, Editor

U.S. Department of Agriculture, Forest Service

Pacific Southwest Research Station

Albany, California

General Technical Report PSW-GTR-237

March 2012

Abstract

North, Malcolm, ed. 2012. Managing Sierra Nevada forests. Gen. Tech. Rep.
PSW-GTR-237. Albany, CA: U.S. Department of Agriculture, Forest Service,
Pacific Southwest Research Station. 184 p.

There has been widespread interest in applying new forest practices based on
concepts presented in U.S. Forest Service General Technical Report PSW-GTR-220,
"An Ecosystem Management Strategy for Sierran Mixed-Conifer Forests." This
collection of papers (PSW-GTR-237) summarizes the state of the science in
some topics relevant to this forest management approach, presents case studies
of collaborative planning efforts and field implementation of these new practices,
and clarifies some of the concepts presented in GTR 220. It also describes a
method for assessing forest heterogeneity at the stand level using the Forest
Vegetation Simulator and a new geographic information system tool for project-
level planning that classifies a landscape into different topographic categories.
While this collection of papers presents information and applications relevant to
implementation, it does not offer standards and prescriptions. Forest management
should be flexible to adapt to local forest conditions and stakeholder interests.
This report does, however, strive to clarify concepts and present examples that
may improve communication with stakeholders and help build common ground
for collaborative forest management.

Keywords: Ecosystem restoration, forest resilience, heterogeneity,
stakeholder collaboration.

Preface

Public forest-land management policy in the Sierra Nevada has gone through substantial changes over the last 20 to 30 years. Policies have tried to incorporate and adapt to public concerns on such issues as sensitive wildlife, high-severity wildfire, and changing climate conditions. Through the 1990s and first decade of the 21st century, Sierra Nevada forest management focused on either mechanical fuels reduction or minimal entry into and maintenance of California spotted owl (*Strix occidentalis occidentalis*) habitat. Recently, many of the 10 national forests in the Sierra Nevada began using concepts found in U.S. Forest Service General Technical Report PSW-GTR-220, "An Ecosystem Management Strategy for Sierran Mixed-Conifer Forests"[1] (hereafter GTR 220) as a foundation to plan and implement projects. Summarizing recent scientific research, GTR 220 suggested revising management practices to actively integrate the provision of wildlife habitat and ecosystem restoration with fuels reduction. The GTR emphasized increasing forest heterogeneity at fine (within-stand) and large (across-landscapes) scales using topography as a guide for varying treatments. It also emphasized the ecological importance of fire, the need to retain suitable structures for sensitive wildlife, and locations where ecosystem restoration might involve thinning intermediate-sized trees. In the initial GTR, the focus was on developing the concepts of ecosystem management for the Sierra Nevada. A second edition of the GTR published in 2010 added an addendum addressing some of the issues frequently raised by forest managers.

Translating GTR 220's concepts into management practices required innovation in collaboration, planning, and implementation. Over the course of many field visits to projects implementing GTR 220 concepts, it became clear that some information gaps still persist, including science summaries of typically problematic topics most projects need to address, conditions that fostered successful stakeholder collaboration, tools for assessing forest heterogeneity, and project examples of GTR 220 implementation and marking options. This GTR is an effort to respond to those needs.

The first section provides a summary of recent research in areas that managers have requested and addresses a specific suite of topics that affect fuels and forest restoration treatments and wildlife habitat in lower and mid-elevation Sierra Nevada forests. Topics include (1) fire and fuels reduction and whether current fire models

---

[1] North, M.; Stine, P.; O'Hara, K.; Zielinski, W.; Stephens, S. 2009. An ecosystem management strategy for Sierran mixed-conifer forests. 2nd ed. with addendum. Gen. Tech. Rep. PSW-GTR-220. Albany, CA: U.S. Department of Agriculture, Forest Service, Pacific Southwest Research Station. 49 p.

can simulate fire response to the fine-scale heterogeneity suggested by GTR 220; (2) bark beetle dynamics—their potential response to different stand structures and how beetles may respond to increased variability in stem density and species composition; and (3) current and future impacts of climate change on Sierra Nevada forests and how important it is to understand the processes shaping historical forests to better manage ecosystems in an uncertain future.

The second section focuses on aspects of wildlife management affecting Sierra Nevada forests. It includes (4) the latest research about two species of concern in lower and mid-elevation forests—fisher and marten; (5) a summary of California spotted owl research that has accumulated since Verner et al. (1992); and (6) some principles of managing for wildlife communities with variable scales, different preferred habitat conditions, and often-unknown responses to management practices.

The next section examines tools that can aid project implementation such as (7) building collaboration and (8) stakeholder involvement. Also addressed are (9) tools for increasing forest heterogeneity at the stand level with general marking guidelines and using the Forest Vegetation Simulator to assess structural heterogeneity in treated stands; and (10) at the landscape level using a geographic information system (GIS) tool developed to classify project landscapes into different topographic categories, which might merit different forest treatments.

The next section focuses on implementation, presenting case studies of projects that have used GTR 220 concepts. It details how the concepts in GTR 220 were (11) translated into project design and marking in the Dinkey North and South project on the Sierra National Forest; were (12) similar to the variable density thinning study at Stanislaus-Tuolumne Experimental Forest; and (13) used in drier eastern Sierra forests on the Sagehen Experimental Forest to meet fuels reduction, forest restoration, and marten habitat improvement objectives.

The final summary sections clarify some GTR 220 concepts and address topics that appear to currently limit management options. Chapter 14 addresses under what conditions GTR 220 concepts apply; what characteristics identify "defect" trees with wildlife value; how canopy conditions can be more accurately assessed given the current standards and guides emphasis on canopy cover targets; and how heterogeneity may influence forest resilience and how it might be assessed. The final chapter (15) suggests changes that may be needed to insure that progress made with GTR 220 continues. Reflecting on lessons learned from field project visits and from these compiled chapters, this last chapter discusses how silviculture practices can adopt principles of heterogeneity, economic constraints and the scale of treatments, and the scientific merit and collaborative importance of committing to question-driven monitoring.

Forest Service managers in the Sierra Nevada have repeatedly mentioned two concerns with GTR 220. The first is an apprehension that practices suggested in the ecosystem management strategy are too time consuming, expensive to implement, difficult for marking crews to interpret, and involve lengthy and costly forums for public involvement. The examples in these chapters suggest that such hurdles appear larger than they really are. With any new forest management strategy, initial implementation will be slower and more complex than current practices. This approach, however, offers a set of ecological restoration principles that are grounded in the latest research findings. Adoption of these principles may help build the trust and transparency necessary before more streamlined projects are attempted. Future workshops and information exchange could help managers communicate what worked and what did not, and avoid each project having to "reinvent the wheel." I hope that what is presented in these chapters will help shorten the learning curve for all of us.

A second concern is balancing the need to clarify concepts while retaining management flexibility. Although managers have requested more detailed definition of GTR 220's concepts, there is also wariness that this detail will lead to prescriptive guidelines that could constrain management practices. This collection of papers, however, is not a prescriptive guide or a set of standards for ecosystem management. Rather it provides examples and information on lessons learned so far, as well as relevant science summaries. Each manager will need to find their own route to implementation that responds to the forest conditions and public constituencies they have. Best management practices require a flexible response to local conditions and needs. Helping to return that flexibility and "art" back to forestry is the essential hope of this second GTR. For stakeholders to support this flexibility, however, there needs to be a common conceptual foundation for understanding how management decisions will be made and how we subsequently learn from the attempts to implement these new approaches. This collection of papers attempts to clarify that conceptual foundation and provide tools and examples of GTR 220 implementation.

There is an apprehension that practices suggested in the ecosystem management strategy are too time consuming, expensive to implement, difficult for marking crews to interpret, and involve lengthy and costly forums for public involvement. The examples in these chapters suggest that such hurdles appear larger than they really are.

Contents

1   **Chapter 1: Fire and Fuels Reduction**
B.M. Collins and S.L. Stephens

1   Introduction
1   Modeling Considerations
4   Landscape Fuel Treatment Design
7   Mixed Fire Severity Across Landscapes
9   Literature Cited

13   **Chapter 2: Forest Health and Bark Beetles**
C.J. Fettig

13   Introduction
13   Host Tree and Bark Beetle Dynamics
14   Factors Associated With Bark Beetle Infestations
15   Managing Stand Density to Reduce Susceptibility to Bark Beetle Infestations
16   Implications of Climate Change on Bark Beetle Dynamics
18   Forest Heterogeneity and Bark Beetles
19   References

23   **Chapter 3: Climate Change and the Relevance of Historical Forest Conditions**
H.D. Safford, M. North, and M.D. Meyer

23   Introduction
25   Recent Trends in Climate and Climate-Driven Processes in the Sierra Nevada
31   Projected Trends in Climate and Climate-Driven Processes
37   Is History Still Relevant?
39   References

47   **Chapter 4: Fishers and American Martens**
K.L. Purcell, C.M. Thompson, and W.J. Zielinski

47   Introduction
47   Habitat Preferences
50   Forest Condition and Management Effects
51   New Analysis Tools
52   Potential Implications of Climate Change
54   Unknowns
56   References

61   **Chapter 5: California Spotted Owls**
S. Roberts and M. North

61   Introduction
61   Population Trends
62   Barred Owl
62   Climate Change Effects
63   Spotted Owl Nesting and Foraging Habitat Characteristics
64   Spotted Owls and Fire
66   References

73 **Chapter 6: Managing Forests for Wildlife Communities**
M. North and P. Manley

73 Introduction

73 Multispecies Habitat Management

74 Vertebrate Conservation and Fuels Reduction

77 Multiscale Monitoring

78 References

81 **Chapter 7: Developing Collaboration and Cooperation**
G. Bartlett

81 Introduction

81 Dinkey Project History

83 Mediator's Role

84 Five Stages of Collaboration

84 Steps That Facilitated Collaboration for the Dinkey Project

87 Additional Steps for Successful Collaboration and Cooperation

88 References

89 **Chapter 8: Using GTR 220 to Build Stakeholder Collaboration**
C. Thomas

89 Introduction

89 Improved Communication

90 Sustainability

91 Perceived Problems

91 Challenges

91 Future Directions

92 References

95 **Chapter 9: Marking and Assessing Forest Heterogeneity**
M. North and J. Sherlock

95 Introduction

96 General Marking Suggestions

97 Stand Visualization Simulator Examples

101 Using FVS to Assess Heterogeneity

104 References

107 **Chapter 10: Geographic Information System Landscape Analysis Using GTR 220 Concepts**
M. North, R.M. Boynton, P.A. Stine, K.F. Shipley, E.C. Underwood, N.E. Roth, J.H. Viers, and J.F. Quinn

107 Introduction

108 Foundations for the GIS Tool

109 Background and Description of the GIS Tool

114 Chapter Summary

114 Literature Cited

117 **Chapter 11: Dinkey North and South Project**
M. North and R. Rojas

117 Introduction

118   Context

118   Information Used

120   Implementation

121   Lessons Learned

124   References

127   **Chapter 12: The Variable-Density Thinning Study at Stanislaus-Tuolumne Experimental Forest**
E. Knapp, M. North, M. Benech, and B. Estes

127   Introduction

129   Context

129   Information Used

132   Implementation

135   Lessons Learned

138   References

141   **Chapter 13: Applying GTR 220 Concepts on the Sagehen Experimental Forest**
P. Stine and S. Conway

141   Introduction

141   Context

143   Information Used

144   Implementation

144   Lessons Learned

147   References

149   **Chapter 14: Clarifying Concepts**
M. North and P. Stine

149   Introduction

150   Forest Types and Landscapes Where GTR 220 Concepts Apply

151   Defect Trees

152   Canopy Cover and Closure

156   Heterogeneity and Resilience

159   References

165   **Chapter 15: A Desired Future Condition for Sierra Nevada Forests**
M. North

165   Introduction

165   The Limitations of Stand-Level Averages

167   Economics and Treatment Scale

169   Monitoring

172   Chapter Summary

172   References

176   **Metric Equivalents**

176   **Acknowledgments**

177   **Appendix: Examples of Forest Structures That May Provide Wildlife Habitat**
D. Walsh and M. North

Chapter 1: Fire and Fuels Reduction

B.M. Collins[1] and S.L. Stephens[2]

Introduction

Fire will continue to be a major management challenge in mixed-conifer forests in the Sierra Nevada. Fire is a fundamental ecosystem process in these forests that was largely eliminated in the 20th century. Fire reintroduction is a critical goal but is subject to constraints such as smoke production, risk of fire moving outside designated boundaries, the expanding wildland-urban interface, and lack of experience in burning large areas of forest. Recent fire and fuels research relevant to planning and implementing forest/fuels treatments revolve around three main topics: (1) potential limitations in the widely used Fire and Fuels Extension (FFE) module of the Forest Vegetation Simulator (FVS), (2) designing effective fuels treatment placement in landscapes under real world constraints, and (3) the size of high-severity burn patches in a landscape with an active mixed-severity fire regime. Although it currently may be difficult to model fire behavior in forests treated for the fine-scale structural and fuel heterogeneity suggested in U.S. Forest Service General Technical Report PSW-GTR-220, "An Ecosystem Management Strategy of Sierran Mixed-Conifer Forests" (hereafter GTR 220) (North et al. 2009a) collectively, the ideas presented may improve fuel treatment implementation and forecasting of wildfire effects on Sierran forests.

Modeling Considerations

Fire behavior predictions from FFE are critical in the evaluation of forest/fuel treatments (North et al. 2009a). These predictions rely heavily on the characterization of surface fuels. It is difficult, however, to both accurately measure all of the key characteristics affecting surface fuel pools (loads by size class, fuel bed depth, surface area to volume ratios by size class, heat content, etc.) and calibrate these values based on observed fire behavior. Therefore, fuels are often represented by established fuel models (Anderson 1982, Scott and Burgan 2005) that contain the collection of fuel properties needed to run the Rothermel surface fire spread model (Rothermel 1972), the basis for much of the fire behavior modeling done in the United States (Andrews et al. 2003; Finney 1998, 2006). Fuel models are determined internally in FFE based on forest structural characteristics, species composition, and, in some cases, site productivity (Rebain 2009, Reinhardt and Crookston 2003). Recent studies have identified some inadequacies with this internal fuel

---

[1] Postdoctoral research fire ecologist, U.S. Department of Agriculture, Forest Service, Pacific Southwest Research Station, 1731 Research Park Dr., Davis, CA 95618.

[2] Associate professor, Mulford Hall, University of California, Berkeley, CA 94720.

Summary of Findings

1. **Potential limitations in the widely-used Fire and Fuels Extension (FFE) module of the Forest Vegetation Simulator (FVS).** We discuss three limitations: (1) FFE's internal fuel model selection based on forest structure, which can lead to underestimation of fire behavior and crown fire potential; (2) problems with FVS's regeneration module, which produces higher live crown base heights over time that may incorrectly reduce torching potential; and (3) FFE's calculation of single stand-level inputs for fire behavior modeling, which may not capture variable fire effects in forests with fine-scale heterogeneity such as those proposed in GTR 220.

2. **Designing effective fuels treatment placement in landscapes under real world constraints.** Past research has provided a theoretical framework in the design of strategically placed landscape fuel treatments, but such designs are constrained by real landscapes. Two recent Sierran landscape fuel treatment projects were evaluated where treatment arrangement was based more on local knowledge than on intensive modeling. Results indicate that such treatments can be quite effective at reducing potential fire behavior.

3. **The size of high-severity burn patches in a landscape with an active mixed-severity fire regime.** Mixed-conifer fire regimes have commonly been characterized as frequent, low-moderate intensity before the onset of fire exclusion. Recent research has identified patches of high-severity fire as integral components of these regimes, but the vast majority of such patches were small. In upper mixed-conifer forests that have been subjected to over 30 years of burning by lightning fires, the median high-severity patch size was about 5 ac, while large patches, those >150 ac, made up <5 percent of the total patches by frequency. Some wildfires today are creating high-severity patches at much larger scales than are desirable to ecologists, managers, and the public.

model logic, particularly when incorporating the 40 Scott and Burgan (2005) fuel models (Collins et al. 2011a, Seli et al. 2008). Collins et al. (2011a) reported that the inclusion of FFE-selected fuel models when simulating fire across their study landscape resulted in a substantial underrepresentation of crown fire potential when modeling under 95th percentile wind and moisture conditions. This assessment of crown fire potential was based on a comparison between modeled crowning within their study area and observed crowning in two nearby wildfires, both of which occurred under wind and moisture conditions similar to those modeled. In a recent study, Cruz and Alexander (2010) pointed out inherent problems in our current fire modeling approaches, whether using FFE or other models such as NEXUS, that lead to the underprediction of crown fire potential. Regardless, model users should critically evaluate both the FFE-chosen fuel model(s) and the fire behavior output from FFE before finalizing modeling results. In instances where predicted fire behavior is noticeably different from observed fire behavior for similar stands/fuel complexes, overriding the FFE fuel model selection with a user-input fuel model is probably necessary.

Another potential problem with FFE model outputs of future fire behavior can result from limitations in the regeneration module in FVS. The FVS variants other than western Montana, central and northern Idaho, and coastal Alaska do not have the "full" regeneration establishment model (Dixon 2002). Consequently, most FVS variants do not model natural regeneration or ingrowth. In the absence of ingrowth, modeled development of undisturbed stands generally results in larger and taller trees with higher stand-level canopy base height. These conditions are modeled to produce self-pruning of the trees' lower limbs. The net effect of this increase in canopy base height over time is reduced crown fire potential. This may or may not reflect reality. For example, Stephens and Moghaddas (2005) reported that 80 to 100-year-old mixed-conifer stands in the central Sierra Nevada, which regenerated naturally after early railroad logging and were subjected to minimal or no silvicultural treatments throughout their development (except full fire suppression), had high canopy base heights, and as a result, low potential for crown fire. Stands with similar structure and management history, however, may be rare in the Sierra Nevada. Many stands managed with either even- or uneven-age systems have higher potential for torching, mainly driven by lower canopy base heights (Stephens and Moghaddas 2005). The user-defined regeneration option in FVS is one way to manipulate the progression of canopy base height over time. The FVS user may need to experiment with different levels of regeneration in FVS to insure that model results are consistent with observational data from the actual stands that are modeled. A more comprehensive solution would be to collect and summarize long-term forest inventory data to support development of a full regeneration module for the western Sierra variant.

The FFE module may have difficulty predicting fire behavior in forests with fine-scale structure and fuels variability that might be created using GTR 220 concepts. … A relatively new output from FFE called P-Torch may help users capture some variability in predicted fire behavior.

Finally, the FFE module may have difficulty predicting fire behavior in forests with fine-scale structure and fuels variability that might be created using GTR 220 concepts. The FFE stand-level fire behavior predictions are based on a single value for each of the fuel/stand structure inputs: fuel model, canopy cover, canopy top height, canopy base height, and canopy bulk density. There can be substantial heterogeneity within many forest stands, whether driven by variability in underlying edaphic conditions or variability induced by management (Collins et al. 2011b, North et al. 2009a). Consequently, the fire behavior predictions may not completely reflect actual fire potential. For example, a stand composed of relatively dense tree clumps with sparser tree spacing between clumps may be predicted to support an active crown fire, when in an actual wildfire, only individual tree and small group torching may occur because of the canopy separations between the tree clumps. A relatively new output from FFE called P-Torch may help users capture some variability in predicted fire behavior (Rebain 2009, app. A). P-Torch is an index that estimates the probability of finding torching of small areas (33 by 33 ft) within a stand. Because it is a probability, which is based on fire behavior calculated for numerous random subplots as opposed to a threshold windspeed value (e.g., torching index), P-Torch may be better able to represent heterogeneous forest stands.

When more standard fire behavior outputs are required (e.g., flame length, fireline intensity), little can be done to correct for the modeling homogenization within FVS-FFE short of acquiring more detailed fuel/stand structure data and modeling at the substand level. A recent study using a detailed network of sensors found significant differences in microclimate, fuel moisture, and fire danger rating with fine-scale, topographically-induced weather variation (Holden and Jolly 2011). The increased acquisition of light detection and ranging (LiDAR) data may aid in capturing fine-scale variability in stand structure. However, these data are expensive, both for acquisition and for processing, and often cannot produce reliable information on surface fuels. Further, it is unclear how much, if any, improvement there is in fire behavior predictions when using higher spatial resolutions (e.g., 5- or 1-m pixels [3.3- or 16.4-ft]) vegetation/fuel inputs.

Landscape Fuel Treatment Design

The occurrence of increasingly large fires from warming climates and fuel accumulations (Miller et al. 2009, Westerling et al. 2006) warrants large planning scales for fuel and restoration treatment projects. In addition, the effort required for planning and analysis of alternatives tends to force larger project areas. However, infrastructure and funding limitations, combined with land management and operational constraints, limit the extent to which fuel and restoration treatments can be implemented across landscapes (Collins et al. 2010). As such, managers are forced to make choices about how to arrange discrete treatment units to collectively limit the spread of high-intensity wildfire across a landscape. Owing to the complexity of modeling fire and fuels treatments across landscapes (data acquisition, data processing, model execution, etc.), fuel treatment project design is often based on local knowledge of both the project area and past fire patterns.

Two recent studies in the northern Sierra Nevada suggest that such landscape fuel treatment projects (i.e., treatment arrangement was based more on local knowledge than on intensive modeling) can be quite effective at reducing potential fire behavior at the landscape scale (Collins et al. 2011a, Moghaddas et al. 2010). Reductions in potential fire behavior in two U.S. Forest Service projects were largely attributed to treatment unit arrangement relative to the dominant high-wind directions that typically occur throughout the fire season in each project area (fig. 1-1). In the Meadow Valley study area (Moghaddas et al. 2010), treatment units were arranged in a somewhat linear fashion with multiple "layers" across the landscape (fig. 1-1, left panel). These "layers" tended to be orthogonal to the "problem" wind direction in that area, which increases the potential for modeled fires to intersect treated areas. This orientation, combined with the multiple layers of treatments, resulted in reductions in modeled fire spread and intensity for "problem" wind-driven fires, which reduced the probability of high-intensity fire across much of the landscape. Aside from predictable reductions in intensity within treatment units, there were also pronounced effects on the downwind or lee side of treatments (fig. 1-1, left panel).

Treatment units in the Last Chance study area (Collins et al. 2011a) were much more clumped and centered about the long axis of the study area. In addition, the treatments were slightly shifted toward the upwind side of the study area (fig. 1-1, right panel). This treatment arrangement was quite different from that for the Meadow Valley area, but very effective at reducing the probability of high-intensity fire (fig. 1-1). Unlike Meadow Valley, Last Chance had multiple "problem" wind directions. By having relatively large, centralized treatment blocks that were placed more toward the upwind edge, Last Chance treatments may have been a good safeguard against modeled wind-driven fires spreading from multiple directions.

Accelerating the rate and extent of fuels reduction is needed because longer fire seasons and warmer temperatures associated with a changing climate (Westerling et al. 2006) may increase the potential for high-severity fire in Sierra Nevada mixed-conifer forests (Miller et al. 2009). Stand- and landscape-level reductions in hazardous fire occurrence can be achieved while incorporating heterogeneity into stand prescriptions (North et al. 2009a). Recent papers found most fuels

Landscape fuel treatment projects based more on local knowledge than on intensive modeling can be quite effective at reducing potential fire behavior at the landscape scale.

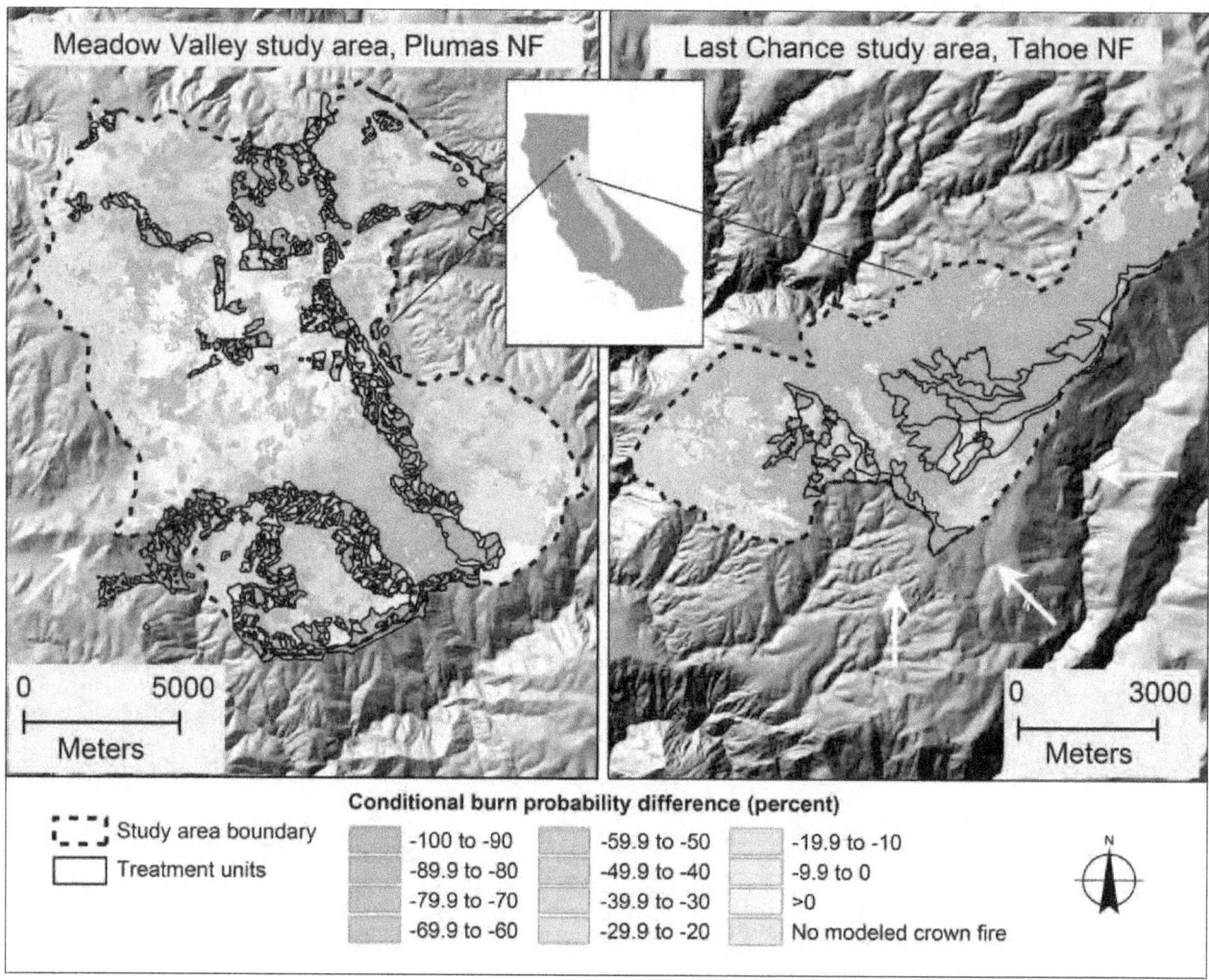

Figure 1-1—Posttreatment minus pretreatment difference in modeled conditional burn probabilities for two landscape fuel treatment projects in the northern Sierra Nevada. Conditional burn probabilities are based on 5,000 randomly placed ignitions simulated using RANDIG. Reported burn probabilities are for flame lengths that are consistent with crown fire initiation (see Collins et al. 2010a for explanation). The arrows represent the modeled "problem" wind direction(s) for each project. Note the different scales for the two projects; the approximate sizes of the study area are Meadow Valley 45,700 ac (18 500 ha); Last Chance 10,600 ac (4300 ha). NF = national forest.

treatments did not adversely affect many ecosystem services (Stephens et al. 2011) and had minimal impact on forest microclimate (Bigelow and North 2011) suggesting treatments may not compound warming trends. Forest resiliency at landscape scales (Collins et al. 2010) needs to be increased before changing fire regimes create conditions that managers and the public find unacceptable. The next one to three decades are a critical period in mixed-conifer forest management and conservation in the Sierra Nevada.

Mixed Fire Severity Across Landscapes

One of the concepts presented in GTR 220 is the ecological importance of fire in Sierran mixed-conifer forest (North et al. 2009a) as it applies to stand-level processes and structures, as well as landscapes. There are numerous studies documenting the historical occurrence of frequent, low-severity fires in mixed-conifer forests throughout the Sierra Nevada (Beaty and Taylor 2008; North et al. 2005, 2009b; Scholl and Taylor 2010; Skinner and Chang 1996; Stephens 2001; Stephens and Collins 2004; Taylor and Beaty 2005). Collectively, these studies suggest that historical forests had a low incidence of high-severity, or stand-replacing fire. However, issues of data availability and data collection associated with these historical reconstructions limit the inferences that can be made regarding more fine-grained stand-replacing fire effects, particularly when attempting to characterize fire over a landscape (Collins and Stephens 2010). These limitations lead to uncertainty in characterizing the "natural" role of stand-replacing fire in Sierra Nevada mixed-conifer forests. This information is important for determining acceptable levels of stand-replacing fire and designing forest/fire management strategies to achieve these levels. Areas that have allowed naturally ignited fires to operate on the landscape for multiple decades, such as the Illilouette Creek basin in Yosemite National Park and Sugarloaf Creek area in Sequoia and Kings Canyon National Parks, are possible points of reference for characterizing more natural forest/fire interactions in the Sierra Nevada. This is not to suggest that these long-term natural fire areas are a proxy for historical forest/fire interactions because despite having multiple decades of natural fire, these areas were affected by fire-exclusion policies for about 90 years prior to initiation of natural fire programs (Collins and Stephens 2007). Although there were noticeable impacts of fire exclusion, these areas represent fire regimes that are largely restored, which has particular relevance to current forest management given differences between historical and current/projected future climates (Collins and Stephens 2010). While both of these long-established natural fire areas are characterized as mixed-conifer forests, they are generally at higher elevations (6,500 to 8,000 ft) than much of the managed mixed-conifer forests throughout the Sierra Nevada. Dominant tree species in these areas are Jeffrey pine (*Pinus jeffreyi* Balf.), white fir (*Abies concolor* (Gord. & Glend.) Lindl. ex Hildebr.), red fir (*A. magnifica* A. Murray), lodgepole pine (*P. contorta murrayana* (Balf.) Engelm.), and to a lesser extent, sugar pine (*P. lambertiana* Douglas).

Collins and Stephens (2010) studied stand-replacing patches within recent fires occurring in the upper elevation, mixed-conifer forests of the Illilouette basin. These fires were predominantly low to moderate severity, with about 15 percent of the fire areas classified as high severity (Collins and Stephens 2010). Patch sizes ranged from 1.3 to 230 ac (0.53 to 93 ha), with small patches (<10 ac)

Median stand-replacing patch size was 5.4 ac … the largest stand-replacing patches in the Illilouette basin (200 to 220 ac) were an order of magnitude or more below those that occurred in recent northern Sierra Nevada wildfires.

(4 ha) accounting for more than 60 percent of the total number of patches (fig. 1-2). Large patches (>150 ac) (60 ha) made up about 5 percent of the total number of patches, but accounted for nearly half the total stand-replacing patch area. Median stand-replacing patch size was 5.4 ac (2.2 ha). Perhaps most importantly, Collins and Stephens (2010) found that the largest stand-replacing patches in the Illilouette basin (200 to 220 ac) (81 to 89 ha) were an order of magnitude or more below those that occurred in recent northern Sierra Nevada wildfires (Antelope Complex and Moonlight Fire; 2,500 to 6,200 ac [1011 to 2509 ha]). The authors suggested three main implications from their study: (1) stand-replacing fire is a component of Sierra Nevada mixed-conifer forests (at least in upper elevation mixed conifer similar to the Illilouette area), but at relatively low proportions across the landscape (15 percent or less); (2) the distribution of stand-replacing patches consists of many small patches and few large patches; and (3) the stand-replacing patch sizes observed in recent Sierra Nevada fires (outside of natural fire areas) often greatly exceed the range of patch sizes reported for the Illilouette basin (Miller et al. 2009).

Figure 1-2—Four-acre high-severity burn patch in the Illilouette basin that provides a high light environment for *Ceanothus* shrubs and pine regeneration.

Literature Cited

Anderson, H.E. 1982. Aids to determining fuel models for estimating fire behavior. Gen. Tech. Rep. INT-122. Ogden, UT: U.S. Department of Agriculture, Forest Service, Intermountain Forest and Range Experiment Station. 22 p.

Andrews, P.L.; Bevins, C.D.; Seli, R.C. 2003. BehavePlus fire modeling system, version 2.0. Gen. Tech. Rep. RMRS-GTR-106WWW. Ogden, UT: U.S. Department of Agriculture, Forest Service, Rocky Mountain Research Station. 132 p.

Beaty, R.M.; Taylor, A.H. 2008. Fire history and the structure and dynamics of a mixed conifer forest landscape in the northern Sierra Nevada, Lake Tahoe Basin, California, USA. Forest Ecology and Management. 255(3–4): 707–719.

Bigelow, S.W.; North, M.P. 2011. Effects of fuels-reduction and group-selection silviculture on understory microclimate in Sierran mixed-conifer forest. Forest Ecology and Management. 264: 51–59.

Collins, B.M.; Everett, R.G.; Stephens, S.L. 2011b. Impacts of fire exclusion and managed fire on forest structure in an old growth Sierra Nevada mixed-conifer forest. Ecosphere. 2(4): art 51.

Collins, B.M.; Stephens, S.L. 2007. Managing natural wildfires in Sierra Nevada wilderness areas. Frontiers in Ecology and the Environment. 5(10): 523–527.

Collins, B.M.; Stephens, S.L. 2010. Stand-replacing patches within a mixed severity fire regime: quantitative characterization using recent fires in a long-established natural fire area. Landscape Ecology. 25(6): 927–939.

Collins, B.M.; Stephens, S.L.; Moghaddas, J.J.; Battles, J. 2010. Challenges and approaches in planning fuel treatments across fire-excluded forested landscapes. Journal of Forestry. 108(1): 24–31.

Collins, B.M.; Stephens, S.L.; Roller, G.B.; Battles, J.J. 2011a. Simulating fire and forest dynamics for a landscape fuel treatment project in the Sierra Nevada. Forest Science. 57(2): 77–88.

Cruz, M.G.; Alexander, M.E. 2010. Assessing crown fire potential in coniferous forests of western North America: a critique of current approaches and recent simulation studies. International Journal of Wildland Fire. 19(4): 377–398.

Dixon, G.E. 2002. Essential FVS: a user's guide to the Forest Vegetation Simulator. Internal Rep. Fort Collins, CO: U.S. Department of Agriculture, Forest Service, Rocky Mountain Research Station. 209 p.

Finney, M.A. 1998. FARSITE: fire area simulator—model development and evaluation. Revised. Res. Pap. RMRS-RP-4. Missoula, MT: U.S. Department of Agriculture, Forest Service, Rocky Mountain Research Station. 47 p.

Finney, M.A. 2006. An overview of FlamMap modeling capabilities. In: Andrews, P.L.; Butler, B.W., eds. Fuels management—how to measure success. Gen. Tech. Rep. RMRS-P-41. Portland, OR: U.S. Department of Agriculture, Forest Service, Rocky Mountain Research Station: 213–220.

Holden, Z.A.; Jolly, W.M. 2011. Modeling topographic influences on fuel moisture and fire danger in complex terrain to improve wildland fire management decision support. Forest Ecology and Management. 262: 2133–2141.

Miller, J.D.; Safford, H.D.; Crimmins, M.; Thode, A.E. 2009. Quantitative evidence for increasing forest fire severity in the Sierra Nevada and southern Cascade Mountains, California and Nevada, USA. Ecosystems. 12: 16–32.

Moghaddas, J.J.; Collins, B.M.; Menning, K.; Moghaddas, E.E.Y.; Stephens, S.L. 2010. Fuel treatment effects on modeled landscape level fire behavior in the northern Sierra Nevada. Canadian Journal of Forest Research. 40(9): 1751–1765.

North, M.; Hurteau, M.; Fiegener, R.; Barbour, M. 2005. Influence of fire and El Niño on tree recruitment varies by species in Sierran mixed conifer forest. Forest Science. 51(3): 187–197.

North, M.; Stine, P.; O'Hara, K.; Zielinski, W.; Stephens, S. 2009a. An ecosystem management strategy for Sierran mixed-conifer forests. 2nd printing, with addendum. Gen. Tech. Rep. PSW-GTR-220. Albany, CA: U.S. Department of Agriculture, Forest Service, Pacific Southwest Research Station. 49 p.

North, M.P.; Van de Water, K.M.; Stephens, S.L.; Collins, B.M. 2009b. Climate, rain shadow, and human-use influences on fire regimes in the eastern Sierra Nevada, California, USA. Fire Ecology. 5(3): 20–34.

Rebain, S.A. 2009. The Fire and Fuels Extension to the Forest Vegetation Simulator. Gen. Tech. Rep. RMRS-GTR-116: Addendum. Ogden, UT: U.S. Department of Agriculture, Forest Service, Rocky Mountain Research Station. 262 p.

Reinhardt, E.; Crookston, N.L. 2003. The Fire and Fuels Extension to the Forest Vegetation Simulator. Gen. Tech. Rep. RMRS-GTR-116. Ogden, UT: U.S. Department of Agriculture, Forest Service, Rocky Mountain Research Station. 209 p.

Rothermel, R.C. 1972. A mathematical model for predicting fire spread in wildland fuels. Res. pap. INT-115. Ogden, UT: U.S. Department of Agriculture, Forest Service, Intermountain Forest and Range Experiment Station. 40 p.

Scholl, A.E.; Taylor, A.H. 2010. Fire regimes, forest change, and self-organization in an old-growth mixed-conifer forest, Yosemite National Park, USA. Ecological Applications. 20(2): 362–380.

Scott, J.H.; Burgan, R.E. 2005. Standard fire behavior models: a comprehensive set for use with Rothermel's surface fire spread model. Gen. Tech. Rep. RMRS-GTR-153. Fort Collins, CO: U.S. Department of Agriculture, Forest Service, Rocky Mountain Research Station. 72 p.

Seli, R.C.; Ager, A.A.; Crookston, N.L.; Finney, M.A.; Bahro, B.; Agee, J.K.; McHugh, C.W. 2008. Incorporating landscape fuel treatment modeling into the Forest Vegetation Simulator. In: Havis, R.N.; Crookston, N.L., eds. Third Forest Vegetation Simulator conference. RMRS-P-54. Fort Collins, CO: U.S. Department of Agriculture, Forest Service, Rocky Mountain Research Station: 27–39.

Skinner, C.N.; Chang, C. 1996. Fire regimes, past and present. In: Sierra Nevada Ecosystem Project: final report to Congress. Vol. II: Assessments and scientific basis for management options. Wildland Resources Center Report No. 37. Davis, CA: University of California, Centers for Water and Wildlands Resources: 1041–1069.

Stephens, S.L. 2001. Fire history differences in adjacent Jeffrey pine and upper montane forests in the eastern Sierra Nevada. International Journal of Wildland Fire. 10(2): 161–167.

Stephens, S.L.; Collins, B.M. 2004. Fire regimes of mixed conifer forests in the north-central Sierra Nevada at multiple spatial scales. Northwest Science. 78(1): 12–23.

Stephens, S.L.; McIver J.D.; Boerner, R.E.J.; Fettig, C.J.; Fontaine, J.B.; Hartsough, B.R.; Kennedy, P.; and Schwilk, D.W. [In press]. Effects of forest fuel reduction treatments in the United States. BioScience.

Stephens, S.L.; Moghaddas, J.J. 2005. Silvicultural and reserve impacts on potential fire behavior and forest conservation: twenty-five years of experience from Sierra Nevada mixed conifer forests. Biological Conservation. 125(3): 369–379.

Taylor, A.H.; Beaty, R.M. 2005. Climatic influences on fire regimes in the northern Sierra Nevada Mountains, Lake Tahoe Basin, Nevada, USA. Journal of Biogeography. 32(3): 425–438.

Westerling, A.L.; Hidalgo, H.; Cayan, D.R.; Swetnam, T. 2006. Warming and earlier spring increases western U.S. forest wildfire activity. Science. 313: 940–943.

Chapter 2: Forest Health and Bark Beetles

C.J. Fettig[1]

Introduction

In recent years, bark beetles have caused significant tree mortality in the Sierra Nevada (http://www.fs.fed.us/r5/spf/publications/pestconditions/index.shtml), rivaling mortality caused by wildfire in some locations. This chapter addresses two important questions: How can managers prepare for and influence levels of bark beetle-caused tree mortality given current forest conditions and future climate uncertainties? and How would the variable forest conditions suggested by U.S. Forest Service General Technical Report PSW-GTR-220, "An Ecosystem Management Strategy for Sierran Mixed-Conifer Forests" (hereafter GTR 220) (North et al. 2009), influence these dynamics?

Host Tree and Bark Beetle Dynamics

Colonization of living hosts by bark beetles requires recruitment of a critical minimum number of beetles to initiate mass attack and overcome host tree defenses (Franceschi et al. 2005). This threshold differs with host tree vigor (i.e., the more "healthy" the tree, the more beetles required to overcome tree defenses) as beetles that initiate host selection are often killed by drowning or immobilization in resin, especially when adequate flow and oleoresin exudation pressure exist (Raffa and Berryman 1983, Vité and Wood 1961). Depending on the bark beetle species and numerous other factors (Fettig et al. 2007), levels of tree mortality attributed to bark beetle attack may be limited to small spatial scales (e.g., single

[1] Research entomologist, U.S. Department of Agriculture, Forest Service, Pacific Southwest Research Station, 1731 Research Park Dr., Davis, CA 95618.

Summary of Findings

1. **Bark beetles are an essential component of forest ecosystems and an important influence on stand dynamics.** Sierra Nevada forests are well recognized for the diversity of tree-killing bark beetle species inhabiting them (table 2-1).

2. **In the absence of frequent understory fire, increases in stand density and tree competition have made many forests more susceptible to bark beetle attack.** Microclimatic influences associated with dense stand conditions may increase beetle success in finding host trees and beetle fecundity and fitness. In addition, drought is one of the more important abiotic factors influencing tree susceptibility in the Sierra Nevada, suggesting changing climatic conditions could significantly alter the amount and distribution of bark beetle-caused tree mortality, particularly in dense stands.

3. **Reductions in stand density are the most effective treatment for reducing bark beetle-caused tree mortality.** Reducing competition improves tree growth and defensive mechanisms while often disrupting pheromone plumes, thus negatively affecting the beetle's ability to locate and successfully mass attack host trees.

4. **Increases in stand- and landscape-level heterogeneity may reduce the occurrence of high levels of bark beetle-caused tree mortality while maintaining endemic (low) levels.** In contrast, forested landscapes that contain little heterogeneity promote the creation of large contiguous areas susceptible to bark beetle outbreaks.

Table 2-1—Bark beetle species that cause significant amounts of tree mortality in the Sierra Nevada

Common name	Scientific name	Primary hosts in the Sierra
California fivespined ips	*Ips paraconfusus*	Ponderosa pine (*Pinus ponderosa* Laws.), lodgepole pine (*Pinus contorta* Loud.), sugar pine (*Pinus lambertiana* Douglas), Jeffrey pine (*Pinus jeffreyi* Grev. & Balf.), and others
Fir engraver	*Scolytus ventralis*	White fir (*Abies concolor* (Gordon & Glend.) Lindl. ex Hildebr.), California red fir (*Abies magnifica* A. Murray bis)
Jeffrey pine beetle	*Dendroctonus jeffreyi*	Jeffrey pine
Mountain pine beetle	*Dendroctonus ponderosae*	Ponderosa pine, lodgepole pine, sugar pine, white bark pine (*Pinus albicaulis* Engelm.), limber pine (*Pinus flexilis* James), western white pine (*Pinus monticola* Douglas ex D. Don), and others
Pine engraver	*Ips pini*	Ponderosa pine, lodgepole pine, sugar pine, Jeffrey pine, and others
Piñon ips	*Ips confusus*	Singleleaf piñon (*Pinus monophylla* Torr. & Frem.) and others
Western pine beetle	*Dendroctonus brevicomis*	Ponderosa pine

trees or small groups of trees) or may affect large areas. When favorable stand and climatic conditions coincide, significant tree mortality may occur. While bark beetle infestations may affect timber and fiber production, water quality and quantity, fuel loadings, fish and wildlife habitat and populations, recreation, grazing capacity, real estate values, biodiversity, carbon storage, endangered species, cultural resources, and other resources (Coulson and Stephen 2006), bark beetles also play a critical role in the functioning of forests.

Factors Associated With Bark Beetle Infestations

After an indepth review of tree and stand factors associated with bark beetle infestations, Fettig et al. (2007) discussed the effectiveness of reducing stand density for preventing bark beetle infestations. Most work has concentrated on forests dominated by ponderosa pine (*Pinus ponderosa* Lawson & C. Lawson) or lodgepole pine (*Pinus contorta* Douglas ex Loud var.). Starting with the earliest research studies, factors such as stand density, tree diameter, and host density have been identified as primary attributes associated with bark beetle infestations. For example, Craighead (1925) and Miller (1926) were among the first to demonstrate that slower growing ponderosa pines were more susceptible to bark beetle attack, specifically by the western pine beetle, a species of primary importance in the Sierra Nevada. Working in the Pacific Northwest, Sartwell (1971) examined the relationship between radial growth and mountain pine beetle attack, another species of concern in the Sierra Nevada. He reported that nearly all trees killed by mountain pine beetle had crown ratios (the ratio of crown length to total tree height) of ≤ 30 percent, suggesting that greater tree competition and slow growth rates increase the likelihood of mountain pine beetle attack. In general, less productive sites experienced higher levels of mountain pine beetle-caused tree mortality than did high-quality sites of similar stocking, a relationship that seems to hold for many bark beetle species.

Hayes et al. (2009) reported that stand density, measured as basal area or stand density index (SDI) (based on the number of trees per unit area and quadratic mean diameter [diameter at breast height of the tree of average basal area]), is the most important predictor of western pine beetle-caused tree mortality at large spatial scales in California. Areas with the highest stand densities experienced the highest levels of tree mortality on both an absolute (trees/ha) and proportion (percentage of mortality) basis. Surprisingly, host density had less predictive power than other measures of stand density, suggesting that tree competition is more important than host tree availability. Because SDI is an indicator of the amount of growing space available (Reineke 1933), and thus well correlated with tree growth, it is not surprising that SDI would be useful in predicting levels of bark beetle-caused tree mortality. Oliver (1995) reported that maximum SDI for even-aged ponderosa pine stands in northern California was regulated by mountain pine beetle and western pine beetle infestations. An SDI value of 230 defined a threshold for a zone of imminent bark beetle-caused tree mortality within which endemic populations kill a few trees but net growth is positive. Maximum (limiting) SDI was defined at 365. Modeling by Hayes et al. (2009) supports these observations and suggests that it might be appropriate to consider lower SDI thresholds under some conditions (e.g., during elevated bark beetle populations as associated with extended drought).

[Tree] host density had less predictive power than other measures of stand density, suggesting that tree competition is more important than host tree availability.

Managing Stand Density to Reduce Susceptibility to Bark Beetle Infestations

Thinning has long been advocated as a preventive measure to alleviate or reduce the amount of bark beetle-caused tree mortality (Fettig et al. 2007). However, thinning prescriptions differ widely, and much of the research concerning the effects of thinning on stand susceptibility to bark beetles has been conducted in stands thinned to achieve other specific objectives (e.g., to reduce wildfire severity). Thinning may have functionally different responses on the abundance and distribution of preferred hosts in the residual stand. Furthermore, thinnings conducted in a careless manner may also result in physical damage to residual trees. Although thinning may reduce stand susceptibility to bark beetle attack, there may be greater potential for increases in subcortical insects and root pathogens (Witcosky et al. 1986). In some cases, root diseases have been shown to increase the susceptibility of trees to bark

Posttreatment tree density may be the best predictor of subsequent levels of bark beetle-caused tree mortality.

beetle attack in the Sierra Nevada (Goheen and Cobb 1980). Furthermore, several bark beetle species (e.g., engraver beetles) are attracted to slash created during thinning operations. Effective guidelines, however, are available to reduce associated risks through proper slash management (DeGomez et al. 2008).

Research suggests that posttreatment tree density may be the best predictor of subsequent levels of bark beetle-caused tree mortality. For example, Fettig et al. (2010) reported significant positive correlations between the percentage of pines killed by bark beetles (several species) and trees/ha, basal area (ft^2/ac), and SDI in the southern Cascades, California. Of these three metrics, trees/ha was the best predictor of levels of tree mortality following fuel reduction and forest restoration treatments (fig. 2-1). Thinning not only affects the vigor of residual trees influencing resin chemistry, flow, and oleoresin exudation pressure, but also the physical environment within treated stands. Increased windspeeds (Bigelow and North 2011) and temperatures are common within thinned stands, and these factors influence bark beetle fecundity, fitness, and survivorship in a variety of ways (Fettig et al. 2007). Thinning also increases wind turbulences that disrupt pheromone plumes used for recruiting conspecifics during initial phases of host tree colonization (Thistle et al. 2004). Low-density stands result in unstable layers and multidirectional traces that dilute pheromone concentrations and could result in reductions in beetle aggregation on individual trees.

Recent work conducted on the Tahoe National Forest, California to determine the impact of thinning on bark beetle infestations in Jeffrey pine (*Pinus jeffreyi* Balf.) forests provides further support for managing stand density to reduce stand susceptibility (Fettig et al. 2012). Treatments included thinning from below (i.e., initiating in the smallest diameter classes) to different residual target basal areas (80.1, 120.2, and 179.9 ft^2/ac [18.4, 27.6, and 41.3 m^2/ha], and an untreated control). Throughout the study, bark beetles killed no pines during the 10-year period in the lowest density treatment. Significantly fewer trees (ac/yr) were killed in the low-density thin than in the high-density thin or untreated control.

Implications of Climate Change on Bark Beetle Dynamics

Bark beetle species indigenous to the Southwestern United States and Mexico have the potential to move northward with climate change.

Climatic changes will significantly affect forest productivity and distribution. For example, Rehfeldt et al. (2006) estimated that by the end of this century, 48 percent of the Western U.S. landscape will have climate profiles incompatible with their current coniferous vegetation. These changes will likely have significant impacts on the frequency and severity of disturbances, such as bark beetle outbreaks, that shape these ecosystems. Bark beetle population success is influenced directly by

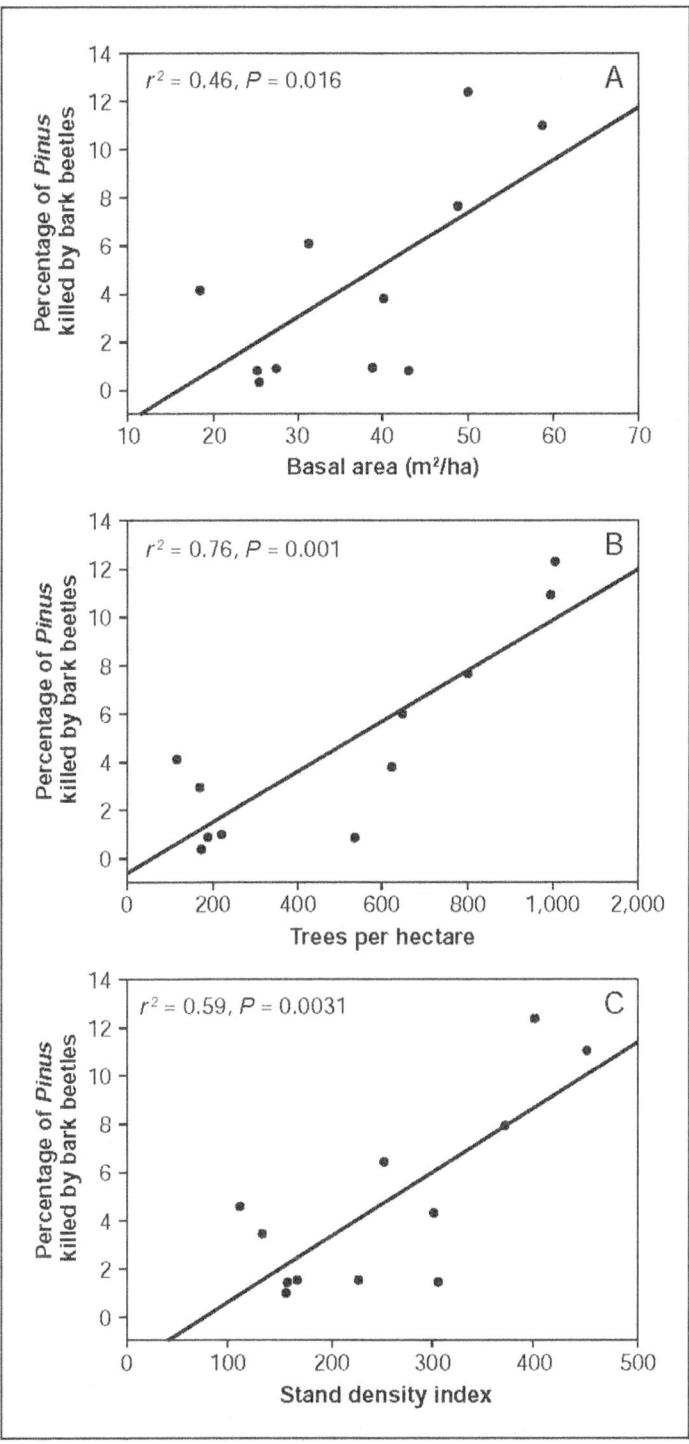

Figure 2-1—Relationship between (A) basal area (m²/ha) (multiply by 4.36 to get ft²/ac), (B) numbers of trees per hectare (trees/ha) (divide by 2.47 to get trees/ac), (C) stand density index and percentage of pines killed by bark beetles pooled across treatments on the Klamath National Forest, California. (Adapted from Fettig et al. 2010.)

temperature effects on developmental timing (Powell and Logan 2005) and mortality (Régnière and Bentz 2007). Warming may allow some species to complete extra generations per year, and adult emergence and flight activity could occur earlier and last longer. Cold-induced mortality during winter may also decrease. Effects of climate change on community associates and host tree vigor will also influence population success indirectly, although little information is available to quantify these relationships. Furthermore, climate-induced changes in carbon assimilation can alter the within-plant allocation of carbohydrates (Grulke et al. 2001) affecting the production of chemical defenses (Herms and Mattson 1992) and a tree's ability to prevent bark beetle colonization.

Based on projected changes in climate, Bentz et al. (2010) suggested that future thermal regimes may be particularly favorable for mountain pine beetle populations, although considerable spatial and temporal variability was modeled. These predictions suggested a movement of temperature suitability to higher latitudes and elevations (e.g., as currently witnessed in whitebark pine (*Pinus albicaulis* Engelm.) in the Sierra Nevada) and identified regions with a high potential for bark beetle outbreaks and associated tree mortality in the coming century. Furthermore, Bentz et al. (2010) expressed a concern that bark beetle species indigenous to the Southwestern United States (e.g., Arizona) and Mexico have the potential to move northward with climate change following range expansions of their current hosts or adaptation to novel hosts.

Forest Heterogeneity and Bark Beetles

In the absence of frequent understory fire, bark beetles have become one of the principle agents of tree mortality in the Sierra Nevada and a strong influence on ecosystem processes. Although bark beetle infestations affect timber and fiber production, and indirectly a range of ecosystem services (Coulson and Stephen 2006), in the past, mortality of individual or small groups of overstory trees may have been a significant influence on the fine-scale spatial heterogeneity characteristic of mixed-conifer forests in California (Savage 1994). Beetles often inflict density-dependent mortality (Smith et al. 2005), and consequently maintain a mix of tree species, ages, sizes, and spatial heterogeneity in these forests. This is accomplished through the opening of canopy gaps that allow for differential reproduction of overstory species.

Tree mortality is often highly episodic (Franklin et al. 1987) making it difficult to determine when rates of beetle-induced tree mortality are uncharacteristically "high." At the Teakettle Experimental Forest, California, cumulative levels of tree mortality (i.e., from all causes, not just bark beetles), as measured by standing dead trees ≥ 2 in (5 cm) d.b.h., was 8.7 percent, (range 5.3 to 13.1 percent) (Smith et al. 2005) compared to 14.0 percent (range 3 to 33 percent) in mixed-conifer, old-growth forests of the Lake Tahoe Basin (Barbour et al. 2002). In the Sierra San Pedro del Martir National Park of Baja, Mexico, where little fire suppression has occurred, cumulative tree mortality in mixed-conifer, old-growth forests was found to be 12.7 percent (range 4 to 15 percent) (Maloney and Rizzo 2002). Ansley and Battles (1998) reported an annual mortality rate of 0.6 percent per year in a Sierran old-growth, fire-suppressed forest, compared to only 0.162 percent per year in an active-fire, old-growth forest in the Sierra San Pedro del Martir (Maloney and Rizzo 2002). Rates in excess of the upper end of these ranges might be considered indicative of "high" levels of tree mortality in mixed-conifer forests.

The forest heterogeneity suggested in GTR 220 is likely to reduce beetle-caused tree mortality below current levels in most fire-suppressed forests. If treatments differ with topography, higher stem densities will be left in the most mesic (and presumably productive) sites that can support these conditions without incurring high levels of tree mortality. Heavier thinning on more xeric sites may be appropriate to reduce competition in areas most prone to drought stress and associated bark beetle attacks. Although measures of density and SDI are usually stand-level means, SDI and potential competitive stress should be assessed at a fine scale (see chapter 9) in areas where microtopography may create localized differences in productivity.

At the landscape scale, the maintenance of a mosaic of different stand structures, densities, and compositions, as suggested in GTR 220, may reduce the frequency and extent of bark beetle outbreaks. Larger scale beetle outbreaks are often associated with more homogeneous forest conditions (i.e., less species diversity and more uniform stem densities). Management that increases spatial diversity of forest conditions with variable tree density, species diversity and growth rates may retain the ecological benefits of chronic bark beetle impacts without facilitating episodic, large-scale tree mortality that historically may have been rare in much of the Sierra Nevada.

In general, bark beetle abundance is a good indicator of tree stress. As climate conditions change and high stem densities increase with fire suppression, beetle mortality can provide some measure of ecosystem response. If patterns change from low-level chronic mortality of scattered individual trees to persistently higher rates, particularly of large clusters, ecosystem resistance and resilience may be compromised.

As climate conditions change and high stem densities increase with fire suppression, beetle mortality can provide some measure of ecosystem response.

References

Ansley, J.S.; Battles, J.J. 1998. Forest composition, structure, and change in an old-growth mixed conifer forest in the northern Sierra Nevada. Journal of the Torrey Botanical Society. 125: 297–308.

Barbour, M.; Kelley, E.; Maloney, P.; Rizzo, D.; Royce, E.; Fites-Kaufmann, J. 2002. Present and past old-growth forests of the Lake Tahoe Basin, Sierra Nevada, US. Journal of Vegetation Science. 13: 461–472.

Bentz, B.J.; Régnière, J.; Fettig, C.J.; Hansen, E.M.; Hayes, J.L.; Hicke, J.A.; Kelsey, R.G.; Negrón, J.F.; Seybold, S.J. 2010. Climate change and bark beetles of the western U.S. and Canada: direct and indirect effects. Bioscience. 60: 602–613.

Bigelow, S.W.; North, M.P. 2011. Effects of fuels-reduction and group-selection silviculture on understory microclimate in Sierran mixed-conifer forest. Forest Ecology and Management. 264: 51–59.

Coulson, R.N.; Stephen, F.M. 2006. Impacts of insects in forest landscapes: implications for forest health management. In: Payne, T.D., ed. Invasive forest insects, introduced forest trees, and altered ecosystems: ecological pest management in global forests of a changing world. New York: Springer-Verlag: 101–126.

Craighead, F.C. 1925. The *Dendroctonus* problems. Journal of Forestry. 23: 340–354.

DeGomez, T.; Fettig, C.J.; McMillin, J.D.; Anhold, J.A.; Hayes, C.J. 2008. Managing slash to minimize colonization of residual leave trees by *Ips* and other bark beetle species following thinning in southwestern ponderosa pine. AZ1448. Tucson, AZ: University of Arizona, College of Agriculture and Life Sciences Bulletin. 21 p.

Fettig, C.J.; Borys, R.R.; Dabney, C.P. 2010. Effects of fire and fire surrogate treatments on bark beetle-caused tree mortality in the Southern Cascades, California. Forest Science. 56: 60–73.

Fettig, C.J.; Hayes, C.J.; Jones, K.J.; McKelvey, S.R.; Mori, S.L.; Smith, S.L. 2012. Thinning Jeffrey pine stands to reduce susceptibility to bark beetle infestations in California, U.S.A. Agricultural and Forest Entomology. 14(1): 111–117.

Fettig, C.J.; Klepzig, K.D.; Billings, R.F.; Munson, A.S.; Nebeker, T.E.; Negrón, J.F.; Nowak, J.T. 2007. The effectiveness of vegetation management practices for prevention and control of bark beetle outbreaks in coniferous forests of the western and southern United States. Forest Ecology and Management. 238: 24–53.

Franceschi, V.R.; Krokene, P.; Christiansen, E.; Krekling, T. 2005. Anatomical and chemical defenses of conifer bark against bark beetles and other pests. New Phytologist. 167: 353–376.

Franklin, J.F.; Shugart, H.H.; Harmon, M.E. 1987. Tree death as an ecological process. Bioscience. 37: 550–556.

Goheen, D.J.; Cobb, F.W., Jr. 1980. Infestation of *Ceratocystis wageneri*-infected ponderosa pine by bark beetles (Coleoptera: Scolytidae) in the central Sierra Nevada. The Canadian Entomologist. 112: 725–730.

Grulke, N.E.; Andersen, C.P.; Hogsett, W.E. 2001. Seasonal changes in carbohydrate pools of ponderosa pine in stands under differing environmental stress. Tree Physiology. 21: 173–184.

Hayes, C.J.; Fettig, C.J.; Merrill, L.D. 2009. Evaluation of multiple funnel traps and stand characteristics for estimating western pine beetle-caused tree mortality. Journal of Economic Entomology. 102: 2170–2182.

Herms, D.A.; Mattson, W.J. 1992. The dilemma of plants: to grow or defend. The Quarterly Review of Biology. 67: 283–335.

Maloney, P.E.; Rizzo, D.M. 2002. Pathogens and insects in a pristine forest ecosystem: the Sierra San Pedro Martir, Baja, Mexico. Canadian Journal of Forest Research. 32: 488–457.

Miller, J.M. 1926. The western pine beetle control problem. Journal of Forestry. 24: 897–910.

North, M.; Stine, P.; O'Hara, K.; Zielinski, W.; Stephens, S. 2009. An ecosystem management strategy for Sierran mixed-conifer forests. 2nd printing, with addendum. Gen. Tech. Rep. PSW-GTR-220. Albany, CA: U.S. Department of Agriculture, Forest Service, Pacific Southwest Research Station. 49 p.

Oliver, W.W. 1995. Is self-thinning in ponderosa pine ruled by *Dendroctonus* bark beetles? In: Proceedings of the 1995 national silviculture workshop. Gen. Tech. Rep. GTR-RM-267. Fort Collins, CO: U.S. Department of Agriculture, Forest Service, Rocky Mountain Research Station: 213–218.

Powell, J.A.; Logan, J.A. 2005. Insect seasonality: circle map analysis of temperature-driven life cycles. Theoretical Population Biology. 67: 161–179.

Raffa, K.F.; Berryman, A.A. 1983. The role of host plant resistance in the colonization behavior and ecology of bark beetles (Coleoptera: Scolytidae). Ecological Monographs. 53: 27–49.

Régnière, J.; Bentz, B. 2007. Modeling cold tolerance in the mountain pine beetle, *Dendroctonus ponderosae*. Journal of Insect Physiology. 53: 559–572.

Rehfeldt, G.E.; Crookston, N.L.; Warwell, M.V.; Evans, J.S. 2006. Empirical analyses of plant climate relationships for the western United States. International Journal of Plant Science. 167: 1123–1150.

Reineke, L.H. 1933. Perfecting a stand-density index for even-aged forests. Journal of Agricultural Research. 46: 627–638.

Sartwell, C. 1971. Thinning ponderosa pine to prevent outbreaks of mountain pine beetle. In: Baumgartner, D.M., ed. Precommercial thinning of coastal and intermountain forests in the Pacific Northwest. Pullman, OR: Washington State University: 41–52.

Savage, M. 1994. Anthropogenic and natural disturbance and patterns of mortality in a mixed-conifer forest in California. Canadian Journal of Forest Research. 24: 1149–1159.

Smith, T.; Rizzo, D.; North, M. 2005. Patterns of mortality in an old-growth mixed-conifer forest of the southern Sierra Nevada, California. Forest Science. 51: 266–275.

Thistle, H.W.; Peterson, H.; Allwine, G.; Lamb, B.K.; Strand, T.; Holsten, E.H.; Shea, P.J. 2004. Surrogate pheromone plumes in three forest trunk spaces: composite statistics and case studies. Forest Science. 50: 610–625.

Vité, J.P.; Wood, D.L. 1961. A study on the applicability of the measurement of oleoresin exudation pressure in determining susceptibility of second growth ponderosa pine to bark beetle infestations. Contributions of Boyce Thompson Institute. 21: 67–78.

Witcosky, J.J.; Schowalter, T.D.; Hansen, E.M. 1986. *Hylastes nigrinus* (Coleoptera: Scolytidae), *Pissodes fasciatus*, and *Steremnius carinatus* (Coleoptera: Curculionidae) as vectors of black-stain root disease of Douglas-fir. Environmental Entomology. 15: 1090–1095.

Chapter 3: Climate Change and the Relevance of Historical Forest Conditions

H.D. Safford,[1] M. North,[2] and M.D. Meyer[3]

Introduction

Increasing human emissions of greenhouse gases are modifying the Earth's climate. According to the Intergovernmental Panel on Climate Change (IPCC), "Warming of the climate system is unequivocal, as is now evident from observation of increases in average air and ocean temperatures, widespread melting of snow and ice, and rising global average sea level" (IPCC 2007). The atmospheric content of carbon dioxide (CO_2) is at its highest level in more than 650,000 years and continues to rise. Mean annual surface air temperatures in California are predicted to increase by as much as 10 °F (5.6 °C) in the next century, creating climatic conditions unprecedented in at least the last 2 million years (IPCC 2007, Moser et al. 2009). Yet climate change is by no means the only stress on forest ecosystems. Growing human populations and economies are dramatically reducing the extent of the Earth's natural habitats. Land use change has reduced the availability of suitable habitat for native plants and wildlife, and, in many places, fragmentation of habitat has led to highly disconnected natural landscapes that are only weakly connected via dispersal and migration. Biotic response to climate and land use change is further complicated by other anthropogenic stressors, including exotic invasives, altered disturbance regimes, air and water pollution, and atmospheric deposition (Noss 2001, Sanderson et al. 2002).

Traditionally, restoration and ecosystem management practices depend on the characterization of "properly functioning" reference states, which may constitute targets or desired conditions for management activities. Because human-caused modifications to ecosystems have been so pervasive, fully functional contemporary reference ecosystems are difficult to find, and reference states must often be defined from historical conditions. One of the implicit assumptions of restoration ecology and ecosystem management is the notion that the historical range of variation (HRV) represents a reasonable set of bounds within which contemporary ecosystems should be managed. The basic premise is that the ecological conditions most likely to preserve native species or conserve natural resources are those that

---

[1] Regional ecologist, U.S. Department of Agriculture, Forest Service, Pacific Southwest Region, 1323 Club Dr., Vallejo, CA 94592.

[2] Research ecologist, U.S. Department of Agriculture, Forest Service, Pacific Southwest Research Station, 1731 Research Park Dr., Davis, CA 95618.

[3] Ecologist, U.S. Department of Agriculture, Forest Service, Southern Sierra Province, Sierra National Forest, 1600 Tollhouse Rd., Clovis, CA 93611.

Summary of Findings

1. **Effects of climate change are already apparent in rising minimum temperatures, earlier snowpack melting, changing stream hydrology, and increased frequency of large, severe wildfires.** Tree mortality rates are increasing in lower and mid-elevation forests but may be decreasing for some subalpine species as well. Some animal species are changing their geographic ranges in response to climatic shifts.

2. **Over the next century, average temperature is predicted to increase by 2 to 4 °F (1.1 to 2.2 °C) in the winter and 4 to 8 °F (2.2 to 4.4 °C) in the summer in the Sierra Nevada.** Changes in precipitation are more difficult to model and may differ between northern and southern California. Models suggest that snowpack in the Sierra Nevada could decrease by 20 to 90 percent. The annual summer drought in California may become more pronounced in its direct and indirect impacts on biota. Changing disturbance regimes (e.g., increases in fire frequency and burned area, and, in some forest types, fire severity) are likely to be the most significant influence on changes in vegetation types and distributions.

3. **In preparing forests for changing climatic conditions, the value of historical ecology is the insight it provides into "the way things work" rather than "the ways things were."** This suggests a management focused on ecological processes (e.g., fire, hydrology, etc.) rather than forest structure. It may be necessary to begin by restoring forest conditions and fuel loadings, but that should not be construed as the final goal.

4. **Management practices may enhance ecosystem resilience and sustainability by removing or reducing other, nonclimate stressors.** A key management focus should be restoration of heterogeneity in forest conditions. In low- and mid-elevation Sierra Nevada forests, such general practices might include reductions of stem densities of smaller fire-intolerant trees and increased use of wildland fire (prescribed fire and managed wildfire).

sustained them in the past, when ecosystems were less affected by people (Egan and Howell 2001; Manley et al. 1995; Wiens et al., in press). However, rapid and profound changes in climate and land use (as well as other anthropogenic stressors) raise questions about the use of historical information in resource management. In the last decade, as the scale and pace of climate change have become more apparent, many scientists have questioned the uncritical application of historical reference conditions to contemporary and future resource management (e.g., Craig 2010, Harris et al. 2006, Millar et al. 2007, Stephenson et al. 2010, White and Walker 1997). What role can historical ecology still play in a world where the environmental baseline is shifting so rapidly?

In this chapter, we review the nature of climate change in the Sierra Nevada, focusing on recent, current, and likely future patterns in climates and climate-driven ecological processes. We then discuss the value of historical reference conditions to restoration and ecosystem management in a rapidly changing world. The climate trend portion of this chapter is drawn from a series of climate change trend summaries that were conducted for the California national forests by the U.S. Forest Service, Pacific Southwest Region Ecology Program in 2010 and 2011 (available at http://fsweb.r5.fs.fed.us/program/ecology/). The historical ecology portion is based on work the first author contributed to Wiens et al. (in press), especially Safford et al. (in press a and b).

What role can historical ecology still play in a world where the environmental baseline is shifting so rapidly?

Recent Trends in Climate and Climate-Driven Processes in the Sierra Nevada

Climate

The Western United States is warming at a faster rate than any other part of the country (Saunders et al. 2008). In the Sierra Nevada, mean annual temperatures have generally increased by around 1 to 2.5 °F (0.5 to 1.4 °C) over the last 75 to 100 years, although some areas of the northern Sierra have experienced slight decreases in temperature (fig. 3-1). Warming temperatures are mostly driven by increases in nighttime minima over the last two to four decades. Over the same period, most weather stations do not show an appreciable increase in mean daily maximum temperatures. At higher elevations, the annual number of days with below-freezing temperatures is dropping, and at lower elevations, there has been an increase in the number of extreme heat days (Moser et al. 2009).

The Sierra Nevada (together with northwestern California) is one of the few places in the Western United States with a positive water balance (precipitation minus potential evapotranspiration) over the last half century. Precipitation has been steady or increasing over much of the area (fig. 3-1), although year-to-year variability in annual precipitation (i.e., higher highs and lower lows) is also increasing at many stations. At higher elevations, the proportion of precipitation falling as rain (vs. snow) is increasing. Over the last 50 years, spring snowpack has decreased by 70 to 120 percent across most of the northern Sierra Nevada, but snowpack is up in much of the southern Sierra Nevada, owing to the combination of higher precipitation and the terrain's higher elevation (fig. 3-2).

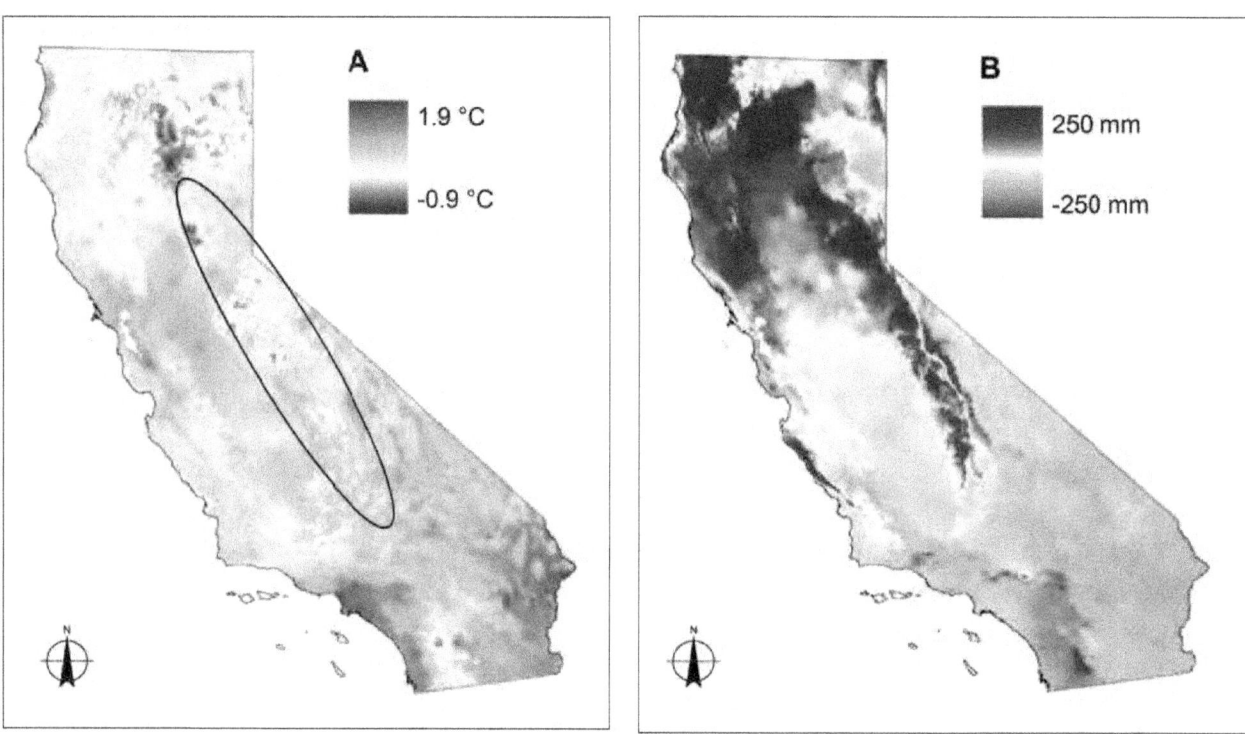

Figure 3-1—Differences in mean annual temperature (A), and mean annual precipitation (B) between the 1930s and 2000s, as derived by the PRISM climate model. Temperatures have risen across most of the Sierra Nevada (with some local areas of decrease), while precipitation has increased along most of the west slope. (Graphic courtesy of S. Dobrowksi, University of Montana.)

Hydrology

Stewart et al. (2005) showed that the onset of spring thaw in most major streams in the central Sierra Nevada occurred 5 to 30 days earlier in 2002 than in 1948, and peak streamflow (measured as the center of mass annual flow) occurred 5 to 15 days earlier. During the same period, March flows in the studied streams were mostly higher by 5 to 20 percent, but June flows were mostly lower by the same amount. Overall spring and early summer streamflow was down in most studied streams. Rising winter and spring temperatures appear to be the primary driver of these patterns (Stewart et al. 2005).

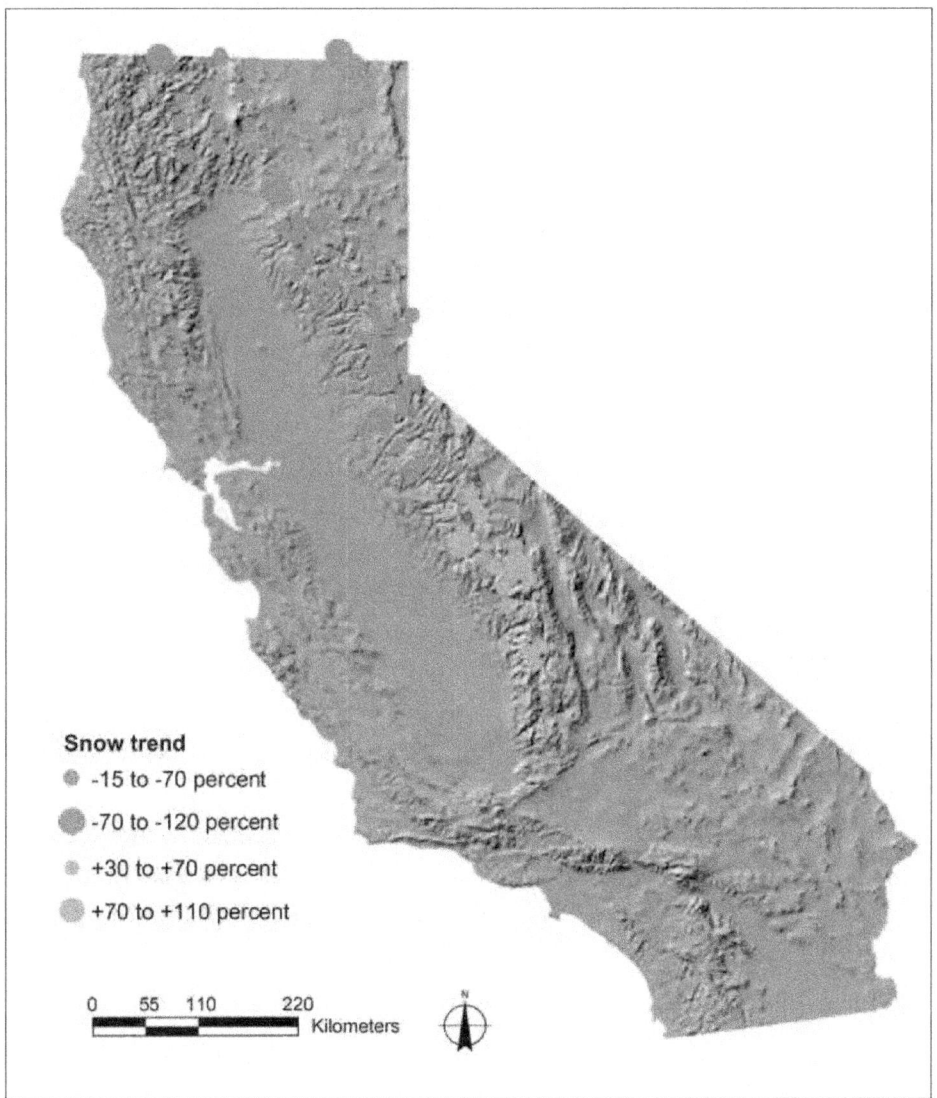

Figure 3-2—Trends in the amount of water contained in the snowpack ("snow water equivalent") on April 1, for the period 1950–1997. Red circles indicate percentage of decrease in snow water; blue circles indicate increase in snow water. (Redrawn from Moser et al. 2009.)

Forest Fires

Data on forest fire frequency, size, total area burned, and severity all show increases in the Sierra Nevada over the last two to three decades. Westerling et al. (2006) found that increasing frequencies of large fires (>1,000 ac) (405 ha) across the Western United States since the 1980s were strongly linked to increasing temperatures and earlier spring snowmelt. The Sierra Nevada was one of two geographic areas of especially increased fire activity, which Westerling et al. (2006) ascribed to an interaction between climate and increased fuels owing to fire suppression. Westerling et al. (2006) also identified the Sierra Nevada as being one of the geographic regions most likely to see further increases in fire activity on account of future increases in temperature. Miller et al. (2009) showed that mean and maximum fire size, and total burned area in the Sierra Nevada, have increased strongly between the early 1980s and 2007. Climatic variables explain very little of the pattern in fire size and area in the early 20th century. In contrast, over the last 25 years, 35 to 50 percent of the pattern in fire size and area can now be explained by spring climate variables (spring precipitation and minimum temperature). The mean size of escaped fires in the Sierra Nevada was about 750 ac (304 ha) until the late 1970s, but the most recent 10-year average has climbed to about 1,100 ac (445 ha). Miller et al. (2009) also showed that forest fire severity (a measure of the effect of fire on vegetation) rose strongly during the period 1984 to 2007, with the pattern concentrated in middle-elevation conifer forests. Fires at the beginning of the record burned at an average of about 17 percent high (stand-replacing) severity, while the average for the last 10-year period was 30 percent. Miller et al. (2009) found that both climate change and increasing forest fuels were necessary to explain the patterns they analyzed.

Forest Structure

Fire suppression has been practiced as a general federal policy since the 1920s. Pre-Euro-American fire frequencies in high-elevation forests such as red fir (*Abies magnifica* (Gordon & Glend.) Lindl. ex Hildebr.) (>40 to 50 years in many places) and subalpine forest (>100 years) were long enough that fire suppression has had little or no impact on ecological patterns or processes (Miller et al. 2009, Van de Water and Safford 2011). Higher elevation forests are also much more remote, less likely to have economic uses, and often protected in wilderness areas and national parks, so impacts from logging or recreation use are generally minimal. Subalpine tree growth is strongly influenced by higher precipitation and warm summers (Graumlich 1991). Long-term changes in stand structure in higher elevation forests are thus more likely to represent responses to changes in exogenous factors like climate.

Mean and maximum fire size, and total burned area in the Sierra Nevada, have increased strongly between the early 1980s and 2007.

Thirty five to 50 percent of the pattern in fire size and area can now be explained by spring climate variables.

Fires at the beginning of the record burned at an average of about 17 percent high severity, while the average for the last 10-year period was 30 percent.

In the early 1930s, the Forest Service mapped vegetation on national forest lands in the Sierra Nevada and sampled thousands of vegetation plots (Wieslander 1935). Bouldin (1999) compared the 1930s plots with the modern Forest Inventory and Analysis plots and described changes in forest structure for the Sierra Nevada from Yosemite National Park to the Plumas National Forest, that is, primarily north of the Sierra National Forest. In red fir forest, Bouldin (1999) found that densities of young trees had increased by about 40 percent between 1935 and 1992, but densities of large trees had decreased by 50 percent during the same period. In old-growth stands, overall densities and basal areas were higher, and the number of plots in the red fir zone dominated by shade-tolerant species increased at the expense of species like Jeffrey pine (*Pinus jeffreyi* Balf.) and western white pine (*Pinus monticola* Douglas ex. D. Don). In old-growth subalpine forests, Bouldin (1999) found that young mountain hemlock (*Tsuga mertensiana* (Bong.) Carriere), a shade-tolerant species, was increasing in density and basal area while larger western white pine was decreasing. In whitebark pine stands, overall density was increasing owing to increased recruitment of young trees, but species composition had not changed. Lodgepole pine (*Pinus contorta* Douglas ex. Louden) appears to be responding favorably to increased warming or increased precipitation throughout the subalpine forest.

Bouldin (1999) also studied mortality patterns in the 1935 and 1992 data sets. He found that mortality rates had increased in red fir (*Abies magnifica* A. Murray bis), with the greatest increases in the smaller size classes. At the same time, in subalpine forests, lodgepole pine, western white pine, and mountain hemlock all showed decreases in mortality. The subalpine zone was the only forest type Bouldin (1999) studied in which mortality had not greatly increased since the 1935 inventory. This suggests that climate change (warming, plus higher precipitation in some cases) is actually making conditions better for some tree species in this stressful environment. Dolanc et al. (2012) recently completed a study that resampled the 1930s Forest Service (Wieslander) plots in the subalpine zone between Yosemite National Park and the Lake Tahoe Basin. Corroborating Bouldin (1999), they found that growing conditions in the subalpine zone were probably better today than in the 1930s, as the density of small trees of almost all species had increased greatly in the 75-year period. Dolanc et al.'s (2012) direct plot-to-plot comparison also found that mortality of large trees had decreased the density of the subalpine forest canopy, but the overall trend was for denser forests with no apparent change in relative tree species abundances.

Van Mantgem et al. (2009) recently documented widespread increases in tree mortality in old-growth forests across the Western United States, including in the

Sierra Nevada. Their plots had not experienced increases in density or basal area during the 15- to 40-year period between first and last census. The highest mortality rates were documented in the Sierra Nevada, and in middle-elevation forests (3,300 to 6,700 ft) (1006 to 2042 m). Higher elevation forests (>6,700 ft) (2042 m) showed the lowest mortality rates, corroborating the Bouldin (1999) findings. Van Mantgem et al. (2009) ascribed the mortality patterns they analyzed to regional climate warming and associated drought stress.

Comparisons of the 1930s Forest Service vegetation inventories and map with modern vegetation maps and inventories show changes in the distribution of many Sierra Nevada vegetation types over the last 70 to 80 years (Bouldin 1999, Moser et al. 2009). The principal trends are (1) loss of yellow pine-dominated forest, (2) increase in the area of forest dominated by shade-tolerant conifers (especially fir species), (3) loss of blue oak woodland, (4) increase in hardwood-dominated forests, (5) loss of subalpine and alpine vegetation, and (6) expansion of subalpine trees into previous permanent snowfields. Trends four through six appear to have a strong connection to climate warming, while trends one through three are mostly the product of human management choices, including logging, fire suppression, and urban expansion.

Wildlife

Between 1914 and 1920, the Museum of Vertebrate Zoology (MVZ) at the University of California Berkeley surveyed the terrestrial vertebrate fauna at 41 sites along a transect that extended from the western slope of Yosemite National Park to an area near Mono Lake (Grinnell and Storer 1924). In the past decade, MVZ resurveyed the Yosemite transect to evaluate the near century-long changes in Yosemite's vertebrate fauna across this elevation gradient, stretching across numerous vegetation types (Moritz et al. 2008). By comparing earlier and recent MVZ small mammal surveys, Moritz et al. (2008) came to several conclusions: (1) the elevation limits of geographic ranges shifted primarily upward, (2) several high-elevation species (e.g., alpine chipmunk [*Tamias alpinus*]) exhibited range contraction (shifted their lower range limit upslope), while several low-elevation species expanded their range upslope, (3) many species showed no change in their elevational range, (4) elevational range shifts resulted in minor changes in species richness and composition at varying spatial scales, (5) closely related species responded idiosyncratically to changes in climate and vegetation, and (6) most upward range shifts for high-elevation species are consistent with predicted climate warming, but changes in most lower to mid-elevation species' ranges are likely the result of landscape-level vegetation dynamics related primarily to changes in fire regimes.

Closely related species responded idiosyncratically to changes in climate and vegetation.

Similar distribution patterns have been observed for other faunal taxa throughout the Sierra Nevada. Forister et al. (2010) tracked 159 species of butterflies over 35 years in the central Sierra Nevada and observed upward shifts in the elevational range of species, a pattern consistent with a warming climate. Tingley et al. (2009) resurveyed bird distributions along the Grinnell transects in the entire Sierra Nevada and concluded that 91 percent of species distributions shifted with changes in temperature or precipitation over time and 26 percent of species tracked both temperature and precipitation. This suggests that birds move in response to changing climates in order to maintain environmental associations to which they are adapted. The authors also suggested that combining climate and niche models may be useful for predicting future changes in regional bird distributions (Tingley et al. 2009). In contrast with other faunal studies, Drost and Fellers (1996) found that most frog and toad species in Yosemite exhibited widespread decline over the past several decades, regardless of elevation. Primary factors that may contribute to this faunal collapse throughout the Sierra Nevada include introduced predators, a fungal pathogen, pesticides, and climate change (Wake and Vredenburg 2008).

Projected Trends in Climate and Climate-Driven Processes

Climate

Currently, no published climate change or vegetation change modeling has been carried out for the Sierra Nevada alone. Indeed, few future-climate modeling efforts have treated areas as restricted as the state of California. The principal limiting factor is the spatial scale of the General Circulation Models (GCMs) that are used to simulate future climate scenarios. Most GCMs produce raster outputs with pixels that are 10,000s of square acres in area. To be used at finer scales, these outputs must be downscaled by using a series of algorithms and assumptions—these finer scale secondary products currently provide the most credible sources we have for estimating potential outcomes of long-term climate change for California. Another complication is the extent to which GCMs disagree with respect to the probable outcomes of climate change. For example, a recent comparison of 21 published GCM outputs that included California found that estimates of future precipitation ranged from a 26 percent increase per 1.8 °F (1 °C) increase in temperature to an 8 percent decrease (Gutowski et al. 2000, Hakkarinen and Smith 2003). That said, there was some broad consensus. All of the reviewed GCMs predicted warming temperatures for California, and 13 of 21 (62 percent) predicted higher precipitation (three showed no change, and five predicted decreases). According to Dettinger (2005), the most common prediction among the most recent models (which are considerably more complex and, ideally, more credible) is temperature warming by about 9 °F (5 °C) by 2100, with precipitation remaining similar or slightly reduced compared to today. Most models agreed that summers will be drier than they are currently, regardless of levels of annual precipitation.

The most widely cited of the recent modeling efforts is probably Hayhoe et al. (2004). They used two contrasting GCMs (much warmer and wetter, vs. somewhat warmer and drier) under low and high greenhouse gas emission scenarios to make projections of climate change impacts for California over the next century. By 2100, under all GCM-emissions scenarios, April 1 snowpack was down by 22 percent to 93 percent in the 6,700- to 10,000-ft (2042 to 3048 m) elevation belt, and the date of peak snowmelt was projected to occur from 3 to 24 days earlier in the season. Average temperatures were projected to increase by 2 to 4 °F (1.1 to 2.2 °C) in the winter and 4 to 8 °F (2.2 to 4.4 °C) in the summer. Finally, three of the four GCM-emissions scenarios employed by Hayhoe et al. (2004) predicted strong decreases in annual precipitation by 2100, ranging from 91 to 157 percent; the remaining scenario predicted a 38 percent increase. Although the southern Sierra Nevada snowpack has generally remained steady (or risen) over the past half-century (fig. 3-2) (Moser et al. 2009), continued warming is likely to erode the temperature buffer that is currently observed in the high southern Sierra Nevada. Most modeling projects a continuous increase in the rain:snow ratio and earlier runoff dates for the next century, with decreased snowpack (late winter snow accumulation decreases by 50 percent by 2100) and growing-season streamflow even in the higher elevation river basins (Miller et al. 2003, Moser et al. 2009).

Most modeling projects a continuous increase in the rain:snow ratio and earlier runoff dates for the next century, with decreased snowpack.

Hydrology

Miller et al. (2003) modeled future hydrological changes in California as a function of two contrasting GCMs (the same GCMs used in Hayhoe et al. [2005] and Lenihan et al. [2003; see below]) and a variety of scenarios intermediate to the GCMs. Miller et al. (2003) found that annual streamflow volumes were strongly dependent on the precipitation scenario, but changes in seasonal runoff were more complex. Predicted spring and summer runoff was lower in all of the California river basins they modeled, except where precipitation was greatly increased, in which case runoff was unchanged from today (Miller et al. 2003). Runoff in the winter and early spring was predicted to be higher under most of the climate scenarios because higher temperatures cause snow to melt earlier. In California rivers that are fed principally by snowmelt (i.e., higher elevation streams), flood potential was predicted to increase under all scenarios of climate change, principally owing to earlier dates of peak daily flows and the increase in the proportion of precipitation falling as rain. These increases in peak daily flows are predicted under all climate change scenarios, including those assuming reduced precipitation (Miller et al. 2003). The predicted increase in peak flow was most pronounced in higher elevation river basins, owing to the greater reliance on snowmelt. If precipitation does increase, streamflow volumes during peak runoff could greatly increase. Under the wettest climate scenario modeled by Miller et al. (2003), by 2100 the volume of flow during the highest flow days could more than double in many Sierra Nevada rivers. This would result in a substantial increase in flood risk in flood-prone areas in the Central Valley. According to Miller et al. (2003), increased flood risk is highly probable under current climate change trends, because temperature, not precipitation, is the main driver of higher peak runoff. If climate change leads not only to an increase in average precipitation but also a shift to more extreme precipitation events, then peak flows would be expected to increase dramatically.

Fire

The combination of warmer climate and increased fuel production (owing to higher CO_2 fertilization) will likely cause more frequent and more extensive fires throughout western North America (Flannigan et al. 2000, Price and Rind 1994). Fire responds rapidly to changes in climate and will likely overshadow the direct effects of climate change on tree species distributions and migrations (Dale et al. 2001, Flannigan et al. 2000, National Research Council 2011). A temporal pattern of climate-driven increases in fire activity is already apparent in the Western United States (Westerling et al. 2006). Modeling studies specific to California expect increased fire activity to persist and possibly accelerate under most future climate scenarios, owing to increased production of fuels under higher CO_2 (and in some cases, precipitation), decreased fuel moistures from warmer dry season temperatures, and possibly increased thundercell activity (Lenihan et al. 2003, 2008; Miller and Urban 1999; Price and Rind 1994; Westerling and Bryant 2006). By 2100, Lenihan et al.'s (2003, 2008) simulations suggest about a 5 to 8 percent increase in annual burned area across California, depending on the climate scenario. Increased frequencies or intensities of fire in coniferous forest in California will almost certainly drive changes in tree species compositions (Lenihan et al. 2003, 2008), and will likely reduce the size and extent of late-successional refugia (McKenzie et al. 2004, USDAFS and USDI 1994). Thus, if fire becomes more active under future climates, there may be significant repercussions for old-growth forest and old-growth-dependent flora and fauna.

A key question is to what extent future fire regimes in montane California will be characterized by either more or less severe fire than is currently (or was historically) the case. Fire regimes are driven principally by the effects of weather/climate and fuel type and availability (Bond and van Wilgen 1996). Seventy years

If fire becomes more active under future climates, there may be significant repercussions for old-growth forest and old-growth-dependent flora and fauna.

of effective fire suppression in the semiarid American West have led to fuel-rich conditions that are conducive to intense forest fires that remove significant amounts of biomass (Arno and Fiedler 2005, McKelvey et al. 1996, Miller et al. 2009). Most future climate modeling predicts climatic conditions that will likely exacerbate these conditions. Basing their analysis on two GCMs under the conditions of doubled atmospheric CO_2 and increased annual precipitation, Flannigan et al. (2000) predicted that mean fire severity in California (measured by difficulty of control) would increase by about 10 percent averaged across the state. Vegetation growth models that incorporate rising atmospheric CO_2 show an expansion of woody vegetation on many Western landscapes (Hayhoe et al. 2004; Lenihan et al. 2003, 2008), which could feed back into increased fuel biomass and connectivity and more intense (and thus more severe) fires. Use of paleoecological analogies also suggests that parts of the Pacific Northwest (including northern California) could experience more severe fire conditions under warmer, more CO_2-rich climates (Whitlock et al. 2003). Fire frequency and severity (or size) are usually assumed to be inversely related (Pickett and White 1985), and a number of researchers have demonstrated this relationship for Sierra Nevada forests (e.g. Miller and Urban 1999, Swetnam 1993). However, if fuels grow more rapidly and dry more rapidly—as is predicted under many future climate scenarios—then both severity and frequency may increase, at least in the short term. In this scenario, profound vegetation-type conversion is likely. Lenihan et al.'s (2003, 2008) results for fire intensity predict that large proportions of the Sierra Nevada landscape may see mean fire intensities increase over current conditions by the end of the century, with the actual change in intensity depending on future precipitation patterns.

Vegetation

Lenihan et al. (2003, 2008) used a dynamic ecosystem model ("MC1") that estimates the distribution and productivity of terrestrial ecosystems such as forests, grasslands, and deserts across a grid of 100 km^2 (38.6 mi^2) cells. To date, this is the highest resolution at which a model of this kind has been applied in California. Based on their modeling results, Lenihan et al. (2003, 2008) projected that forest types and other vegetation dominated by woody plants in California would migrate to higher elevations as warmer temperatures make those areas suitable for colonization and survival. For example, with higher temperatures and a longer growing season, the area occupied by subalpine and alpine vegetation was predicted to decrease as evergreen conifer forests and shrublands migrate to higher altitudes (fig. 3-3). Under their "wetter" future scenarios (i.e., slightly wetter or similar to today), Lenihan et al. (2003, 2008) projected a general expansion of forests in the Sierra Nevada, especially in the north and at higher elevations. With higher rainfall and

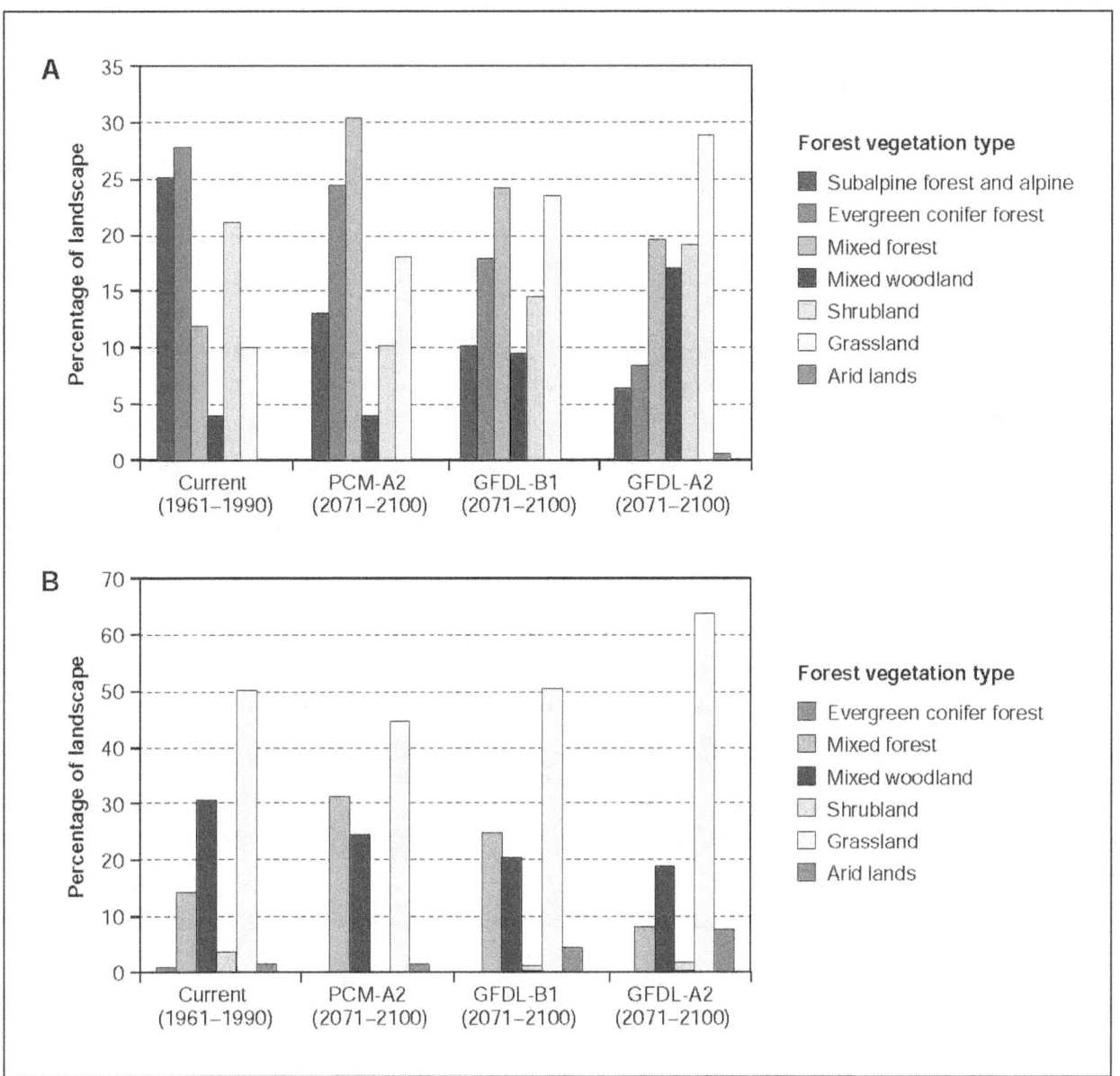

Figure 3-3—MC1 outputs for the Sierra Nevada (A) and Sierra Nevada Foothills (B) ecological sections, current vs. future projections of vegetation extent. These ecological sections include most of the Sierra Nevada west slope. The PCM-A2 scenario = similar precipitation to today, with <5.5 °F (<3.1 °C) temperature increase; GFDL-B1 = moderately drier than today, with a moderate temperature increase (<5.5 °F) (<3.1 °C); GFDL-A2 = much drier than today and much warmer (>7.2 °F) (>4 °C). All scenarios project significant loss of subalpine and alpine vegetation. Most scenarios project lower cover of shrubland (including west-side chaparral and east-side sagebrush), resulting principally from increasing frequencies and extent of fire. Large increases in the hardwood component of forests are projected in all scenarios except for the hot-dry scenario in the foothills. Large increases in cover of grassland are projected for the Sierra Nevada section. The drier scenarios project moderate expansion of arid lands. In the Sierra Nevada section, conifer forest decreases in cover under all scenarios. (Graphic developed using data from Lenihan et al. 2008.)

higher nighttime minimum temperatures, broadleaf trees (especially oak species) were predicted to replace conifer-dominated forests in many parts of the low- and middle-elevation Sierra Nevada. Under their drier future scenarios, Lenihan et al. (2003, 2008) predicted that grasslands would expand, and that increases in the extent of tree-dominated vegetation would be minimal. An expansion of shrublands into conifer types was also predicted, owing to drought and increases in fire frequency and severity, but increasing fire frequency in the Sierra Nevada may replace much low- to middle-elevation shrubland with grassland (fig. 3-3). Hayhoe et al. (2004) also used the MC1 ecosystem model to predict vegetation and ecosystem changes under a number of different future greenhouse gas emissions scenarios. Their results were qualitatively similar to the Lenihan et al. (2003, 2008) results.

Wildlife

Projected changes in California's terrestrial fauna and flora are expected over the next century. Stralberg et al. (2009) developed current and future species distribution models for 60 focal bird species and found that novel avian assemblages with no modern analogy could occupy over half of California. This implies a dramatic reshuffling of avian communities and altered pattern of species interactions, even in the upper elevations of the Sierra Nevada, where only a modest proportion of novel avian communities were projected. Using species distribution modeling, the California Avian Data Center (2011) projected that approximately 60 percent of coniferous forest bird species in the Sierra Nevada will exhibit substantial range reductions within the next 40 to 90 years (using 21 focal avian species). Based on bioclimatic models, Lawler et al. (2009a,b) projected high (>50 percent) turnover and vulnerability of California's amphibian fauna and moderate (10 to 40 percent) turnover in California's mammalian fauna under a high greenhouse gas emissions scenario by the end of the century. In a similar study, Loarie et al. (2008) projected that 66 percent of California's native flora will experience >80 percent reduction in range size within a century. Their study identified the southern Sierra Nevada and the coastal mountains of northwest California as climate change refugia, defined as areas projected to harbor species with shrinking ranges (presumably retaining subsets of regional species assemblages over time). Authors from these studies recommended novel adaptive management approaches and large-scale planning efforts that promote landscape/regional habitat connectivity. Loarie et al. (2008) also recommended serious consideration of human-assisted dispersal of California's flora and prioritization of climate change refugia for conservation and restoration.

Loarie et al. (2008) projected that 66 percent of California's native flora will experience >80 percent reduction in range size within a century. Their study identified the southern Sierra Nevada and the coastal mountains of northwest California as climate change refugia.

Is History Still Relevant?

In the Sierra Nevada, much has been made of the drastic ecosystem changes wrought by Euro-Americans since their arrival en masse in California in the mid-19th century. Numerous scientific studies have documented these changes, which result from—among other things—changed fire regimes, logging, livestock grazing, mining, agriculture, hunting, growing human populations and their infrastructure, air and water pollution, species introductions, water diversion, and, most recently, climate warming. In lower and middle-elevation forests of the Sierra Nevada, the combined impacts of these human influences have resulted in significant habitat loss in some forest types (oak woodlands and low-elevation riparian forests, for example), and major changes in forest composition and structure in others (e.g., in many conifer-dominated forest types at lower and middle elevations, especially yellow pine [ponderosa and Jeffrey pine] and mixed-conifer forests). Higher elevation forests, especially in the subalpine zone, have suffered much less from human impacts.

In the face of this ecosystem degradation, there is an understandable tendency to "get back to the good old days." In this school of thought, ecosystem status before the arrival of Euro-Americans is assumed to be optimal, while current conditions are impaired. The goal then is to return the ecosystem to its historical state, trajectory, or range of variation (HRV) before Euro-Americans arrived. This approach has been a foundation for conservation, preservation, and restoration management in the United States, but rapidly and profoundly shifting environmental baselines threaten our ability to continue this approach (Craig 2010; Harris et al. 2006; Millar et al. 2007; Stephenson et al. 2010; White and Walker 1997; Wiens et al., in press).

The major concern is that intrinsic assumptions of environmental "stationarity" that pervade traditional conservation, preservation, and restoration practices are no longer valid (if they really ever were) (Craig 2010; Milly et al. 2008; Wiens et al., in press). "Stationarity" is the idea that:

> "...the long-term mean is more or less invariant and the range of past conditions encompasses current and future conditions as well. The reasoning is that, although true environmental stationarity may not exist over the long term, the periodicity or rate of change may be slow enough compared to human experience to permit the useful assumption of stationarity" (Safford et al., in press).

With environmental conditions changing as rapidly and as extensively as they are, critics question the relevance of applying historically based targets in environments that are fundamentally different from what they were in the past.

Conservation and resource management often focuses on preservation of specific species, species assemblages, or a relatively static notion of the habitat required to maintain populations. In light of rapid global change, an alternative perspective is developing, one that is more focused on management of ecosystem structure and process rather than specific species or their habitat.

Given all of this change, are historical forest conditions irrelevant? Absolutely not! However, the way that history is used in ecosystem management, restoration or conservation should change. For example, the HRV concept was developed to ensure that ecosystem functions, especially disturbance processes, were incorporated into management (Landres et al. 1999, Morgan et al. 1994). However, as currently practiced, conservation and resource management often focuses on preservation of specific species, species assemblages, or a relatively static notion of the habitat required to maintain populations. In light of rapid global change, an alternative perspective is developing, one that is more focused on management of ecosystem structure and process rather than specific species or their habitat (Harris et al. 2006, Hunter et al. 1988, Stephenson et al. 2010). This perspective emphasizes the ecological function or ecological integrity of a site, and is less concerned with the identities, numbers, or arrangements of biota.

In this changed management environment, the role of historical ecology is to inform a management response to global change rather than resisting global change. Historical ecology can, among other things, identify important broad-scale and long-term processes that influence local ecological outcomes under different climate conditions or disturbance regimes. Historical conditions also can provide clues to mechanisms underlying ecosystem dynamics and resilience (i.e., Why have some systems persisted through climatic changes in the past?), guide the development and validation of predictive models, suggest appropriate future trajectories, define parameters by which we will recognize "properly functioning" ecosystems, help us to operationally define concepts like "ecological integrity" and "resilience," allow us to determine expected levels of ecosystem services, and inform us if current conditions are anomalous and worthy of management intervention (Landres et al. 1999; Millar and Woolfenden 1999; Safford et al., in press a and b; Swetnam et al. 1999). In essence, historical ecology represents our clearest window into ecological patterns and processes that occur at temporal scales beyond the scope of human observation.

Forest Heterogeneity and Climate Change

Given the uncertainties associated with climate change, focusing on the reduction or removal of nonclimate stressors can be prudent management. Historical conditions in active-fire forests suggest burning created fine- and large-scale heterogeneity in stand structure, wildlife habitat, fuel loads, and understory conditions. Human management of Sierra Nevada forests over the last century and a half has greatly reduced this heterogeneity. It is difficult to quantify forest heterogeneity from limited historical data, and unlikely that frequent fire would reproduce the same forest structure under current conditions. However, management practices following those in U.S. Forest Service General Technical Report PSW-GTR-220 that increase variation in forest conditions may help increase forest resilience to changes in climate and climate-related processes such as fire. For example, variation in stem density and fuel loads can limit the extent and severity of drought stress and high-severity fire, such that resulting mortality contributes to forest heterogeneity. Many fire-suppressed forests are now in an "alternative stable state" where disturbance, whether a result of beetle, drought, or fire mortality, tends to reinforce current structural and compositional homogeneity. Such uniform conditions promote low resilience to disturbances and projected changes in climate. A goal of current management could be to alter forest conditions past a threshold where disturbance processes act to increase rather than reduce forest heterogeneity. Heterogeneity in structure, function, and composition can provide ecosystems with the ecological "flexibility" (Holling 1973) to withstand and persist through both expected and unexpected environmental stresses.

References

Arno, S.F.; Fiedler, C.E. 2005. Mimicking nature's fire: restoring fire-prone forests in the West. Washington, DC: Island Press. 256 p.

Bond, W.J.; van Wilgen, B.W. 1996. Fire and plants. London, England: Chapman and Hall. 263 p.

Bouldin, J. 1999. Twentieth-century changes in forests of the Sierra Nevada, California. Davis, CA: University of California, Davis. 222 p. Ph.D. dissertation.

California Avian Data Center. 2011. Modeling bird distribution responses to climate change: a mapping tool to assist land managers and scientists in California. Data obtained from California Avian Data Center, http://data.prbo.org/cadc2/ (November 22, 2011).

Craig, R.K. 2010. "Stationarity is dead"—long live transformation: five principles for climate change adaptation law. Harvard Environmental Law Review. 34: 9–75.

Dale, V.H.; Joyce, L.A.; McNulty, S.; Neilson, R.P.; Ayres, M.P.; Flannigan, M.D.; Hanson, P.J.; Irland, L.C.; Lugo, A.E.; Peterson, C.J.; Simberloff, D.; Swanson, F.J.; Stocks, B.J.; Wotton, B.W. 2001. Climate change and forest disturbances. BioScience. 51: 723–734.

Dettinger, M.D. [N.d.]. From climate-change spaghetti to climate-change distributions for 21st century California. San Francisco Estuary and Watershed Science. 3(1): Article 4. http://repositories.cdlib.org/jmie/sfews/vol3/iss1/art4.

Dolanc, C.R.; Thorne, J.H.; Safford, H.D. 2012. Widespread shifts in the demographic structure of Sierra Nevada subalpine forests over the last 80 years. Global Ecology and Biogeography. DOI: 10.1111/j.1466-8238.2011.00748.x.

Drost, C.A.; Fellers, G.M. 1996. Collapse of a regional frog fauna in the Yosemite Area of the California Sierra Nevada, USA. Conservation Biology. 10: 414–425.

Egan, D.; Howell, E.A., eds. 2001. The historical ecology handbook: a restorationist's guide to reference ecosystems. Washington, DC: Island Press. 457 p.

Flannigan, M.D.; Stocks, B.J.; Wotton, B.M. 2000. Climate change and forest fires. Science of the Total Environment. 262: 221–229.

Forister, M.L.; McCall, A.C.; Sanders, N.J.; Fordyce, J.A.; Thorne, J.H.; O'Brien, J.; Waetjen, D.P.; Shapiro, A.M. 2010. Compounded effects of climate change and habitat alteration shift patterns of butterfly diversity. Proceedings of the National Academy of Sciences. 107: 2088–2092.

Graumlich, L.J. 1991. Subalpine tree growth, climate, and increasing CO_2: an assessment of recent growth trends. Ecology. 72: 1–11.

Grinnell, J.; Storer, T. 1924. Animal life in the Yosemite. Berkeley, CA: University of California Press. [Not paged].

Gutowski, W.J.; Pan, Z.; Anderson, C.A.; Arritt, R.W.; Otieno, F.; Takle, E.S.; Christensen, J.H.; Christensen, O.B. 2000. What RCM data are available for California impacts modeling? Sacramento, CA: California Energy Commission workshop on climate change scenarios for California. California Energy Commission.

Hakkarinen, C.; Smith, J. 2003. Appendix I: Climate scenarios for a California Energy Commission study of the potential effects of climate change on California: summary of a workshop. In: Global climate change and California: potential implications for ecosystems, health, and the economy. Palo Alto, CA: Electric Power Research Institute. 38 p.

Harris, J.A.; Hobbs, R.J.; Higgs, E.; Aronson, J. 2006. Ecological restoration and global climate change. Restoration Ecology. 14: 170–176.

Hayhoe, K.; Cayan, D.; Field, C.B.; Frumhoff, P.C.; Maurer, E.P.; Miller, N.L.; Moser, S.C.; Schneider, S.H.; Cahill, K.N.; Cleland, E.E.; Dale, L.; Drapek, R.; Hanemann, R.M.; Kalstein, L.S.; Leniahn, J.; Lunch, C.K.; Neilson, R.P.; Sheridan, S.C.; Verville, J.H. 2004. Emissions pathways, climate change, and impacts on California. Proceedings of the National Academy of Sciences. 101: 12422–12427.

Holling, C.S. 1973. Resilience and stability of ecological systems. Annual Review of Ecology and Systematics. 4: 1–23.

Hunter, M.L., Jr.; Jacobson, G.L., Jr.; Webb, T., III. 1988. Paleoecology and the coarse-filter approach to maintaining biological diversity. Conservation Biology. 2: 375–385.

Intergovernmental Panel on Climate Change [IPCC]. 2007. Climate change 2007: synthesis report. Contribution of working groups I, II and III to the Fourth Assessment Report of the Intergovernmental Panel on Climate Change. [Pachauri, R.K; Reisinger, A., eds.]. Geneva, Switzerland: 104 p.

Landres, P.B.; Morgan, P.; Swanson, F.J. 1999. Overview of the use of natural variability concepts in managing ecological systems. Ecological Applications. 9: 1179–1188.

Lawler, J.J.; Shafer, S.L.; Bancroft, B.A.; Blaustein, A.R.. 2009a. Projected climate impacts for the amphibians of the Western Hemisphere. Conservation Biology. 24: 38–50.

Lawler, J.J.; Shafer, S.L.; White, D.; Kareiva, P.; Maurer, E.P.; Blaustein, A.R.; Bartlein, P.J. 2009b. Projected climate-induced faunal change in the Western Hemisphere. Ecology. 90: 588–597.

Lenihan, J.M.; Bachelet, D.; Neilson, R.P.; Drapek, R. 2008. Response of vegetation distribution, ecosystem productivity, and fire to climate change scenarios for California. Climate Change. 87(Suppl. 1): S215–S230.

Lenihan, J.M.; Drapck, R.; Bachelet, D.; Neilson, R.P. 2003. Climate change effects on vegetation distribution, carbon, and fire in California. Ecological Applications. 13: 1667–1681.

Loarie, S.R.; Carter, B.E.; Hayhoe, K.; McMahon, S.; Moe, R.; Knight, C.A.; Ackerly, D.D. 2008. Climate change and the future of California's endemic flora. PLoS One. 3(6): e2502: 1–10.

Manley, P.N.; Brogan, G.E.; Cook, C.; Flores, M.E.; Fullmer, D.G.; Husari, S.; Jimerson, T.M.; Lux, L.M.; McCain, M.E.; Rose, J.A.; Schmitt, G.; Schuyler, J.C.; Skinner, M.J. 1995. Sustaining ecosystems: a conceptual framework. Publ. R5-EM-TP-001. San Francisco, CA: U.S. Department of Agriculture, Forest Service, Pacific Southwest Region. 216 p.

McKelvey, K.S.; Skinner, C.N.; Chang, C.; Erman, D.C.; Husari, S.J.; Parsons, D.J.; van Wagtendonk, J.W.; Weatherspoon, C.W. 1996. An overview of fire in the Sierra Nevada. In: Sierra Nevada Ecosystem Project: final report to Congress. Vol. II, Assessments and scientific basis for management options. Davis, CA: University of California, Centers for Water and Wildland Resources: 1033–1040.

McKenzie, D.; Gedalof, Z.; Peterson, D.L.; Mote, P. 2004. Climatic change, wildfire, and conservation. Conservation Biology. 18: 890–902.

Millar, C.I.; Stephenson, N.L.; Stephens, S.L. 2007. Climate change and forests of the future: managing in the face of uncertainty. Ecological Applications. 17: 2145–2151.

Millar, C.I.; Woolfenden, W.B. 1999. The role of climate change in interpreting historical variability. Ecological Applications. 9: 1207–1216.

Miller, C.; Urban, D. 1999. Forest pattern, fire and climatic change in the Sierra Nevada. Ecosystems. 2: 76–87.

Miller, J.D.; Safford, H.D.; Crimmins, M.; Thode, A.E. 2009. Quantitative evidence for increasing forest fire severity in the Sierra Nevada and southern Cascade Mountains, California and Nevada, USA. Ecosystems. 12: 16–32.

Miller, N.L.; Bashford, K.E.; Strem, E. 2003. Potential impacts of climate change on California hydrology. Journal of the American Water Resources Association. 39: 771–784.

Milly, P.C.D.; Betancourt, J.; Falkenmark, M.; Hirsch, R.M.; Kundzewicz, Z.W.; Lettenmaier, D.P.; Stouffer, R.J. 2008. Stationarity is dead: whither water management? Science. 319: 573–574.

Morgan, P.; Aplet, G.H.; Haufler, J.B.; Humphries, H.C.; Moore, M.M.; Wilson, W.D. 1994. Historical range of variability: a useful tool for evaluating ecosystem change. Journal of Sustainable Forestry. 2: 87–111.

Moritz, C.; Patton, J.L.; Conroy, C.J.; Parra, J.L.; White, G.C.; Beissinger, S.R. 2008. Impact of a century of climate change of small-mammal communities in Yosemite National Park, USA. Science. 322: 261–264.

Moser, S.; Franco, G.; Pittiglio, S.; Chou, W.; Cayan, D. 2009. The future is now: an update on climate change science impacts and response options for California. California Climate Change Center Report CEC-500-2008-071. Sacramento, CA: California Energy Commission. 91 p.

National Research Council. 2011. Climate stabilization targets: emissions, concentrations, and impacts over decades to millennia. Washington, DC: The National Academies Press. 298 p.

North, M.; Stine, P.; O'Hara, K.; Zielinski, W.; Stephens, S. 2009. An ecosystem management strategy for Sierran mixed-conifer forests. 2nd printing, with addendum. Gen. Tech. Rep. PSW-GTR-220. Albany, CA: U.S. Department of Agriculture, Forest Service, Pacific Southwest Research Station. 49 p.

Noss, R.F. 2001. Beyond Kyoto: forest management in a time of rapid climate change. Conservation Biology. 15: 578–590.

Pickett, S.T.A.; White, P.S. 1985. The ecology of natural disturbance and patch dynamics. New York, NY: Academic Press. 472 p.

Price, C.; Rind, D. 1994. The impact of a $2 \times CO_2$ climate on lightning-caused fires. Journal of Climate. 7: 1484–1494.

Safford, H.D.; Hayward, G.; Heller, N.; Wiens, J.A. [In press a]. Climate change and historical ecology: can the past still inform the future? In: Wiens, J.A.; Hayward, G.; Safford, H.D.; Giffen, C. eds. Historical environmental variation in conservation and natural resource management: past, present and future. New York, NY: John Wiley and Sons.

Safford, H.D.; Wiens, J.A.; Hayward, G. [In press b]. Conclusion: the growing importance of the past in managing ecosystems of the future. In: Wiens, J.A.; Hayward, G.; Safford, H.D.; Giffen, C. eds. Historical environmental variation in conservation and natural resource management: past, present and future. New York, NY: John Wiley and Sons.

Sanderson, E.W.; Jaiteh, M.; Levy, M.A.; Redford, K.H.; Wannebo, A.V.; Woolmer, G. 2002. The human footprint and the last of the wild. BioScience. 52: 891–904.

Saunders, S.; Montgomery, C.; Easley, T.; Spencer, T. 2008. Hotter and drier. The West's changed climate. New York, NY: The Rocky Mountain Climate Organization and the Natural Resources Defense Council. 54 p.

Stahlberg, D.; Jongsomjit, D.; Howell, C.A.; Snyder, M.A.; Alexander, J.D.; Wiens, J.A.; Root, T.L. 2009. Re-shuffling of species with climate disruption: a no-analog future for California birds. PLoS One. 4(9) e6825: 1–8.

Stephenson, N.L.; Millar, C.I.; Cole, D.N. 2010. Shifting environmental foundations: the unprecedented and unpredictable future. In: Cole, D.N.; Yung, L., eds. Beyond naturalness: rethinking park and wilderness stewardship in an era of rapid change. Washington, DC: Island Press: 50–66.

Stewart, I.T.; Cayan, D.R.; Dettinger, M.D. 2005. Changes toward earlier streamflow timing across western North America. Journal of Climate. 18: 1136–1155.

Swetnam, T.W. 1993. Fire history and climate change in giant sequoia groves. Science. 262: 885–889.

Swetnam, T.W.; Allen, C.D.; Betancourt, J.L. 1999. Applied historical ecology: using the past to manage for the future. Ecological Applications. 9: 1189–1206.

Tingley, M.W.; Monahan, W.B.; Beissinger, S.R.; Moritz, C. 2009. Birds track their Grinnellian niche through a century of climate change. Proceedings of the National Academy of Sciences. 106: 19367–19643.

U.S. Department of Agriculture, Forest Service and U.S. Department of the Interior, Bureau of Land Management [USDA and USDI]. 1994. Record of decision for amendment to Forest Service and Bureau of Land Management planning documents within the range of the northern spotted owl. [Place of publication unknown]. 74 p. (plus attachment A: standards and guidelines].

Van de Water, K.M.; Safford, H.D. 2011. A summary of fire frequency estimates for California vegetation before Euroamerican settlement. Fire Ecology. 7: 26–58.

Van Mantgem, P.J.; Stephenson, N.L.; Byrne, J.C.; Daniels, L.D.; Franklin, J.F.; Fulé, P.Z.; Harmon, M.E.; Larson, A.J.; Smith, J.M.; Taylor, A.H.; Veblen, T.T. 2009. Widespread increase of tree mortality rates in the western United States. Science. 323: 521–524.

Wake, D.B.; Vrendenburg, V.T. 2008. Are we in the midst of the sixth mass extinction? A view from the world of amphibians. Proceedings of the National Academy of Sciences. 105: 11466–11473.

Westerling, A.L.; Bryant, B. 2006. Climate change and wildfire in and around California: fire modeling and loss modeling. Report from the California Climate Change Center to the California Energy Commission. CEC-500-2006-190-SF. Sacramento, CA, California Energy Commission publishing. 28 p.

Westerling, A.L.; Hidalgo, H.; Cayan, D.R.; Swetnam, T. 2006. Warming and earlier spring increases western U.S. forest wildfire activity. Science. 313: 940–943.

White, P.S.; Walker, J.L. 1997. Approximating nature's variation: selecting and using reference information in restoration ecology. Restoration Ecology. 5: 338–349.

Whitlock, C.; Shafer, S.L.; Marlon, J. 2003. The role of vegetation change in shaping past and future fire regimes in the northwest U.S. and the implications for ecosystem management. Forest Ecology and Management. 178: 5–21.

Wiens, J.A.; Hayward, G.; Safford, H.D., Giffen, C., eds. [In press]. Historical environmental variation in conservation and natural resource management: past, present and future. New York, NY: John Wiley and Sons.

Wieslander, A.E. 1935. A vegetation type map of California. Madroño. 3: 140–144.

Western Regional Climate Center. 2010. California climate data archive. Western Regional Climate Center. http://www.calclim.dri.edu/ccacoop.html. (21 May 2010).

Chapter 4: Fishers and American Martens

K.L Purcell,[1] C.M. Thompson,[2] and W.J. Zielinski[3]

Introduction

Fishers (*Martes pennanti*) and American martens (*M. americana*) are carnivorous mustelids associated with late-successional forests. The distributions of both species have decreased in the Sierra Nevada and southern Cascade region (Zielinski et al. 2005). Fishers occur primarily in lower elevation (3,500 to 7,000 ft) (1067 to 3134 m) Sierran mixed-conifer and ponderosa pine forests, while marten distribution overlaps that of fishers but extends to much higher elevation (4,500 to 10,000 ft) (1372 to 3048 m) red fir and lodgepole pine forests. Fishers and martens have disproportionately large home ranges for their body sizes. Home ranges for male and female fishers average 9,960 ac (4031 ha) and 2,456 ac (994 ha), respectively. Martens have home ranges that average 1,413 ac (572 ha) and 877 ac (355 ha) for males and females, respectively.

Habitat Preferences

Habitat selection occurs at multiple spatial scales. For martens, the strength of habitat selection varies with scale (Minta et al. 1999); selection appears to be strongest at the microhabitat (e.g., resting and denning sites [generally 0.1 to 1 ac] [0.04 to 0.4 ha]) and the landscape scales (> 2,000 ac (809 ha). Fishers are expected to show similar patterns at larger scales, relative to their larger home ranges; however, documentation is lacking. Resting and denning structures are likely the most limiting habitat elements (Martin and Barrett 1991, Porter et al. 2005, Purcell et al. 2009, Spencer et al. 1983, Zielinski et al. 2004), and understanding resting habitat characteristics may be particularly important for conserving both species. The majority of fisher resting sites are cavities or platforms in live trees or snags, whereas martens more often use snags, logs, and stumps (Martin and Barrett 1991, Purcell et al. 2009, Spencer 1987, Zielinski et al. 2004). Trees and snags used as rest sites are typically among the largest available, often >35 in diameter at breast height (d.b.h.) (range 13 to 71 in) (89 cm; range 34 to 180 cm) (Martin and Barrett 1991, Purcell et al. 2009, Spencer 1987, Zielinski et al. 2004). Live trees used by fishers are often of declining health, with resting locations found in cavities caused by heartwood decay or platforms resulting from diseases such as mistletoe and

---

[1] Research wildlife biologist, U.S. Department of Agriculture, Forest Service, Pacific Southwest Research Station, 2081 E. Sierra Ave., Fresno, CA 93710.

[2] Postdoctoral research wildlife ecologist, U.S. Department of Agriculture, Forest Service, Pacific Southwest Research Station, 2081 E Sierra Ave., Fresno, CA 93710.

[3] Research wildlife biologist, U.S. Department of Agriculture, Forest Service, Pacific Southwest Research Station, 1700 Bayview Dr., Arcata, CA 95521.

Summary of Findings

1. **The distributions of American martens and fishers in the Sierra Nevada and southern Cascade region have decreased, and both species are expected to suffer additional habitat loss under changing climatic conditions.** Habitat selection by both species occurs at multiple spatial scales, ranging from microsite conditions to landscape configuration.

2. **Resting and denning structures are probably the most limiting habitat element for fishers and martens.** Because fishers and martens are nomadic within defined ranges (i.e., they move between rest sites on a daily basis outside the denning season), they require resting structures and resting habitat that are well distributed across the landscape and are sensitive to changes in landscape configuration.

3. **High canopy cover and large trees and snags are important components in both fisher and marten resting habitat.** Results suggest a minimum canopy cover target of approximately 60 percent for fishers and 30 percent for martens. Fishers prefer shade-intolerant species such as oaks and pines while martens use firs and lodgepole pines. Both species select sites characterized by complex vertical and horizontal structure.

4. **Recent findings support recommendations for focusing habitat management for fishers and martens in areas where fire would have burned less frequently historically, such as north-facing slopes, canyon bottoms, and riparian areas.**

5. **Two new analysis tools may be helpful for predicting management impacts on fisher populations.** One tool allows the quantitative evaluation of proposed treatments on fisher resting habitat using FIA data (Zielinski et al. 2006, 2010). A second analysis tool uses growth and disturbance models, combined with landscape trajectory analysis, to provide a visual, intuitive representation of the predicted risk of potential management actions on fisher habitat at the home-range scale (Thompson et al. 2011).

rust brooms. The use of both live trees and snags by these species suggests that, if sufficient numbers of large trees are present over the landscape, requirements for large snags will likely also be met over time (Smith et al. 2005). These findings are consistent with North et al. (2009) regarding the importance of large trees and snags, especially those with defects such as disease or damage. Suitable structures need to be well-distributed throughout their home ranges because reuse of resting sites is typically low. Research shows that fishers prefer to rest in shade-intolerant trees such as pines and oaks (Purcell et al. 2009), which are now less abundant than they were historically (McDonald 1990, Minnich et al. 1995, Roy and Vankat 1999). The North et al. (2009) approach encouraged the retention of oaks and pines, and stressed the importance of hardwoods, especially California black oaks (*Quercus kelloggii* Newberry). Black oaks require openings for regeneration (McDonald 1990), suggesting that the creation of small openings around mature productive trees would aid establishment of young trees needed to replace dying oaks. This should be balanced with retaining smaller trees around oaks that are potential dens for hiding cover. Fishers seldom use oak snags for resting. Most oaks used by fishers are live trees, although dead portions of otherwise healthy trees are important. In the northern Sierra Nevada, martens frequently use large red firs (*Abies magnifica* Andr. Murray), white firs (*Abies concolor* (Gordon & Glend.) Lindley) and lodgepole pines (*Pinus contorta* Douglas ex. Loudon) for resting (Spencer 1987).

Habitat conditions in the immediate vicinity of resting structures (resting sites) are characterized by complex vertical and horizontal structure, dense canopy cover, large trees, and snags (Purcell et al. 2009, Spencer et al. 1983, Zielinski et al. 2004). Canopy cover is consistently the most important variable distinguishing resting sites from available sites for fishers, with results suggesting a minimum canopy cover target of approximately 60 percent (Purcell et al. 2009). Cover is also influential for martens, which generally do not occur in areas where canopy cover is less than 30 percent (Spencer et al. 1983). The typically high diversity of tree sizes surrounding fisher resting sites suggests the need for complex vertical structure, but may be an artifact of past logging practices and fire suppression, which altered forest conditions from stands dominated by large trees and snags to dense stands with size class distributions that include more small stems and fewer large stems (Goforth and Minnich 2008, Minnich et al. 1995). Smaller trees may provide the requisite canopy cover, if a suitably large resting structure is available (Poole et al. 2004, Purcell et al. 2009). The small-diameter tree component of canopy cover may explain why the basal area of small-diameter trees is an important predictor for fisher resting sites (Zielinski et al. 2004).

Habitat conditions in the immediate vicinity of resting structures are characterized by complex vertical and horizontal structure, dense canopy cover, large trees, and snags.

Forest Condition and Management Effects

Recent research findings support the validity of the North et al. (2009) recommendations for focusing habitat management for fishers and martens in areas where, historically, fires would have burned less frequently, such as north-facing slopes, canyon bottoms, and riparian areas. Resting sites are often found close to streams and on relatively steep slopes (Bull et al. 2001, Purcell et al. 2009, Zielinski et al. 2004), and fisher telemetry locations include more observations in canyons and fewer observations on ridges than expected (Underwood et al. 2010). Marten habitat typically occurs at elevations where natural fire-return rates are low (e.g., red fir forest) compared to the elevations where fishers occur (McKelvey et al. 1996); consequently, there is generally less need for fuels treatment in marten habitat.

Our knowledge of habitat needs of fishers and martens at larger spatial scales is based largely on studies of martens conducted in other regions. At the landscape scale, martens' preference for mature forest has been well established. Martens rarely occupy landscapes where 25 to 30 percent of mature forests have been removed (Bissonette et al. 1997, Chapin et al. 1998, Hargis et al. 1999, Potvin et al. 1999). In Oregon, Bull et al. (2001) showed that martens preferentially selected unharvested stands compared to stands subjected to regeneration, partial, or selection cuts. Buskirk and Ruggiero (1994) reviewed marten responses to anthropogenic habitat alteration, and found that martens made little use of regenerating clearcuts for several decades after harvest, and that marten populations declined after clearcut logging. Thompson (1994) documented that martens in uncut forests had significantly higher density, survival, and reproduction than in surrounding logged, regenerating forests. These responses may also be occurring in the Sierra Nevada, where a long-term study site in the Tahoe National Forest has documented a significant decline in marten abundance during the last few decades, possibly because of the cumulative effects of timber harvests on forest landscape configuration (e.g., decreases in patch size of mature forest with an increase in interpatch distance) (Moriarty et al. 2011). These studies reinforce the sensitivity of martens, and presumably fishers, to changes in landscape composition and configuration.

At the same time, martens are known to inhabit younger or managed forests as long as some of the structural elements found in older forests remain, particularly those required for resting and denning. In British Columbia, Porter et al. (2005) reported that martens were capable of persisting in a young, manipulated forest as long as structural features characteristic of older forests were retained. On the Lassen National Forest, martens preferentially used shelterwood stands during the summer, when chipmunks and ground squirrels were available in these relatively open areas; however, females showed strong year-round selection for old-growth stands (Ellis 1998). Habitat conditions for martens appear best in old-growth stands, particularly red fir and lodgepole pine in proximity to meadows or riparian areas (Simon 1980, Spencer et al. 1983).

New Analysis Tools

A research need identified in North et al. (2009) was an assessment of proposed treatments on wildlife habitat features of interest. For fisher resting habitat, these predictive models would use either a predictive microhabitat model or a habitat model based on Forest Inventory and Analysis (FIA) data. The effects of forest practices on fisher resting habitat can now be quantitatively evaluated with the development of a model for the southern Sierra Nevada that predicts resting habitat value from plot data (Zielinski et al. 2006, 2010). The model can use FIA data or other types of fixed-area plot data and the Forest Vegetation Simulator (FVS) to forecast future effects of proposed activities on fisher resting habitat. Similar models have not yet been developed for martens.

In general, we still know little about the risks associated with different forest management actions, particularly for fishers. A specific research need identified in North et al. (2009) entailed examination of potential outcomes of proposed forest treatments based on modeling habitat in female fisher home ranges. This shortcoming has been partially addressed through the recent development of an analytical tool that predicts the relative impacts of management actions on fisher habitat (Thompson et al. 2011). Lacking more explicit information, this approach is essentially a form of ecological risk management. We quantified the range of variation in currently occupied female fisher home ranges and assumed that, if we managed landscapes to resemble those occupied home ranges, there is a high likelihood the landscape will remain functional fisher habitat and minimize the risk of negative population impacts. By following the trajectory of the landscape through time, we demonstrate how certain management prescriptions, including "no action," may involve greater risk to fishers owing to the greater divergence from the reference conditions. Results also indicate that female fishers use landscapes with relatively high proportions of large trees and snags, and where patches of high-quality habitat are connected in a heterogeneous mix of forest ages and conditions. This suggests that some level of management to reduce fire risk may be consistent with the maintenance of landscapes capable of supporting fishers as long as sufficient resting/denning structures are retained. This finding is in agreement with results from other recent efforts that modeled the effects of wildfires and fuels management on fisher

Certain management prescriptions, including "no action," may involve greater risk to fishers owing to the greater divergence from the reference conditions.

Management to reduce fire risk may be consistent with the maintenance of landscapes capable of supporting fishers as long as sufficient resting/denning structures are retained.

populations (Scheller et al. 2011, Spencer et al. 2008). These studies found that, although fuels treatments had direct negative effects on habitat suitability, those effects were mitigated by the potential benefits of reducing the likelihood of large wildfires that would eliminate or severely degrade available fisher habitat. This may especially be true if future fire regimes prove to be more extreme than past regimes (Carroll et al., in press; Spencer et al. 2008).

Potential Implications of Climate Change

Climate change is expected to have profound effects on the distributions of animal and plant species. In general, we expect upward shifts in latitude and elevation as warming occurs and species move to areas that suit their metabolic temperature tolerances (Root et al. 2003). Climate change will lead directly to shifts in the abundance and distribution of plant species, which could take decades to centuries to unfold (Davis 1990). Although the potential impacts of climate change have not been evaluated quantitatively in the southern Sierra Nevada, they are likely to alter species and structural composition. Overall, the extent of forested landscape is not expected to change appreciably during the 21st century, but the biggest predicted change is the reduction in area of conifer-dominated forest types, which are generally replaced by mixed woodland and hardwood-dominated forest types. (Lawler et al., in press; Lenihan et al. 2003). Because oaks, especially California black oaks, are a key component of fisher habitat, floristic changes may benefit fishers as long as temperature effects do not result in upward range shifts.

Lawler et al. (in press) recently published a study investigating the possible direct and indirect effects of climate change on selected species of the genus *Martes*. They found that macroclimate conditions closely correlated with Pacific fisher presence in California were likely to change greatly over the next century, resulting in a possibly pronounced loss of suitable habitat. Their results suggested that martens and fishers will be highly sensitive to climate change, and would probably experience the largest climate impacts at their southernmost latitudes (i.e., in the southern Sierra Nevada). The authors noted that fisher habitat is driven to a great extent by mesotopographic and local vegetation features that could not be incorporated into their climatic models. However, since fire occurrence and behavior have substantial effects on local vegetation and these factors are driven to a large extent by climate/weather, they also looked at stand-level implications of fire under a series of future fire scenarios. Lawler et al. (in press) recommended protecting fisher habitat through targeted forest-fuel treatment, and applying more liberal fire-management policies to naturally ignited fires during moderate weather conditions.

Interactions between climate and fire generate further changes in projected vegetation (see Safford et al. this volume). Climate-driven changes in fire regimes are projected to include increases in fire frequency, area, and intensity (Flannigan et al. 2000). Changes in fire regimes are expected to result in loss of late-seral habitat, increasing the probability of local extinction of species—such as fishers and martens—associated with these habitats (McKenzie et al. 2004). Decreases in the density of large conifer and hardwood trees and canopy cover are projected as fire severity increases. As these factors are closely related to fisher rest site and home range use in the southern Sierra Nevada (Purcell et al. 2009; Zielinski et al. 2004, 2005), the expectation is for an overall decrease in the availability of fisher habitat.

Other indirect, complex, interacting, and largely unpredictable effects may also play important roles. Predator-prey relationships may be altered if shifts in prey do not track those of martens and fishers. Reductions in snowpack could alter competitive relationships between martens and fishers, as snow potentially mitigates competitive interactions between the species (Krohn et al. 1997). Increased overlap between martens and fishers is expected to lead to increased competition between the two species, with fishers the likely beneficiary.

For martens, a shift in distribution to higher elevations would drive them toward the limit of forested habitats, which could limit their distribution and lead to decreases in population size. The marten range in the Cascades of California may already be demonstrating such effects (Kirk and Zielinski 2009, Zielinski et al. 2005). At high elevations, martens currently occupy areas with small trees and reduced forest cover (Green 2007), and have also been documented to use boulder fields, talus slopes, and rock slides (Green 2007, Grinnell et al. 1937). While use of these habitats may be more than transitory, they may not provide for year-round habitat needs (Green 2007).

Perhaps the biggest challenge related to climate change lies not simply in the changes per se, but in the rate of increase. Change is expected to occur at a rate and order of magnitude greater than rates of change experienced previously, and beyond the capability of species to adaptation through evolutionary responses (Root and Schneider 1993, Root et al. 2003). Although predictions based on various model projections differ, taken as a whole, martens and fishers are expected to be highly sensitive to climate change.

Martens and fishers are expected to be highly sensitive to climate change.

Unknowns

At present there is a great deal of uncertainty around predicting impacts on marten and fisher habitat, particularly cumulative effects. This is largely because our knowledge of how habitat change influences survival and reproduction is limited, and because we do not yet understand the importance of landscape heterogeneity to these species. Owing in part to the large home ranges of fishers and martens, multiple spatial scales must be considered in forest management planning. In particular, managers should consider the extent and connectivity of older forest patches, and the heterogeneity and composition of the remaining landscape. For fishers in particular, maintaining habitat in riparian areas and on topographic positions that normally did not burn frequently or severely (North et al. 2009) may help provide connectivity without significantly reducing the effectiveness of fuel reduction efforts. New analytical tools (i.e., Thompson et al. 2011, Zielinski et al. 2010) should be evaluated to assess projected effects at home range and landscape scales.

We still lack important information about reproductive site characteristics for these species, including their requirements for den trees and denning habitat at multiple spatial scales. As suggested in North et al. (2009), one way to help ensure the retention of key forest structures would be to provide a list of attributes and representative photos of resting and denning structures for use by marking crews (fig. 4-1) (see Lofroth et al. 2010 for descriptions of the specific types of structures used by fishers for resting and denning). Because most disturbances in fisher and marten habitat will be the result of treatments to reduce fuels and control forest pathogens, it is important to conduct rigorous studies on the effects of fuel treatments on fishers, martens, and their prey. Also, we know very little about the effects of management activities on important fisher and marten prey species or foraging behavior (Martin 1987). Addressing these information needs will lead to better informed management decisions and a greater likelihood that forest managers can provide the habitat conditions needed to support viable fisher and marten populations.

Figure 4-1—Examples of structures used as resting and denning sites by fishers in the Sierra National Forest, California. (A) cedar log (rest), (B) cavity in the base of a black oak (rest), (C) mistletoe broom in a sugar pine (*Pinus lambertiana* Dougl.) (rest), (D) deformity in a white fir (rest), (E) cedar snag with fisher looking out (rest), (F) cedar snag (rest), (G) woodpecker hole in a live ponderosa pine (den), and (H) cavity entrance in a black oak (den).

References

Bissonette, J.A.; Harrison, D.J.; Hargis, C.D.; Chapin, T.G. 1997. The influence of spatial scale and scale-sensitive properties on habitat selection by American marten. In: Bissonette, J.A., ed. Wildlife and landscape ecology. New York: Springer-Verlag: 368–385.

Bull, E.L.; Aubry, K.B.; Wales, B.C. 2001. Effects of disturbance on forest carnivores of conservation concern in eastern Oregon and Washington. Northwest Science. 75: 180–184.

Buskirk, S.W.; Ruggiero, L.F. 1994. American marten. In: Ruggiero, L.F.; Aubry, K.B.; Buskirk, S.W.; Lyon, L.J.; Zielinski, W.J., tech. eds. The scientific basis for conserving forest carnivores: American marten, fisher, lynx, and wolverine in the Western United States. Gen. Tech. Rep. RM-GTR-254. Fort Collins, CO: U.S. Department of Agriculture, Forest Service, Rocky Mountain Research Station: 38–73.

Carroll, C.; Spencer, W.; Lewis, J. [In press]. Use of habitat and viability models in Martes conservation and restoration. In: Aubry, K.; Zielinski, W.; Raphael, M.; Proulx, G.; Buskirk, S., eds. Biology and conservation of martens, sables, and fishers: a new synthesis. Ithaca, NY: Cornell University Press.

Chapin, T.G.; Harrison, D.J.; Katnik, D.D. 1998. Influence of landscape pattern on habitat use by American marten in an industrial forest. Conservation Biology. 12: 96–227.

Davis, M.B. 1990. Climatic change and the survival of forest species. In: Woodwell, G.M., ed. The earth in transition: patterns and processes of biotic impoverishment. Cambridge, England: Cambridge University Press: 99–110.

Ellis, L.M. 1998. Habitat use pattern of the American marten in the southern Cascade mountains of California. Arcata, CA: Humboldt State University. 95 p. M.S. thesis.

Flannigan, M.D.; Stocks, B.J.; Wottom, B.M. 2000. Climate change and forest fires. Science of the Total Environment. 262: 221–229.

Green, R.E. 2007. Distribution and habitat associations of forest carnivores and an evaluation of the California wildlife habitat relationships model for American marten in Sequoia and Kings Canyon National Parks. Arcata, CA: Humboldt State University. 90 p. M.S. thesis.

Grinnell, J.; Dixon, J.S.; Linsdale, J.M. 1937. Fur-bearing mammals of California: their natural history, systematic status, and relations to man. Volumes 1, 2. Berkeley, CA: University of California. 265 p.

Goforth, B.R.; Minnich, R.A. 2008. Densification, stand-replacement wildfire, and extirpation of mixed conifer forest in Cuyamaca Rancho State Park, southern California. Forest Ecology and Management. 256: 36–45.

Hargis, C.D.; Bissonette, J.A.; Turner, D.L. 1999. The influence of forest fragmentation and landscape pattern on American martens. Journal of Applied Ecology. 36: 157–172.

Kirk, T.A.; Zielinski, W.J. 2009. Developing and testing a landscape habitat suitability model for the American marten (*Martes americana*) in the Cascades mountains of California. Landscape Ecology. 24: 759–773.

Krohn, W.B.; Zielinski, W.J.; Boone, R.B. 1997. Relations among fishers, snow, and martens in California: results from small-scale spatial comparisons. In: Proulx, G.; Bryant, H.N.; Woodard, P.M., eds. Martes: taxonomy, ecology, techniques, and management. Edmonton, AB: Provincial Museum of Alberta: 211–232.

Lawler, J.J.; Safford, J.D.; Girvetz, E.H. [In press]. Martens and fishers in a changing climate. In: Aubry, K.; Zielinski, W.; Raphael, M.; Proulx, G.; Buskirk, S., eds. Biology and conservation of martens, sables, and fishers: a new synthesis. Ithaca, NY: Cornell University Press.

Lenihan, J.M.; Drapek, R.; Bachelet, D.; Neilson, R.P. 2003. Climate change effects on vegetation distribution, carbon, and fire in California. Ecological Applications. 13: 1667–1681.

Lofroth, E.C.; Raley, C.M.; Higley, J.M.; Truex, R.L.; Yaeger, J.S.; Lewis, J.C.; Happe, P.J.; Finley, L.L.; Naney, R.H.; Hale, L.J.; Krause, A.L.; Livingston, S.A.; Myers, A.M.; Brown, R.N. 2010. Conservation of fishers (*Martes pennanti*) in south-central British Columbia, western Washington, western Oregon, and California. Volume I: Conservation assessment. Denver, CO: U.S. Department of the Interior, Bureau of Land Management. 163 p.

Martin, S.K. 1987. The ecology of the pine marten (*Martes americana*) at Sagehen Creek, California. Berkeley, CA: University of California. 223 p. Ph.D. dissertation.

Martin, S.K.; Barrett, R.H. 1991. Rest site selection by marten at Sagehen Creek, California. Northwestern Naturalist. 72: 37–42.

McDonald, P.M. 1990. *Quercus kelloggii* Newb. California black oak. In: Burns, R.M.; Honkala, B.H., tech. coords. Silvics of North America. Volume 2. Agric. Handb. 654. Washington, DC: U.S. Department of Agriculture: 661–671.

McKelvey, K.L.; Skinner, C.N.; Chang, C.; Erman, D.C.; Husari, S.J.; Parsons, D.J.; van Wagtendonk, J.W.; Weatherspoon, C.P. 1996. An overview of fire in the Sierra Nevada. Sierra Nevada Ecosystem Project: Final report to Congress. Volume II: assessments and scientific basis for management options. Water and Resources Center Report No. 37. Davis, CA: Centers for Water and Wildland Resources, University of California, Davis: 1033–1040.

McKenzie, D.; Gedalof, Z.; Peterson, D.L.; Mote, P. 2004. Climate change, wildfire, and conservation. Conservation Biology. 18: 890–902.

Minnich, R.A.; Barbour, M.G.; Burk, J.H.; Fernau, R.F. 1995. Sixty years of change in Californian conifer forests of the San Bernardino Mountains. Conservation Biology. 9: 902–914.

Minta, S.C.; Kareiva, P.M.; Peyton, A.C. 1999. Carnivore research and conservation: learning from history and theory. In: Clark, T.W.; Peyton Curlee, A.; Minta, S.C.; Kareiva, P.M., eds. Carnivores in ecosystems: The Yellowstone experience. New Haven, CT: Yale University Press: 323–404.

Moriarty, K.M.; Zielinski, W.J.; Forsman, E. 2011. Decline in American marten occupancy rates at Sagehen Experimental Forest, California. Journal of Wildlife Management. 75: 1774–1787.

North, M.; Stine, P.; O'Hara, K.; Zielinski, W.; Stephens, S. 2009. An ecosystem management strategy for Sierran mixed-conifer forests. 2nd printing, with addendum. Gen. Tech. Rep. PSW-GTR-220. Albany, CA: U.S. Department of Agriculture, Forest Service, Pacific Southwest Research Station. 49 p.

Poole, K.G.; Porter, A.D.; de Vries, A.; Maundrel, C.; Grindal, S.G.; St. Clair, C.C. 2004. Suitability of a young deciduous-dominated forest for American marten and the effects of forest removal. Canadian Journal of Zoology. 82: 423–435.

Porter, A.D.; St. Clair, C.C.; de Vries, A. 2005. Fine-scale selection by marten during winter in a young deciduous forest. Canadian Journal of Forest Research. 35: 901–909.

Potvin, F.; Belanger, L.; Lowell, K. 1999. Marten habitat selection in a clearcut boreal landscape. Conservation Biology. 14: 844–857.

Purcell, K.L.; Mazzoni, A.K.; Mori, S.; Boroski, B.B. 2009. Resting structures and resting habitat of fishers in the southern Sierra Nevada, CA. Forest Ecology and Management. 258: 2696–2706.

Root, T.L.; Schneider, S.H. 1993. Can large-scale climatic models be linked with multiscale ecological studies? Conservation Biology. 7: 256–270.

Root, T.L.; Price, J.T.; Hall, K.R.; Schneider, S.H.; Rosenzweig, C.; Pounds, J.A. 2003. Fingerprints of global warming on wild animals and plants. Nature. 421: 57–60.

Roy, D.G.; Vankat, J.L. 1999. Reversal of human-induced vegetation changes in Sequoia National Park, California. Canadian Journal of Forest Research. 29: 399–412.

Scheller, R.M.; Spencer, W.D.; Rustigian-Romsos, H.; Syphard, A.D.; Ward, B.C.; Strittholt, J.R. 2011. Using stochastic simulation to evaluate competing risks of wildfires and fuels management on an isolated forest carnivore. Landscape Ecology. 26: 1491–1504.

Simon, T.L. 1980. An ecological study of the pine marten in the Tahoe National Forest. Sacramento, CA: California State University. 143 p. M.S. thesis.

Smith, T.F.; Rizzo, D.M.; North, M. 2005. Patterns of mortality in an old-growth mixed-conifer forest of the Southern Sierra Nevada, California. Forest Science. 51: 266–275.

Spencer, W.D.; Barrett, R.H.; Zielinski, W.J. 1983. Marten habitat preferences in the northern Sierra Nevada. Journal of Wildlife Management. 47: 1181–1186.

Spencer, W.D. 1987. Seasonal rest-site preferences of pine martens in the northern Sierra Nevada. Journal of Wildlife Management. 51: 616–621.

Spencer, W.D.; Rustigian, H.L.; Scheller, R.M.; Syphard, A.; Strittholt, J.; Ward, B. 2008. Baseline evaluation of fisher habitat and population status and effects of fires and fuels management on fishers in the southern Sierra Nevada. Unpublished report. http://consbio.org/products/reports/4. (February 8, 2012.)

Thompson, I.D. 1994. Marten populations in uncut and logged boreal forests in Ontario. Journal of Wildlife Management. 58: 272–280.

Thompson, C.M.; Zielinski, W.J.; Purcell, K.L. 2011. The use of landscape trajectory analysis to evaluate management risks: a case study with the Pacific fisher in the Sierra National Forest. Journal of Wildlife Management. 75: 1164–1176.

Underwood, E.C.; Viers, J.H.; Quinn, J.F.; North, M. 2010. Using topography to meet wildlife and fuels treatment objectives in fire-suppressed landscapes. Environmental Management. 46: 809–819.

Zielinski, W.J.; Truex, R.L.; Schmidt, G.A.; Schlexer, F.V.; Schmidt, K.N.; Barrett, R.H. 2004. Resting habitat selection by fishers in California. Journal of Wildlife Management. 68: 475–492.

Zielinski, W.J.; Truex, R.L.; Schlexer, F.V.; Campbell, L.A.; Carroll, C. 2005. Historical and contemporary distributions of carnivores in forests of the Sierra Nevada, California, USA. Journal of Biogeography. 32: 1385–1407.

Zielinski, W.J.; Truex, R.L.; Dunk, J.R.; Gaman, T. 2006. Using forest inventory data to assess fisher resting habitat suitability in California. Ecological Applications. 16: 1010–1025.

Zielinski, W.J.; Gray, A.; Dunk, J.R.; Keyser, C.; Sherlock, J.; Dixon, G. 2010. Using Forest Inventory and Analysis (FIA) data and the Forest Vegetation Simulator (FVS) to predict wildlife habitat suitability: resting habitat for the fisher (*Martes pennanti*). Gen. Tech. Rep. PSW-GTR-232. Albany, CA: U.S. Department of Agriculture, Forest Service, Pacific Southwest Research Station. 31 p.

Chapter 5: California Spotted Owls

S. Roberts[1] and M. North[2]

Introduction

California spotted owls (*Strix occidentalis occidentalis*) are habitat specialists that are strongly associated with late-successional forests. For nesting and roosting, they require large trees and snags embedded in a stand with a complex forest structure (Blakesley et al. 2005, Gutiérrez et al. 1992, Verner et al. 1992b). In mixed-conifer forests of the Sierra Nevada, California spotted owls typically nest and roost in stands with high canopy closure (≥75 percent) [Note: when citing studies, we use terminology consistent with Jennings et al. (1999), however, not all studies properly distinguish between canopy cover and closure and often use the terms interchangeably (see chapter 14 for clarification)] and an abundance of large trees (>24 in (60 cm) diameter at breast height [d.b.h.]) (Bias and Gutiérrez 1992, Gutiérrez et al. 1992, LaHaye et al. 1997, Moen and Gutiérrez 1997, Verner et al. 1992a). The California spotted owl guidelines (Verner et al. 1992b) effectively summarized much of the information about nesting and roosting habitat. Since that report, research on the California spotted owl has continued with much of the new information concentrated in five areas: population trends, barred owl (*Strix varia*) invasion, climate effects, foraging habitat, and owl response to fire.

Population Trends

A rangewide investigation from 1990 to 2005 into the population dynamics of the California spotted owl showed that subpopulations at four studied locations were declining or remaining steady (mean λ = 1.007, 95 percent confidence interval (CI) = 0.952 to

Summary of Findings

1. **Spotted owls select habitat at multiple scales**, with less flexibility in the nesting and roosting habitat requirements, and more flexibility in the foraging habitat.

2. **Foraging habitat appears to have more moderate canopy closure and is still associated with large trees**, possibly because of their importance as nest sites for northern flying squirrels, an important prey species for spotted owls in mesic Sierra Nevada forests.

3. **Low- to moderate-severity fire does not reduce the probability of spotted owl occupancy** if numerous large trees and areas of high canopy closure remain after a fire.

4. **Dense understory of regenerating trees can interfere with owl foraging.** Low- to moderate-severity fire reduces the density of small trees and may improve the habitat quality of spotted owl nesting or foraging habitat.

5. **Forest heterogeneity, with various vegetation communities or fire severities infused into late-successional forest, may improve spotted owl fitness.**

6. **Fire effects on foraging habitat are not well understood,** and future research needs to be directed toward owl foraging use patterns in a burned landscape.

[1] Wildlife ecologist, U.S. Geological Survey, Western Ecological Research Center, Yosemite Field Station, 7799 Chilnualna Falls Rd., Box 2163, Wawona, CA 95389.

[2] Research ecologist, U.S. Department of Agriculture, Forest Service, Pacific Southwest Research Station, 1731 Research Park Dr., Davis, CA 95618.

1.066) (Blakesley et al. 2010). Apparent survival was similar between the sexes and increased with owl age. The subpopulation residing in the only national park included in the meta-analysis, Sequoia-Kings Canyon (SEKI), showed the highest survival rates. Mean annual reproductive output (number of young fledged per territorial female) ranged from 0.988 (± 0.154) in the El Dorado National Forest to 0.555 (± 0.110) in SEKI. El Dorado showed the highest annual variation, with higher reproduction every second year, while SEKI had low annual variation. Although reproductive output varied between the four subpopulations, the El Dorado showed a declining trend. This declining trend is probably related to recent low annual reproduction and a consistent decrease in recruitment in the El Dorado. The high annual variation and decreasing trend observed in the El Dorado subpopulation indicate that habitat quality is not stable and probably decreasing over time. As with the northern spotted owl, reproductive output was highest with adults, followed by second-year subadults, and then first-year subadults. Population viability analyses indicated that the probability of a >10 percent decline in 7 years was lowest at 0.41 (95 percent CI = 0.09 to 0.78) for the Sierra National Forest subpopulation and highest at 0.64 (95 percent CI= 0.27 to 0.94) for the Lassen National Forest, and inconclusive for the El Dorado and SEKI (Blakesley et al. 2010).

Barred Owl

The barred owl, an aggressive competitor, has invaded the Sierra Nevada from the north and started reproducing as far south as the El Dorado National Forest (Keane 2007). This invasion appears to be a natural biogeographical process (Dark et al. 1998). Once barred owls establish a population adjacent to spotted owls, there are negative effects on spotted owl metapopulation dynamics (Olson et al. 2005). Barred owls are habitat and diet generalists (Livezey 2007) and appear to outcompete spotted owls during the breeding season, displacing spotted owls from territories that they occupy (Hamer et al. 2007). Ishak et al. (2008) found that many spotted owls had a blood parasite not found in barred owls, which may further reduce spotted owl competiveness with the recent invader. In the Pacific Northwest, scientists and managers are currently trying to rapidly formulate methods for reducing the barred owls' negative impacts on spotted owls (Buchanan et al. 2007).

Climate Change Effects

In the Pacific Northwest, Glenn et al. (2010) showed that the rate of population change (λ) for the northern spotted owl was positively influenced by wetter-than-normal growing seasons, which they speculated improved owl prey availability. However, cold, wet winter and spring (early nesting season), as well as the number of hot summer days, negatively affected the rate of population change. The influence of climate data on the rate of population change (λ) was highly variable, explaining 3 to 85 percent of the total variability seen in λ, across six different study areas. Adult survival, which was closely related to regional climate conditions, had a stronger influence on the rate of population change than recruitment, which was associated with local weather. As climate change models project warmer winters with higher variability in winter precipitation, and hotter, drier summers across the Pacific Northwest and northern California, climate could potentially have a rangewide negative effect on spotted owl survival, recruitment, and population growth rates. North et al. (2000) suggested that regional weather during the nesting season influenced reproductive success and nest-site canopy structure was important in mitigating the effects of detrimental weather. Carroll (2010) advised that models used for spotted owl conservation planning should incorporate habitat variables along with climate information.

Spotted Owl Nesting and Foraging Habitat Characteristics

Generally, spotted owl survival increases with increasing area of late-successional forest (Dugger et al. 2005, Franklin et al. 2000, Olson et al. 2004) and decreases with increasing area of early successional forests (Dugger et al. 2005). However, because owls use a variety of habitats for foraging and nesting, forest heterogeneity across the landscape can improve spotted owl viability. Spotted owl survival and reproductive rates were higher in owl territories that included a mosaic of vegetation types infused within late-successional forest (Franklin et al. 2000), presumably because there was a greater diversity or abundance of prey within this mosaic (Ward et al. 1998, Zabel et al. 1995).

Spotted owls select habitat at multiple spatial and temporal scales, with less flexibility in nesting and roosting habitat requirements than foraging habitat. Blakesley et al. (2005) used remote sensing vegetation data to investigate the importance of spatial scale for spotted owl occupancy on a landscape scale. Between the two scales (500 and 2,000 ac) (202 to 809 ha) they found that the forest structure at the 500-ac (202-ha) scale was the most important. Within that scale, studies agree that both high overstory canopy closure and cover and an abundance of large trees are major influences in owl habitat selection (Bias and Gutiérrez 1992, Blakesley et al. 2005, Gutiérrez et al. 1992, LaHaye et al. 1997, Moen and Gutiérrez 1997, Roberts et al. 2011, Verner et al. 1992a). Reproduction can be associated with foraging habitat quality, because owls appear to fledge young more often as prey availability increases (Carey et al. 1992, Rosenberg et al. 2003). In northeastern California,

Because owls use a variety of habitats for foraging and nesting, forest heterogeneity across the landscape can improve spotted owl viability.

spotted owl reproduction was negatively correlated to nonforested areas and forest types not used for nesting or foraging within the nest area (500 acres) (Blakesley et al. 2005).

While foraging has been better studied for the northern spotted owl (*Strix occidentalis caurina* ex. Forsman et al. 2004), there are several emerging patterns applicable to California spotted owl foraging. For example, northern spotted owls may forage in or near edge habitat (Clark 2007, Folliard et al. 2000, Ward et al. 1998), but California spotted owls did not locate their nests close to edges (Phillips et al. 2010). For California spotted owls, foraging habitat appears to be more open (≥40 percent) than nesting habitat (≥70 percent) with respect to canopy closure (Call et al. 1992, Zabel et al. 1992), basal area (Roberts et al. 2011), and stand density (Irwin et al. 2007). Additionally, spotted owl foraging habitat is associated with large trees, possibly because of their importance as nest sites for northern flying squirrels (*Glaucomys sabrinus*) (Meyer et al. 2005, Waters and Zabel 1995), an important prey species for spotted owls in mesic or closed-canopied Sierra Nevada forests (Williams et al. 1992). Irwin et al. (2007) found owl foraging associated with forests in proximity to nest sites and small streams. In an analysis of owl locations including many foraging locations in the southern Sierra Nevada, owls used canyon/stream bottoms significantly more than expected (Underwood et al. 2010). Riparian area use may be related to preferred forest structural conditions (i.e., large trees and high canopy closure) or possibly higher abundance of northern flying squirrels (Meyer et al. 2005, 2007). In northern Sierra Nevada mixed-conifer forests, Innes et al. (2007) found higher densities of dusky-footed woodrats (*Neotoma fuscipes*), another preferred owl prey species, in areas with large black oaks (*Quercus kelloggii* Newberry). In general, these studies suggest that foraging habitat is (1) more open (less vegetation biomass) than nesting habitat, (2) often located close to nest sites, (3) associated with large trees and snags, and (4) infused with other vegetation types (e.g., riparian forests, black oak-dominated patches).

Spotted Owls and Fire

The late-successional, and often dense, forests favored by spotted owls for nesting and roosting are at risk to stand-replacing fires because of heavy fuel loading (Agee et al. 2000). Accumulated dead biomass and down woody debris can carry fire horizontally through the forest and vertically into the upper canopy (Tappeiner and McDonald 1996, Weatherspoon and Skinner 1995). Such high fuel loading and vertically continuous ladder fuels put structurally complex, mature forests at greater risk of stand-replacing fire (Agee, 1993, North and Hurteau 2011, Weatherspoon et al. 1992). However, forest landscapes exposed to repeated burning are often buffered from the effects of future wildfires and characterized by a mosaic of forest patches with high structural heterogeneity at multiple spatial scales (Collins et al. 2009, Stephens et al. 2008). This heterogeneity can improve spotted owl persistence by protecting late-successional patches from stand-replacing fire and potentially enhancing the abundance or diversity of prey species within an individual territory (resulting from greater habitat diversity) (fig. 5-1).

Figure 5-1—A California spotted owl nest in a mixed-conifer forest that burned in a prescribed fire with mixed fire severity in 1997 in Yosemite National Park. Note the nest (shown by arrow) is in an area that burned at low severity and has high canopy closure. The nest is adjacent (<50 ft away) (<15.2 m) to an area (left one third of the photo) with lower closure that experienced moderate fire severity.

High fuel loading and ladder fuels can reduce foraging or nesting habitat quality for California spotted owls in Sierra Nevada forests. In a fire-suppressed forest, Blakesley et al. (2005) found that increasing the proportion of smaller trees (<23 in d.b.h.) (<60 cm) around the nest, even with high overstory canopy cover (>70 percent), can negatively influence owl occupancy. Decades of fire suppression created a dense understory of regenerating white fir (*Abies concolor* (Gordon & Glend.) Lindley), and these thickets of young trees could interfere with owl foraging in high-use areas. Roberts et al. (2011) found that scattered small trees did not negatively affect owl occupancy in forests where managers allowed low- to moderate-severity fire to periodically clear out these thickets and leave behind large, live trees while retaining high overstory canopy closure. Scattered pockets of small- and medium-diameter trees (4 to 20 in d.b.h.) (10 to 50 cm) can contribute to a multilayered canopy that may allow for efficient thermoregulation for spotted owls, which are not well adapted to heat exposure (Barrows 1981, Weathers et al. 2001). In contrast, Clark (2007) showed that northern spotted owl occupancy and annual survival rates declined (Clark et al. 2011), and annual home range and local extinction increased immediately following (1 to 4 years) wildfire. Clark (2007) also found that annual home range size increased with increasing amount of hard edge (e.g., logging or fire boundaries) within the home range, suggesting lower

Scattered pockets of small- and medium-diameter trees can contribute to a multilayered canopy that may allow for efficient thermoregulation for spotted owls.

quality habitat within fragmented sites. Postfire salvage logging and large areas of early-seral forests in his study area, however, may have confounded his observed occupancy rates.

Fire effects on foraging habitat are not well understood. Clark (2007) observed 23 northern spotted owls using all types of fire severity in southern Oregon. However, within burned areas, owls strongly selected low-severity or unburned areas with minimal overstory canopy mortality. In this burned landscape, owl high-use areas were characterized by lower fire severity and greater structural diversity. Clark (2007) also found that postfire salvage logging reduced owl habitat quality. In contrast, Bond et al. (2009) followed seven owls (three pairs and an individual) using a 4-year-old burned forest in southern Sierra Nevada and found higher than expected owl foraging in high-severity burn areas. The study, however, is limited by its small sample size, brief period of study (12 weeks), and nonrandom owl selection. Additionally, studies of deer mice (*Peromyscus maniculatus*) and other spotted owl prey in Yosemite National Park indicate that deer mouse abundance was negatively associated with increasing fire severity (Roberts et al. 2011). Collectively, these studies suggest the presence of large trees and high overstory canopy closure are the most important pre- and postfire conditions associated with spotted owl occupancy.

References

Agee, J.K. 1993. Fire ecology of Pacific Northwest forests. Washington, DC: Island Press. 505 p.

Agee, J.K.; Bahro, B.; Finney, M.A.; Omi, P.N.; Sapsis, D.B.; Skinner, C.N.; van Wagtendonk, J.W.; Weatherspoon, C.P. 2000. The use of fuel breaks in landscape fire management. Forest Ecology and Management. 127: 55–66.

Barrows, C.W. 1981. Roost selection by spotted owls: an adaptation to heat stress. The Condor. 83: 302–309.

Bias, M.A.; Gutiérrez, R.J. 1992. Habitat association of California spotted owls in the central Sierra Nevada. Journal of Wildlife Management. 56: 584–595.

Blakesley, J.A.; Noon, B.R.; Anderson, D.R. 2005. Site occupancy, apparent survival, and reproduction of California spotted owls in relation to forest stand characteristics. Journal of Wildlife Management. 69: 1554–1654.

Blakesley, J.A.; Seamans, M.E.; Conner, M.M.; Franklin, A.B.; White, G.C.; Gutiérrez, R.J.; Hines, J.E.; Nichols, J.D.; Munton, T.E.; Shaw, D.W.H.; Keane, J.J.; Steger, G.N.; McDonald, T.L. 2010. Population dynamics of spotted owls in the Sierra Nevada, California. Wildlife Monographs. 174: 1–36.

Bond, M.L.; Lee, D.E.; Siegel, R.B.; Ward, J.P. 2009. Habitat use and selection by California spotted owls in a postfire landscape. Journal of Wildlife Management. 73: 1116–1124.

Buchanan, J.B.; Gutiérrez, R.J.; Anthony, R.G.; Cullinan, T.; Diller, L.V.; Forsman, E.D.; Franklin, A.B. 2007. A synopsis of suggested approaches to address potential competitive interactions between barred owls (*Strix varia*) and spotted owls (*S. occidentalis*). Biological Invasions. 6: 679–691.

Call, D.R.; Gutiérrez, R.J.; Verner, J. 1992. Foraging habitat and home-range characteristics of California spotted owls in the Sierra Nevada. Condor. 94: 880–888.

Carey, A.B.; Horton, S.P.; Biswell, B.L. 1992. Northern spotted owls: influence of prey base and landscape character. Ecological Monographs. 62: 223–250.

Carroll, C. 2010. Role of climatic niche models in focal-species-based conservation planning: assessing potential effects of climate change on northern spotted owl in the Pacific Northwest, USA. Biological Conservation. 143: 1432–1437.

Clark, D.A. 2007. Demography and habitat selection of northern spotted owls in post-fire landscapes of southwestern Oregon. Corvallis, OR: Oregon State University. 202 p. M.S. thesis.

Clark, D.A.; Anthony, R.G.; Andrews, L.S. 2011. Survival rates of northern spotted owls in post-fire landscapes of southwest Oregon. Journal of Raptor Research. 45: 38–47.

Collins, B.M.; Miller, J.D.; Thode, A.E.; Kelly, M.; van Wagtendonk, J.W.; Stephens, S.L. 2009. Interactions among wildland fires in a long-established Sierra Nevada natural fire area. Ecosystems. 12: 114–128.

Dark, S.J.; Gutiérrez, R.J.; Gould, G.I., Jr. 1998. The barred owl (*Strix varia*) invasion in California. The Auk. 115: 50–56.

Dugger, K.M.; Wagner, F.; Anthony, R.G.; Olson, G.S. 2005. The relationship between habitat characteristics and demographic performance of northern spotted owls in southern Oregon. Condor. 107: 863–878.

Folliard, L.B.; Reese, K.; Diller, L.V. 2000. Landscape characteristics of northern spotted owl nest sites in northwestern California. Journal of Raptor Research. 34: 75–84.

Forsman, E.D.; Anthony, R.G.; Meslow, E.C.; Zabel, C.J. 2004. Diet and foraging behavior of northern spotted owls in Oregon. Journal of Raptor Research. 38: 214–230.

Franklin, A.B.; Gutiérrez, R.J.; Burnham, K.P. 2000. Climate, habitat quality, and fitness in northern spotted owl populatoin in northwest California. Ecological Monographs. 70: 539–590.

Glenn, E.M.; Anthony, R.G.; Forsman, E.D. 2010. Population trends in northern spotted owls: associations with climate in the Pacific Northwest. Biological Conservation. 143: 2543–2552.

Gutiérrez, R.J.; Verner, J.; McKelvey, K.S.; Noon, B.R.; Steger, G.N.; Call, D.R.; LaHaye, W.S.; Bingham, B.B.; Senser, J.S. 1992. Habitat relations of the California spotted owl. In: Verner, J.; McKelvey, K.S.; Noon, B.R.; Gutiérrez, R.J.; Gould, G.I., Jr.; Beck, T.W., tech. coords. The California spotted owl: a technical assessment of its current status. Gen. Tech. Rep. PSW-GTR-133. Albany, CA: U.S. Department of Agriculture, Forest Service, Pacific Southwest Research Station: 79–98.

Hamer, T.E.; Forsman, E.D.; Glenn, E.M.; Elizabeth, M. 2007. Home range attributes and habitat selection of barred owls and spotted owls in an area of sympatry. The Condor. 109: 750–768.

Innes, R.J.; Van Vuren, D.H.; Kelt, D.A.; Johnson, M.L.; Wilson, J.A.; Stine, P.A. 2007. Habitat associations of dusky-footed woodrats (*Neotonia fuscipes*) in mixed-conifer forest of the northern Sierra Nevada. Journal of Mammalogy. 88: 1523–1531.

Irwin, L.L.; Clark, L.A.; Rock, D.C.; Rock, S.L. 2007. Modeling foraging habitat of California spotted owls. Journal of Wildlife Management. 71: 1183–1191.

Ishak, H.D.; Dumbacher, J.P.; Anderson, N.L.; Keane, J.J.; Valkiunas, G.; Haig, S.M.; Tell, L.A.; Sehgal, R.N.M. 2008. Blood parasites in owls with conservation implications for the spotted owl (*Strix occidentalis*). PLOS One. 3: e2304.

Keane, J. 2007. Personal communication. Research wildlife biologist, U.S. Department of Agriculture, Forest Service, Pacific Southwest Research Station, 1731 Research Park Dr., Davis, CA 95618.

LaHaye, W.S.; Gutiérrez, R.J.; Call, D.R. 1997. Nest-site selection and reproductive success of California spotted owls. Wilson Bulletin. 109: 42–51.

Livezey, K.B. 2007. Barred owl habitat and prey: a review and synthesis of the literature. Journal of Raptor Research. 41: 177–201.

Meyer, M.D.; Kelt, D.A.; North, M.P. 2005. Nest trees of northern flying squirrels in the Sierra Nevada. Journal of Mammalogy. 86: 275–280.

Meyer, M.D.; Kelt, D.A.; North, M.P. 2007. Microhabitat associations of northern flying squirrels in burned and thinned forest stands of the Sierra Nevada. American Midland Naturalist. 157: 202–211.

Moen, C.A.; Gutiérrez, R.J. 1997. California spotted owl habitat selection in the central Sierra Nevada. Journal of Wildlife Management. 61: 1281–1287.

North, M.P.; Steger, G.N.; Denton, R.; Eberlein, G.; Munton, T.E.; Johnson, K. 2000. Association of weather and nest-site structure with reproductive success in California spotted owls. Journal of Wildlife Management. 64: 797–807.

North, M.P.; Hurteau, M.D. 2011. High-severity wildfire effects on carbon stocks and emissions in fuels treated and untreated forest. Forest Ecology and Management. 261: 1115–1120.

Olson, G.S.; Glenn, E.M.; Anthony, R.G.; Forsman, E.D.; Reid, J.A.; Loschl, P.J.; Ripple, W.J. 2004. Modeling of demographic performance of northern spotted owls relative to forest habitat in Oregon. Journal of Wildlife Management. 68: 1039–1053.

Olson, G.S.; Anthony, R.G.; Forsman, E.D.; Ackers, S.H.; Loschl, P.J.; Reid, J.A.; Dugger, K.M.; Glenn, E.M.; Ripple, W.J. 2005. Modeling of site occupancy dynamics for northern spotted owls, with emphasis on the effects of barred owls. Journal of Wildlife Management. 69: 918–932.

Phillips, C.E.; Tempel, D.J.; Gutiérrez, R.J. 2010. Do California spotted owls select nest trees close to forest edges? Journal of Raptor Research. 44: 311–314.

Roberts, S.L.; van Wagtendonk, J.W.; Miles, A.K.; Kelt, D.A. 2011. Effects of fire on spotted owl site occupancy in a late-successional forest. Biological Conservation. 144: 610–619.

Rosenberg, D.K.; Swindle, K.A.; Anthony, R.G. 2003. Influence of prey abundance on spotted owl reproductive success in western Oregon. Canadian Journal of Zoology. 81: 1715–1725.

Stephens, S.L.; Fry, D.; Franco-Vizcano, E. 2008. Wildfire and forests in northwestern Mexico: the United States wishes it had similar fire problems. Ecology and Society. 13: 10.

Tappeiner, J.C.; McDonald, P.M. 1996. Regeneration of Sierra Nevada forests. In: Sierra Nevada Ecosystem Project; final report to Congress. Vol. II: Assessments and scientific basis for management options. Davis, CA: University of California, Center for Water and Wildland Resources: 501–512.

Underwood, E.C.; Viers, J.H.; Quinn, J.F.; North, M.P. 2010. Using topography to meet wildlife and fuels treatment objectives in fire-suppressed landscapes. Journal of Environmental Management. 46: 809–819.

Verner, J.; Gutiérrez, R.J.; Gould, G.I., Jr. 1992a. The California spotted owl: general biology and ecological relations. In: Verner, J.; McKelvey, K.S.; Noon, B.R.; Gutiérrez, R.J.; Gould, G.I., Jr.; Beck, T.W., tech. coords. The California spotted owl: a technical assessment of its current status. Gen. Tech. Rep. PSW-GTR-133. Albany, CA: U.S. Department of Agriculture, Forest Service, Pacific Southwest Research Station: 55–77.

Verner, J.; McKelvey, K.S.; Noon, B.R.; Gutiérrez, R.J.; Gould, G.I., Jr.; Beck, T.W. 1992b. Assessment of the current status of the California spotted owl, with recommendations for management. In: Verner, J.; McKelvey, K.S.; Noon, B.R.; Gutiérrez, R.J.; Gould, G.I., Jr.; Beck, T.W., tech. coords. The California spotted owl: a technical assessment of its current status. Gen. Tech. Rep. PSW-GTR-133. Albany, CA: U.S. Department of Agriculture, Forest Service, Pacific Southwest Research Station: 3–26.

Ward, J.P., Jr.; Gutiérrez, R.J.; Noon, B.R. 1998. Habitat selection by northern spotted owls: the consequences of prey selection and distribution. The Condor. 100: 79–92.

Waters, J.R.; Zabel, C.J. 1995. Northern flying squirrel densities in fir forests of northeastern California. Journal of Wildlife Management. 59: 858–866.

Weathers, W.W.; Hodum, P.J.; Blakesley, J.A. 2001. Thermal ecology and ecological energetics of California spotted owls. The Condor. 103: 678–690.

Weatherspoon, C.P.; Husari, S.J.; van Wagtendonk, J.W. 1992. Fire and fuels management in relation to owl habitat in forests of the Sierra Nevada and southern California. In: Verner, J.; McKelvey, K.S.; Noon, B.R.; Gutiérrez, R.J.; Gould, G.I., Jr.; Beck, T.W., tech. coords. The California spotted owl: a technical assessment of its current status. Gen. Tech. Rep. PSW-GTR-133. Albany, CA: U.S. Department of Agriculture, Forest Service, Pacific Southwest Research Station: 247–260.

Weatherspoon, C.P.; Skinner, C.N. 1995. An assessment of factors associated with damage to tree crowns from the 1987 wildfires in northern California. Forest Science. 41: 430–451.

Williams, D.F.; Verner, J.; Sakai, H.F.; Waters, J.R. 1992. General biology of prey species of the California spotted owl. In: Verner, J.; McKelvey, K.S.; Noon, B.R.; Gutiérrez, R.J.; Gould, G.I., Jr.; Beck, T.W., tech. coords. The California spotted owl: a technical assessment of its current status. Gen. Tech. Rep. PSW-GTR-133. Albany, CA: U.S. Department of Agriculture, Forest Service, Pacific Southwest Research Station: 207–221.

Zabel, C.J.; Steger, G.N.; McKelvey, K.S.; Eberlein, G.P.; Noon, B.R.; Verner, J. 1992. Home-range size and habitat-use patterns of California spotted owls in the Sierra Nevada. In: Verner, J.; McKelvey, K.S.; Noon, B.R.; Gutiérrez, R.J.; Gould, G.I., Jr.; Beck, T.W., tech. coords. The California spotted owl: a technical assessment of its current status. Gen. Tech. Rep. PSW-GTR-133. Albany, CA: U.S. Department of Agriculture, Forest Service, Pacific Southwest Research Station: 149–163.

Zabel, C.J.; McKelvey, K.S.; Ward, J.P., Jr. 1995. Influence of primary prey on home-range size and habitat-use patterns of northern spotted owls (*Strix occidentalis caurina*). Canadian Journal of Zoology. 73: 433–439.

Chapter 6: Managing Forests for Wildlife Communities

M. North[1] *and P. Manley*[2]

Introduction

Forest management to maintain native wildlife communities is an important, yet complex objective. The complexities stem from two primary sources: habitat requirements for native species are diverse and span multiple spatial scales and seral stages, and habitat is a species-specific concept making multispecies community response difficult to predict. Given these uncertainties, restoration objectives frequently lack target conditions for the multitude of species that comprise the various vertebrate communities, and monitoring plans fail to integrate across multiple scales and habitats.

Multispecies Habitat Management

Habitat can be defined as the environmental conditions needed to support essential food, resting, and breeding requirements of an individual species (Morrison et al. 2006). Habitat suitability is a function of the degree to which an environment can support these requirements. Detailed habitat requirements are not known for many vertebrate species associated with Sierra Nevada forests. Most habitat models are limited to species of conservation concern, which are often habitat specialists associated with forest conditions that are uncommon or declining in extent. The California spotted owl (*Strix occidentalis occidentalis*), northern goshawk (*Accipiter gentilis*), and Pacific fisher (*Martes pennanti*) are among the highest profile species of concern in the Sierra Nevada, and they are all associated with old-forest elements or structural conditions, such as large trees, snags, and logs, and some areas with high

Summary of Findings

1. It is difficult to predict the effects of forest management on multiple species, which have different habitat requirements and respond to forest conditions at different scales. **Current models for assessing wildlife habitat, such as the California Wildlife-Habitat Relations, should be viewed with caution** as they generally fail to account for the different spatial and temporal scales at which species may respond to forest conditions or assess habitat features other than large trees and canopy cover.

2. For a few species of interest, there is stand-level information on habitat associations, but little information on how to optimize the spatial arrangement of different forest conditions, or how to "knit" the pieces together at the landscape level. In the absence of better information, **a cautious approach is to increase habitat that is currently rare, or underrepresented compared to active-fire forest conditions, avoid creating forest conditions that do not have a historical analog**, and emulate the spatial heterogeneity of forest conditions that would have been created by topography's influence on fire frequency and intensity.

3. **Monitoring may be the best means of overcoming some of these limitations**, if it is rigorously designed and leverages existing inventory and sampling effort.

[1] Research ecologist, U.S. Department of Agriculture, Forest Service, Pacific Southwest Research Station, 1731 Research Park Dr., Davis, CA 95618.

[2] Program manager, U.S. Department of Agriculture, Forest Service, Pacific Southwest Research Station, 60 Nowelo St., Hilo, HI 96720.

Managers may examine what forest conditions currently are rare compared to historical active-fire conditions, and then treat stands to increase underrepresented habitat conditions

canopy closure. To provide habitat for a broad array of species, managers will need to consider other seral conditions and forest structures. For example, some songbirds are strongly associated with shrub patches (Burnett et al. 2009) that have become increasingly rare in the low-light understory of fire-suppressed forests. In addition to old-forest conditions, some habitats (e.g., aspen stands, meadows, open large pine-dominated forests, shrub fields) and some "special habitat elements" (e.g., "defect" trees, downed logs, large snags) have clearly declined in abundance (Bouldin 1999). In the absence of better information, managers may examine what forest conditions currently are rare compared to historical active-fire conditions, and then treat stands to increase underrepresented habitat conditions.

A second concern is that many wildlife species respond to forest conditions at multiple spatial and temporal scales. This suggests that management practices should be based on careful consideration of the amounts and configurations of current and target habitat conditions within landscapes. In many cases, however, potential management impacts on wildlife are examined only at the stand scale or over relatively short timeframes. Temporal considerations can be particularly important because decades of stand development may be needed to create some desired habitat conditions. Management plans should be explicit about maintaining current high-value habitat in sufficient amounts and distribution while at the same time treating other areas more heavily to accelerate development of desired future habitat conditions. For large-scale assessments of landscapes, it is often difficult to determine the optimal size and distribution of different forest conditions that would improve current and future habitat conditions for the local vertebrate community. There are few reference landscapes with active fire regimes, and the spatial configuration of habitat conditions in such landscapes has yet to be examined (fig. 6-1). While research can suggest general principles for landscape-scale wildlife management, such as providing for connectivity and a mosaic of forest conditions (Hilty et al. 2006, Lindenmayer and Fisher 2006, Lindenmayer et al. 2008), specifics are generally lacking and will differ with different species and existing forest conditions. Lacking better information, a prudent approach may be to emulate the variation in forest conditions that could be expected to occur given the influence of local topographic conditions on fire frequency and intensity (North et al. 2010).

Vertebrate Conservation and Fuels Reduction

Fuels reduction commonly focuses on reducing the amount and connectivity of woody material on the forest floor, from the forest floor to the canopy, and across the canopy. Two of the primary challenges associated with reducing the risk of high-intensity wildfire and maintaining native vertebrate species are (1) inadequate

Figure 6-1—Illilouette Basin, Yosemite National Park, which has burned several times since being designated a wildland-fire use area in the 1970s. Note the diversity and complexity of different forest types and conditions resulting in part from different fire severity patterns and changes in edaphic conditions.

tools for characterizing wildlife habitat relationships and assessing impacts of fuels treatments to these habitats, and (2) the inherent conflict between maintaining existing species while changing forest structure and composition.

Currently, models for assessing how different types of treatments affect the wildlife community lack precision. The California Wildlife-Habitat Relationships (CWHR) database is often used to approximate how treatments will alter habitat based on general changes in tree size and canopy cover (Mayer and Laudenslayer 1988). The forest is broadly categorized using the dominant tree size class, and canopy cover is approximated through interpretation of aerial photographs or modeled indirectly with the Forest Vegetation Simulator into broad cover classes (see limitations of this approach in chapter 14 under "Canopy Cover and Closure"). These are rough estimates of a forest's habitat taken at a fixed point in time and do not consider features such as snags, down wood, or understory diversity that are often linked to wildlife use. The CWHR is a set of broad-scale habitat associations and general life history traits for the 694 species in its database that is based largely on expert opinion. Consequently, the use of CWHR for making reliable, project-level predictions on the potential habitat impacts of forest management activities on a wildlife community is limited. In addition, CWHR does not account for area size and landscape context in its habitat designations (George and Zack 2001). Furthermore, tests of CWHR (Block et al. 1994, Laymon 1989, Laymon and Halterman

1989, Purcell et al. 1992) have found high rates of omission (species detected but not listed in CWHR) and commission (species predicted but not present), prompting the authors of one study (Block et al. 1994) to suggest that CWHR not be used "as the sole source of information in land-use decisions." Variation in forest community types (e.g., CALVEG) has also been used to estimate landscape-scale biodiversity, but research suggests it may fail to explain variation in species abundances or account for spatial variability (Cushman et al. 2008, Noon et al. 2003). For some sensitive wildlife species, quantitative models have been developed to examine how treatments may impact habitat quality more explicitly (e.g., Thompson et al. 2011). However, the use of such models to infer impacts on the entire vertebrate community should be viewed with caution. Recent assessments of the effectiveness of "keystone," "umbrella," "indicator," "top predator," and "flagship" species suggest that management activities that are based on such surrogate species generally fail to capture the needs of the ecosystem's broader array of species (Caro 2010, Sergio et al. 2008).

Fuels treatments alter habitat conditions for wildlife species that currently occupy the treatment area, benefiting some but reducing habitat quality for others (Stephens et al., in press). Managers should be cautious when applying prescriptions that result in the simplification and homogenization of stand structures, creating relatively novel habitat conditions to which few native vertebrate species are adapted. These include significantly reducing or eliminating crown overlap, vertical canopy complexity, and small tree and understory cover (fig. 6-2). Fuels reduction that removes all understory cover, sometimes called "clearcutting from below,"

Assessments of the effectiveness of "keystone," "umbrella," "indicator," "top predator," and "flagship" species suggest that management activities that are based on such surrogate species generally fail to capture the needs of the ecosystem's broader array of species.

Figure 6-2—Example of a fuels treatment that removes all understory and ladder fuels, a condition sometimes referred to as a "clearcut from below."

Pat Manley

may eliminate habitat for many species of the vertebrate community. For example, a diverse array of understory shrubs may serve a variety of ecological functions including the provision of wildlife forage and protective cover, soil stabilization, nitrogen fixation, barriers to invasive plant establishment, and sources of nectar for pollinators. Yet because of their potential role as a fuel and their competition with tree seedlings, some treatments specifically strive to dramatically reduce or eliminate shrub cover. Eliminating these conditions probably moderately increases forest resistance to crown fire and may have value close to communities and in strategic locations. However models suggest retaining these stand features may not significantly increase high-severity fire risk if care is taken to create vertical diversity in vegetation cover without creating ladder fuels. An alternative approach in fuels reduction projects would be to manage for wildlife habitat heterogeneity: (1) increase the frequency of underrepresented habitat conditions (e.g., late-seral structures, canopy gaps, open, low-density forests, rare or uncommon tree and shrub species), (2) promote variable forest conditions based on natural topography and fire regimes, and (3) facilitate both overstory and understory vegetation diversity.

Multiscale Monitoring

Effective monitoring is needed to understand the complex response of wildlife communities to forest management. There is a perception that resources and expertise are too limited to initiate a multispecies, multiscale monitoring program. Manley et al. (2006), however, introduced a protocol to serve as a consistent and efficient method for obtaining basic presence/absence and habitat data for several species at sites using a probabilistic sample. The Multiple Species Inventory and Monitoring (MSIM) protocol is designed to be implemented in association with Forest Inventory and Analysis grid points. The protocol uses a base monitoring approach on which national forests can build to meet their specific monitoring needs with the greatest efficiency of effort and cost. The MSIM protocol could be used as a basis for developing plans to monitor treatments following U.S. Forest Service General Technical Report PSW-GTR 220 "An Ecosystem Management Strategy for Sierran Mixed-Conifer Forests" (North et al 2009) concepts and to assess how management strategies may better meet desired conditions.

References

Block, W.M.; Morrison, M.L.; Verner, J.; Manley, P.N. 1994. Assessing wildlife-habitat-relationships models: a case study with California oak woodlands. Wildlife Society Bulletin. 22: 549–561.

Bouldin, J. 1999. Twentieth-century changes in forests of the Sierra Nevada, California. Davis, CA: University of California, Davis. 222 p. Ph.D. dissertation.

Burnett, R.; Jongsomjit, D.; Stralberg, D. 2009. Avian monitoring in the Lassen and Plumas National Forest: 2008 annual report. Point Reyes Bird Observatory Contribution. 1684: 104–186.

Caro, T. 2010. Conservation by proxy: indicator, umbrella, keystone, flagship, and other surrogate species. Washington, DC: Island Press. 374 p.

Cushman, S.A.; McKelvey, K.S.; Flather, C.H.; McGarigal, K. 2008. Do forest community types provide a sufficient basis to evaluate biological diversity? Frontiers in Ecology and the Environment. 6: 13–17.

George, T.L.; Zack, S. 2001. Spatial and temporal considerations in restoring habitat for wildlife. Restoration Ecology. 9: 272–279.

Hilty, J.; Lidicker, W.Z., Jr.; Merenlender, A.; Dobson, A.P. 2006. Corridor ecology: the science and practice of linking landscapes for biodiversity conservation. Washington, DC: Island Press. 344 p.

Laymon, S.A. 1989. A test of the California wildlife-habitat relationship system for breeding birds in valley-foothill riparian habitat. In: Abell, D.L., tech. coord. Proceedings of the California riparian systems conference: protection, management, and restoration for the 1990s. Gen. Tech. Rep. PSW-GTR-110. Berkeley, CA: U.S. Department of Agriculture, Forest Service, Pacific Southwest Forest and Range Experiment Station: 307–313.

Laymon, S.A.; Halterman, M.D. 1989. A proposed habitat management plan for yellow-billed cuckoos in California. In: Abell, D.L., tech. coord. Proceedings of the California riparian systems conference: protection, management, and restoration for the 1990s. Gen. Tech. Rep. PSW-GTR-110. Berkeley, CA: U.S. Department of Agriculture, Forest Service, Pacific Southwest Forest and Range Experiment Station: 272–277.

Lindenmayer, D.B.; Fischer, J. 2006. Landscape change and habitat fragmentation. Washington, DC: Island Press. 352 p.

Lindenmayer, D.; Hobbs, R.J.; Montague–Drake, R.; Alexandra, J., Bennett, A.; Burgman, M.; Cale, P.; Calhoun, A.; Cramer, V.; Cullen, P.; Driscoll, D.; Fahrig, L.; Fisher, J.; Franklin, J.; Haila, Y.; Hunter, M.; Gibbons, P.; Lake, S.; Luck, G.; MacGregor, C.; McIntyre, S.; Mac Nally, R.; Manning, A.; Miller, J.; Mooney, H.; Noss, R.; Possingham, H.; Saunders, D.; Schmiegelow, F.; Scott, M.; Simberloff, D.; Sisk, T.; Tabor, G.; Walker, B.; Wiens, J.; Woinarski, J.; Zavaleta, E. 2008. A checklist for ecological management of landscapes for conservation. Ecology Letters. 11: 78–91.

Manley, P.N.; Van Horne, B.; Roth, J.K.; Zielinski, W.J.; McKenzie, M.M.; Weller, T.J.; Weckerly, F.W.; Vojta, C. 2006. Multiple species inventory and monitoring technical guide. Gen. Tech. Rep. WO-73. Washington, DC: U.S. Department of Agriculture, Forest Service, Washington Office. 204 p.

Mayer, K.E.; Laudenslayer, W.F. 1988. Guide to wildlife habitats of California. Sacramento, CA: State of California, Resources Agency, Department of Fish and Game. 166 p.

Morrison, M.; Marcot B.G.; Mannan, R.W. 2006. Wildlife-habitat relationships: concepts and applications. Washington, DC: Island Press. 435 p.

Noon, B.; Murphy, D.; Beissinger, S.; Shaffer, M.; Dellasala, D. 2003. Conservation planning for U.S. national forests: conducting comprehensive biodiversity assessments. Bioscience. 53.

North, M.; Stine, P.; O'Hara, K.; Zielinski, W.; Stephens, S. 2009. An ecosystem management strategy for Sierran mixed-conifer forests. 2nd printing, with addendum. Gen. Tech. Rep. PSW-GTR-220. Albany, CA: U.S. Department of Agriculture, Forest Service, Pacific Southwest Research Station. 49 p.

North, M.; Stine, P.; Zielinski, W.; O'Hara, K.; Stephens, S. 2010. Harnessing fire for wildlife. The Wildlife Professional. 4: 30–33.

Purcell, K.L.; Hejl, S.J.; Larson, T.A. 1992. Evaluating avian-habitat relationships models in mixed-conifer forests of the Sierra Nevada. Transactions of the Western Section of the Wildlife Society. 28: 120–136.

Stephens, S.L.; McIver, J.D.; Boerner, R.E.J.; Fettig, C.J; Fontaine, J.B.; Hartsough, B.R.; Kennedy, P.; Schwilk, D.W. [In press]. Effects of forest fuel reduction treatments in the United States. BioScience.

Sergio, F.; Caro, T.; Brown, D.; Clucas, B.; Hunter, J.; Ketchum, J.; McHugh, K.; Hiraldo, F. 2008. Top predators as conservation tools: ecological rationale, assumptions and efficacy. Annual Review of Ecology, Evolution, and Systematics. 39: 1–19.

Thompson, C.M.; Zielinski, W.J.; Purcel, K.L. 2011. The use of landscape trajectory analysis to evaluate management risks: a case study with the Pacific fisher in the Sierra National Forest. Journal of Wildlife Management. 75: 1164–1176.

Chapter 7: Developing Collaboration and Cooperation

G. Bartlett[1]

Introduction

Good forestry practices require onsite flexibility. A core concept in U.S. Forest Service General Technical Report PSW-GTR-220 "An Ecosystem Management Strategy for Sierran Mixed-Conifer Forests" (North et al. 2009) is that management treatments and thinning intensity should differ depending on local forest conditions and topographic location. In the absence of restricted forestry practices (e.g., stream exclusion zones, upper diameters for thinning, etc.), managers have to effectively communicate where and how different treatment decisions will be made. Using GTR 220 concepts requires effective outreach and project transparency. No single blueprint exists to achieve cooperation and trust as social context differs between projects, national forests, and stakeholders involved.

The objective of this chapter is to provide an example and analysis of a successful collaboration that may help projects find their own path to building public cooperation. Other forest management projects many not need professional mediation, yet some of the principles discussed here may be of value in any project involving public outreach. This chapter's example is a summary of how mediation and group collaboration led to settlement of one of the more litigated forest management projects in the Sierra Nevada—fuels treatments around the Dinkey Creek area on the Sierra National Forest.

For 15 years, conflict and litigation had stalled management practices on the Kings River project, which contains habitat used by a subpopulation of fisher. In 2009, with the help of an outside mediator, the Sierra National Forest Project Planning Forum successfully developed a proposed 5,000-ac (2023-ha) project—Dinkey Creek North and South based on GTR 220's conceptual framework. Subsequent to the successful project collaboration, the Sierra National Forest received significant Collaborative Forest Landscape Restoration funding. Currently, the Sierra National Forest is proceeding with the environmental analysis, and is expanding the collaborative group's membership and project area.

Dinkey Project History

In 2007, the Center for Collaborative Policy, a program of California State University, Sacramento, that provides impartial mediation services, conducted an assessment of the mediation potential of several forest management projects, including

---

[1] Staff mediator, Center for Collaborative Policy, 815 S Street., 1st floor, Sacramento State University, Sacramento, CA 95811.

Summary of Findings

1. **Collaboration involves five stages: assessment, organization, education, negotiation, and implementation:** Assessing the issues, organizing the collaborative group, and educating stakeholders about each other's interests and technical issues lay the foundation for negotiation. During negotiation, the parties work through all the issues, building agreements over time. Stakeholders then monitor the project and adapt during implementation.

2. **Early engagement of a broad range of participants is essential to robust agreements:** For stakeholders to have meaningful dialogue and an effect on issues, stakeholders need to engage early in project planning. Engaging a broad range of stakeholder participants can create a project that balances fire, wildlife, and silviculture perspectives, making final agreements more robust.

3. **Site visits support decisionmaking and agreements:** Site visits illustrate existing variability and contribute to clarifying project objectives. Site visits help ground stakeholder discussion over desired conditions, providing a specific context in which decisions need to be made rather than a principled argument over management practices.

4. **An impartial mediator can promote trust and problemsolving:** The mediator's essential role is to organize the process, create trust, normalize conflict, develop a problemsolving environment, manage the timeframe, and orient the group to reach outcomes. A key element to trust building is the mediator's independence and ability to speak to all parties confidentially.

Kings River, in the Southern Sierra Nevada. At that time, the center did not recommend the parties meet to resolve project issues because the conditions necessary for success were not present. The center did, however, make some recommendations to correct these conditions. The first recommendation was for the parties to engage in joint factfinding to establish consensus on the scientific foundations from which projects could be developed. Joint factfinding is a process in which stakeholders engage with scientific experts to frame research questions and interpret research results (Ehrman and Stinson 1999, Karl et al. 2007). In the southern Sierra projects, stakeholders often cited conflicting studies to justify their proposed management recommendations. As a result, the Forest was "paralyzed by science." The center also recommended that the Sierra National Forest engage the public early in any project development. During the assessment, stakeholders complained that they only learned about projects once they were in such late stages of development that the Forest Service did not have flexibility to modify or significantly change the project because of the professional and resource investment, which had already occurred.

Between the 2007 assessment and March 2009, a group of Forest Service and university scientists developed GTR 220 (North et al. 2009) summarizing recent research on forest and fire ecology, ecosystem restoration, silviculture, and wildlife species (particularly the Pacific fisher) (*Martes pennanti*) in the Sierra Nevada. There was substantial research relevant to forest management that had been completed since the last major summary of Sierra Nevada science (SNEP 1996), but much of it was technical and scattered among many different journals. Using the North et al. (2009) paper as a starting point for finding scientific common ground, the U.S. Institute for Environmental Conflict Resolution invited the Center for Collaborative Policy to speak with the parties and consider organizing a collaborative effort to develop a project.

Mediator's Role

The center appointed a mediator to the project with the assigned task of facilitating meetings and being impartial to the substance or content of outcomes. The mediator's essential role was to organize the process, create trust, normalize the conflict, develop a problemsolving environment, manage the timeframe, and orient the group to reach outcomes. A key element to building trust was the condition that the mediator had the planning forum's permission to speak confidentially with all of the participants to discuss their interests, concerns, and negotiation strategies. In turn, participants were able to call the mediator when they were upset or worried about something. This trust helped the parties overcome hurdles and allowed the mediator to reframe conflict as a problem to be solved. For example, early in the process, during the development of one of the signature documents, the mediator was able to combine significant comments from several stakeholders into one document, getting permission from several key parties to share it as a straw proposal for group consideration. She never disclosed who submitted comments, and one person's contribution might have been viewed as controversial within the person's organization. However, this version was substantially better and the parties' accepted it without question, largely because the draft better reflected the intent they wanted to convey.

Five Stages of Collaboration

As practiced by the center, collaborative policymaking typically involves five stages: assessment, organization, education, negotiation, and implementation (table 7-1). The Dinkey collaborative went through these stages and is now in the implementation process. The first three stages lay the foundation for getting to negotiation. In the assessment stage, the mediator meets with the parties to determine whether they would like to negotiate and if they have enough interests in common to support a negotiated outcome. In this stage, it is important to identify participants willing to collaborate and consider others' perspectives. Next the organizational structure is developed. The mediator works with the parties to set the agenda and a decisionmaking rule for the collaborative process, and to define how agreements and outcomes will link to agency decisionmaking. In the third stage, education, the parties develop a common understanding of the project's scientific and technical issues, and also the interests and goals of each of the interest groups.

During negotiations, the parties first identify all the key issues that need to be addressed. Then the group works through the issues, building agreements over time. The parties' interests are used to develop criteria for decisionmaking. As areas of potential disagreement emerge, they are put on the table and treated as issues that the parties need to resolve. During implementation, stakeholders initiate and monitor the project, modifying the approach as data indicate.

Steps That Facilitated Collaboration for the Dinkey Project

- **Include a broad range of participants.** The initial inclination was for the Forest Service to meet with a singular environmental organization that had engaged on the original larger Kings River project. However, the success of the process was ultimately rooted in having a diversity of perspectives represented. For each "small" agreement, stakeholders had to grapple with balancing fire, wildlife, and silviculture perspectives, a process that made final agreements more robust. Expanding participation diffused tensions that had developed over the long history of the conflict and litigation. Additional parties brought expertise, problemsolving, and humor.

- **Establish a conceptual framework, purpose and need, and long-term desired condition.** There is often a tendency to immediately start evaluating the project without first finding common ground on current forest conditions and long-term objectives. General Technical Report 220 helped establish a conceptual framework around which the purpose and need was developed.

The parties first identify all the key issues that need to be addressed. The parties' interests are used to develop criteria for decisionmaking. As areas of potential disagreement emerge, they are put on the table and treated as issues that the parties need to resolve.

Table 7-1—Progressive steps in collaborative decisionmaking

Five stages of collaborative decisionmaking on public issues				
Assessment/planning	Organization	Education	Negotiation/ resolution	Implementation
Conflict analysis and assessment • Do the parties want to negotiate? • Are the issues negotiable? Can the parties get a better deal elsewhere? What are the chances for success? Identify: • What is the problem • Mission goals • Range of issues to be addressed • Preliminary process design Representation issues (stakeholder analysis): • Who are the dealmakers and dealbreakers? • What groups should be represented? • Who can legitimately speak for each group? Assess adequacy of staffing: • Process • Policy • Administrative Assess adequacy of commitment: • Time • Financial resources	Training in interest-based collaboration Meeting logistics and schedule Settle representation issue Settle mission goals Develop ground rules: • Decisionmaking • Press/observers • Roles/responsibilities • Other Dealbreaker analysis Determine ongoing communication and accountability systems with: • Constituents • Elected/appointed boards • General public • Other important players Agenda setting for education phase: • Initial discussion of issues • Initial issue framework Finalize process design	Review history, context, and legal/statutory framework Develop common understanding of problem and issues Thorough understanding of one's interests and adversaries' interests Thorough understanding of most likely alternatives to a negotiated agreement Develop common information base: • What information do we have? • What portion of that information is accepted by all? • What new information is needed and how to get it (data gaps) Educate constituency to issues and interests Develop framework for negotiation, including range and order of issues to be addressed	Turn interests into decisionmaking criteria Option generation/ brainstorming Inventing without deciding Developing/refining trial balloons Linking and packaging agreements Agreements in principle Agreements in detail If get stuck: • Revisit underlying interests • Revisit alternatives to a negotiated agreeement Constant feedback from one's constituency Develop agreements with: • Quid pro quo linkages • Assurances for mutual commitments	Linking agreements to external decisionmaking Monitoring implementation to assure compliance and respond to changing conditions
Key challenges by stage				
Can problem be successfully addressed through negotiation? Not excluding any party that could undermine negotiated agreements	Determining how group makes its decisions	Agreeing to devote sufficient time to this stage Postponing judgment to learn about other parties' interests	Reconciling conflicting interests Bringing constituents along Development of assurances	A test of how well implementation was integrated into the agreement

Determining desired future conditions involved evaluating current conditions using forest measurement data, discussion, and selection of desired future conditions, and developing management practices to get there. Given the time commitment and expertise required, a subcommittee was formed and tasked with developing recommendations to bring back to the full group.

- **Scientific experts served as technical resources during meetings.** In the organization phase, the mediator vetted scientists with relevant expertise with each of the stakeholders who were going to participate in the collaborative planning forum. The planning forum participants essentially approved each technical expert. The technical experts participated in most planning forum meetings: they were able to answer scientific questions immediately, keeping the workflow and dialogue moving. This proved invaluable to moving forward and reaching agreements. In cases where questions arose requiring analytical work, the scientists were able to clarify the analytical questions first hand and then conduct analytical work or provide data with a clear understanding of what was needed.

> The parties were unable to reach agreement on the definition of forest health... [However, they] were still able to negotiate the details of the Dinkey project by dealing with the specifics of the particular project rather than the philosophy or values around forest health.

- **Some intractable issues moved forward without complete consensus.** For example, the parties were unable to reach agreement on the definition of forest health because they had different philosophical approaches to forest management. However, the parties were still able to negotiate the details of the Dinkey project by dealing with the specifics of the particular project rather than the philosophy or values around forest health. The negotiations forced parties to evolve from individuals challenging each other to a collaborative team seeking solutions.

- **Site visits used to develop decision priorities and the initial mark.** The subcommittee went out into the field and looked at parts of the project area. After the site visit, the group developed a set of decision priorities to clarify how project objectives varied with location (e.g., forest in defense zones versus riparian areas). This priorities document continued to evolve and serve as the repository for agreements. Working with the silviculturists, the group developed targets that were translated into preliminary marking guidelines. After stands in different priority zones were marked, the group and the GTR authors visited the sites and discussed the mark and the reasoning used to make decisions. This field visit was particularly useful for grounding discussions over desired conditions, providing a specific context in which decisions needed to be made rather than a principled argument over management practices.

Additional Steps for Successful Collaboration and Cooperation

- **Timely engagement.** For stakeholders to have meaningful dialogue and an effect on issues, the Forest Service needs to engage potential participants early in project planning. While stakeholders can be nimble, in cases of low trust and high conflict, having adequate time is essential for conflict resolution. Working with a stakeholder group, a deliberative initial pace can be frustrating, but is often needed to build the foundation for long-term collaboration and may potentially reduce project approval time during the environmental analysis and review.

- **Building trust.** Many issues can come up to derail collaboration, but one of the most common is starting off with the most difficult and contentious issues first. In the long-term it may be more productive to first build general agreement on ecological principles. For example, does the group agree that low-intensity fire is a critical ecological process that management actions should attempt to mimic where possible? General agreements on ecological principles tied to topographic feature can help determine if the parties share concepts for current and future desired conditions for the planning landscape. If there is conceptual agreement, do the parties also understand and trust the data being used to examine treatment levels and impacts to resources. Information used to understand the landscape, descriptions of existing conditions, historical reference conditions, and estimates of effects of actions (alternatives, no action) taken to achieve desired conditions need to be supported by the group. Next, where possible (i.e., outside defense zones), the planning process and marking prescriptions should balance and move multiple objectives forward (e.g., fuels reduction, ecosystem restoration, and provision of wildlife habitat) rather than using single or primary objectives for different landscape locations. Finally, project monitoring is essential to demonstrating a commitment to understanding what worked and what did not. Greater management flexibility will only improve forest conditions if it commits to assessing and adapting from what it learns. As climate changes, all management practices will be experimental. Monitoring is essential to building trust in an uncertain future.

Many issues can come up to derail collaboration, but one of the most common is starting off with the most difficult and contentious issues first. In the long-term it may be more productive to first build general agreement on ecological principles.

- **Testing implementation.** Heterogeneity marking is less about right or wrong and more about moving in a new direction. Sharing ideas, trying different approaches, and making mistakes will be part of developing a new approach. The marking crew leader and crews should understand the design features and preliminarily mark several acres to test design measures as they are transferred to the ground. The collaborative group should review this phase with the Forest Service since the marking crews are the people who will actually cover all the ground in the project area.

- **Patience.** These collaborative projects may initially require more time and resources before a particular method or "tool box" application is developed. One potential benefit would be to try GTR 220-based collaboration in several more areas and then analyze commonalities across all the projects. This would help fine tune procedures and provide insights that could streamline project development efforts and develop a set of tools that might be applicable in other landscapes.

References

Ehrman, J.R.; Stinson, B.L. 1999. Joint fact-finding and the use of technical experts. In: Susskind, L.; McKearnan, S.; Thomas-Larmer, J., eds. The Consensus Building Handbook. Thousand Oaks, CA: Sage Publications: 375–398.

Karl, H.A.; Susskind, L.E.; Wallace, K.H. 2007. A dialogue, not a diatribe: effective integration of science and policy through joint fact finding. Environment. 49: 20–34.

North, M.; Stine, P.; O'Hara, K.; Zielinski, W.; Stephens, S. 2009. An ecosystem management strategy for Sierran mixed-conifer forests. 2nd printing, with addendum. Gen. Tech. Rep. PSW-GTR-220. Albany, CA: U.S. Department of Agriculture, Forest Service, Pacific Southwest Research Station. 49 p.

Sierra Nevada Ecosystem Project [SNEP]. 1996. Sierra Nevada Ecosystem Project: final report to Congress. Davis, CA: University of California, Davis Centers for Water and Wildland Resources. Volumes 1–4.

Chapter 8: Using GTR 220 to Build Stakeholder Collaboration

C. Thomas[1]

Introduction

Since 2008, Sierra Forest Legacy, a nonprofit conservation organization, has increased its participation in the design of projects on national forest lands in the Sierra Nevada. Our interest has been to engage scientists, managers, and other stakeholders in the design of projects that integrate the best available scientific information. Our second interest has been to explore the possibilities for "up-front" collaboration between these parties to bridge disagreements over the scope of natural resource impacts. We have observed, and, in some cases, actively participated in, the application of principles outlined in U.S. Forest Service General Technical Report GTR 220, "An Ecosystem Management Strategy for Sierran Mixed-Conifer Forests," (North et al. 2009) in approximately 12 project-level planning efforts since its 2009 publication. These projects included various levels of collaborative efforts between land managers, scientists, and stakeholders grounded in GTR 220 principles. Previously, questions about "whose science," where to take risks, and with what resources have sometimes been settled in the courtroom. The value of GTR 220 for all groups is its provision of a conceptual model to use as a starting point for fresh dialog after a decade of conflict.

Summary of Findings

1. **GTR 220 provides a conceptual model to use as a starting point for new dialog about forest management.** Exploring the principles of GTR 220 in a collaborative setting provides the basis for joint fact finding and mutual learning.

2. **Future applications of GTR 220 should strive to more fully address wildlife ecology at the microsite, stand, home range and landscape scales.**

3. **Successful GTR 220 application may require capacity changes** such as organized information exchange, standardized short- and long-term monitoring, and facilitating stakeholder group participation.

Improved Communication

Because GTR 220 is not prescriptive, practitioners have shared ideas, mostly in field settings, about how to identify, mark, and describe desired microsite and project-level heterogeneity. This information exchange has been crucial as the flow of new research on fisher (*Martes pennanti*) rest sites, fire ecology, topographical influences, climate change effects, carbon storage, and pest dynamics has significantly accelerated. Through collaborative factfinding, diverse interests can explore and expand a communal knowledge base and support adaptive management and incorporation of new information while conducting ongoing restoration efforts.

---

[1] Executive Director, Sierra Forest Legacy, P.O. Box 244, Garden Valley, CA 95633.

There is a marked improvement in project planning that is building stronger relationships, more trust, and improved projects.

The social implications of using GTR 220 are also significant. There is now more emphasis on interdisciplinary team integration, stakeholder involvement, and collaboration in project design. In project planning, where GTR 220 is a centerpiece, it is not uncommon to find conservation groups, scientists, mill owners, Forest Service staff, and others discussing protection of wildlife trees, clumping strategies and variable density, snag retention, oak structural decadence, the importance of shrub species, and size of openings for pine regeneration. There is a marked improvement in project planning that is building stronger relationships, more trust, and improved projects. While the GTR 220 approach is still a work in progress with no pat formulas for success and little to judge yet in terms of monitored outcomes, it suggests intensive, science-based collaboration has a future in project and landscape planning. There is a growing body of scientific knowledge, significant experience, and a deep interest in restoring the Sierra mixed-conifer forests that is driving a stronger concept of sustainability.

Sustainability

Questions regarding the sustainability of natural resources have been at the core of these conflicts in a period where stakeholders and managers debated the relative merits of proposed treatments affecting fire behavior, forest health, and wildlife in the Sierra Nevada. Sustainability has often been conceived as a "three-legged stool" (fig. 8-1) suggesting that social and economic issues exist outside of an ecological foundation (e.g., Dawe and Ryan 2003). Weak sustainability can result in local economy boom-and-bust cycles, weakened social structures, and damaged landscapes. In contrast, strong sustainability (Hart 1998) defines a much closer connection between our socioeconomic activities and the environment—a vision where

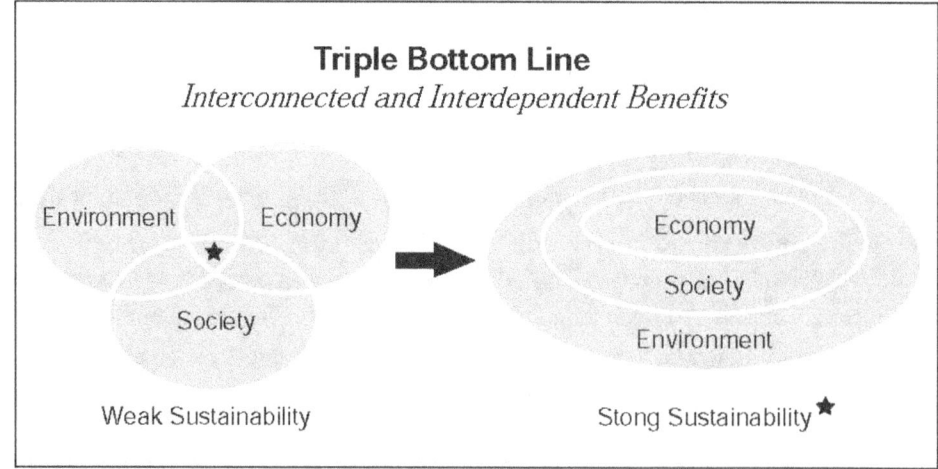

Figure 8-1—Schematics of weak and strong sustainability concepts. (Adapted from Hart 1998.)

economic activities, communities and society are based within and supported by the environment. Callicott and Mumford (1998) further refined the connection between human use of resources and the ecosystem by defining ecological sustainability "as meeting human needs without compromising the health of ecosystems." General Technical Report 220 provides a foundation for discussing the ecological needs of a healthy mixed-conifer ecosystem and our sustainable interaction with this environment.

Perceived Problems

One objection to the use of GTR 220 is the additional time and costs associated with designing and marking ecologically appropriate and more complicated prescriptions. When taking a holistic approach, the success rate of cooperatively designed projects in achieving agreed-upon goals should be tracked over time so this monitoring can support improved approaches. While these projects do develop slowly, they may still come out ahead when compared to projects that are appealed or litigated.

Challenges

We believe wildlife ecology, in a broad sense, should be expanded in future applications of GTR 220. Concerns about wildlife need to be extended beyond Pacific fisher to include principles for sustaining the whole wildlife community in these landscapes through ongoing restoration efforts. Designing projects that sustain key attributes associated with occupancy was identified as a future research need in the 2009 publication (North et al., p. 32) and represents a fundamental aspect of wildlife conservation. Biodiversity protection and ecological resilience are at the heart of Sierra Nevada restoration. This linkage is supported in a recent synthesis on forests and climate change by the United Nations' Convention on Biodiversity and co-authored by the U.S. Forest Service: "The available scientific evidence strongly supports the conclusion that the capacity of forests to resist change, or to recover from disturbance, is dependent on biodiversity at multiple scales" (Thompson et al. 2009). Key concepts that foster biodiversity, including promoting landscape connectivity, heterogeneity, and reducing human impacts, need to be addressed in landscape- and project-level planning.

Future Directions

For successful collaboration to continue in the Sierra Nevada, we believe three principle capacity issues need to be addressed: organized information exchange, standardized short- and long-term monitoring, and stakeholder group capacity to

At present, there are multiple projects based on GTR 220 concepts, yet no centralized forum for exchanging information and learning from other projects.

meaningfully participate. At present, there are multiple projects based on GTR 220 concepts, yet no centralized forum for exchanging information and learning from other projects. The region might consider establishing a Web site, newsletter, or workshops to support expanded use of GTR 220 in planning and design efforts across the Sierra Nevada. Another approach might be a Web-based "living" seminar to support information exchange for practitioners.

A second concern is the need for monitoring to understand the impacts of these new management practices on species and ecosystems. Monitoring of forest stands is necessary to understand how the treatments alter stand conditions and how wildlife responds. Monitoring protocols that build on existing inventory and assessment approaches (i.e., Manley et al. 2006) may be the most efficient means to develop monitoring plans. Effective monitoring plans need to integrate the results from multiple scales and should feed into a decision-support framework for implementing adaptive management in a transparent and collaborative manner.

The third concern can be best addressed by Forest Service support for ongoing facilitation services, collaboration with the University of California, and other institutions that can offer scientific expertise and exploring foundation interest in capacity building within stakeholder groups.

For many of the GTR 220 principles to be fully implemented, fire will have to become more widely used as an ecological tool. We encourage establishing regional direction that promotes returning fire as a key component of forest restoration. This would include appropriate staffing at the forest and district levels, public education, collaboration with air quality regulators, and strong commitments to the use of managed fire.

References

Callicott, J.B.; Mumford, K. 1997. Ecological sustainability as a conservation concept. Conservation Biology. 11: 32–40.

Dawe, N.K.; Ryan, K.L. 2003. The faulty three-legged-stool model of sustainable development. Conservation Biology. 17: 1458–1460.

Hart, M. 1998. Triple bottom line sustainability graphic. From Sustainable Community Indicators Trainer's Workshop, Courtesy of Maureen Hart, Hart Environmental Data, and U.S. Environmental Protection Agency Office of Sustainable Ecosystems and Communities. http://www.sustainablemeasures.com. (September 15, 2011).

Manley, P.N.; Van Horne, B.; Roth, J.K.; Zielinski, W.J.; McKenzie, M.M.; Weller, T.J.; Weckerly, F.W.; Vojta, C. 2006. Multiple species inventory and monitoring technical guide. Gen. Tech. Rep. WO-73. Washington, DC: U.S. Department of Agriculture, Forest Service, Washington Office. 204 p.

North, M.; Stine, P.; O'Hara, K.; Zielinski, W.; Stephens, S. 2009. An ecosystem management strategy for Sierran mixed-conifer forests. 2nd printing, with addendum. Gen. Tech. Rep. PSW-GTR-220. Albany, CA: U.S. Department of Agriculture, Forest Service, Pacific Southwest Research Station. 49 p.

Thompson, I.; Mackey, B.; McNulty, S.; Mosseler, A. 2009. Forest resilience, biodiversity, and climate change. A synthesis of the biodiversity/resilience/stability relationship in forest ecosystems. Secretariat of the Convention on Biological Diversity, Montreal. Technical Series no. 43. 67 p.

Chapter 9: Marking and Assessing Forest Heterogeneity

M. North[1] and J. Sherlock[2]

Introduction

Marking guidelines commonly use stocking level, crown class, and species preferences to meet management objectives. Traditionally, these guidelines were applied across the extent of the stand. Current marking guidelines are more flexible, responding to within-stand variability with different stocking level, crown class, and species preference guidelines in response to fine-scale variability in forest structure and composition. By varying marking guidelines within stands, managers can meet potentially conflicting prescription objectives such as reducing crown bulk density while maintaining an average target canopy cover (Sherlock 2007). In this chapter, we discuss marking guidelines that may help explicitly implement a fine-scale response to within-stand variability and provide ways of measuring and assessing posttreatment heterogeneity. The emphasis in U.S. Forest Service General Technical Report PSW-GTR-220 "An Ecosystem Management Strategy for Sierran Mixed-Conifer Forests" (North et al. 2009) is still on using topography to help vary treatments, but silviculturists also need to respond to the stand conditions they have to work with.

In forests with frequent, low-intensity fire regimes, fine-scale heterogeneity makes it difficult to identify and demarcate stands ("group(s) of trees and associated vegetation having similar structures and growing under similar soil and climatic conditions" [Oliver and Larson 1996]). Structure analysis at the Teakettle Experimental Forest found that mixed conifer was made up of three

[1] Research ecologist, U.S. Department of Agriculture, Forest Service, Pacific Southwest Research Station, 1731 Research Park Dr., Davis, CA 95618.

[2] Assistant regional silviculturist, U.S. Department of Agriculture, Forest Service, Pacific Southwest Region, 1323 Club Dr., Vallejo, CA 94592.

Summary of Findings

1. **GTR 220 suggests creating three general patch conditions: tree groups, gaps, and a matrix with a low density of large, preferably pine, trees.** The relative proportion of these three patch conditions may change with topographic position and in response to the forest conditions managers have to work with.

2. **It may help marking crews to first identify tree groups and gaps as anchor points around which to mark the remainder of the treatment area.** Reconstruction studies suggest most tree groups and gaps were 0.1 to 0.5 ac (0.04 to 0.2 ha). It may be most difficult to develop prescriptions and mark stands lacking large legacy trees or that have fairly uniform spacing.

3. **The Forest Vegetation Simulator (FVS) and stand exam plots may be used to assess forest heterogeneity** by classing plots by patch type, using the "process plots as stands" option and then comparing the mean and coefficient of variation between all plots and plots by patch type. Details are provided on using "Suppose" within FVS to model current and future conditions, and outputting results to Excel® to calculate the coefficient of variation.

dominant vegetation conditions: tree groups, gaps, and shrub patches. An average "stand" in Teakettle's mixed-conifer forest supports about 70 percent of the stand area in tree groups or scattered large trees, 16 percent in gaps, and 14 percent in shrub patches (North et al. 2002). Teakettle studies also found that ecological processes were best understood at this patch scale, before and after fuels reduction treatments were applied (Ma et al. 2010, North and Chen 2005, Wayman and North 2007, Zald et al. 2008). These patches differed in size but most were between 0.02 to 0.3 ac, fitting the general patch size pattern noted by Knapp et al. (chapter 12). For ecological restoration and the provision of habitat and microclimate variability, marking and measuring forest structure at finer patch scales may be an important complement to stand average assessments.

Within stands, GTR 220 describes three general conditions: (1) high-density, closed-canopy groups of trees; (2) open gaps; and (3) a matrix of low-density areas dominated by large, preferably pine, trees.

General Marking Suggestions

Within stands, GTR 220 describes three general conditions: (1) high-density, closed-canopy groups of trees; (2) open gaps; and (3) a matrix of low-density areas dominated by large, preferably pine, trees. These three conditions were also found in a recent meta-analysis of all studies of tree patterns in fire-frequent forests of western North America (Larson and Churchill 2012). With these conditions, one approach to marking might be to start with the areas that most easily fit either a group or gap as anchor points. Both groups and gaps could have a range of sizes anywhere from 0.1 to 1.0 ac (0.04 to 0.4 ha), but reconstructions suggest that before fire suppression, size more commonly ranged from 0.1 to 0.5 ac (0.04 to 0.2 ha).

If a stand lacks gaps, the goal in creating them is to produce a high-light environment favoring both regeneration of shade-intolerant trees and some shrub patches. Areas currently lacking pine, and fir groups with evidence of root disease, could be recognized as priority locations for gaps. Some gaps may be created by enlarging existing openings or low-density areas, particularly if the higher light environment may benefit a struggling shade-intolerant such as a remnant black oak (*Quercus kelloggii* Newberry). Gaps may occasionally include a large pine that would act as a seed source. If a tree were left in a gap, it would ideally be located near the edge or the northern end of the opening to maximize the amount of light available to regenerating pines in the remaining area. To increase light, the gap edge may also be "feathered" by thinning trees, particularly those on the gap's southern edge. Groups of tree may be identified by focusing on the attributes that make them potential wildlife habitat such as the presence of large, old trees and higher levels of canopy closure. Particular priority for retaining a group is when it has additional attributes that may enhance habitat value such as broken stems, evidence of heart rot organisms, mistletoe brooms, etc. (see defect tree section in chapter 14 and the appendix). The size and shape of groups should depend on obvious breaks in composition or size of trees in the existing stand.

After groups and gaps are identified, low-density areas may be marked with the intent of restoring a more open, pine-dominated forest condition in topographic locations where historical fire would have produced these conditions (see Stand Visualization System examples below). Most leave trees would be selected based on size, species, and vigor, but also on important habitat features.

As the climate changes and temperatures increase, water stress will increase on trees. If trees are left in groups, will they experience increased water stress and a higher rate of mortality? Any increase in tree density will increase competition for resources and generally reduce growth. However, it is clear in all reconstruction studies in the Sierra Nevada that large trees have historically been clumped, and this pattern existed even during past periods of extended drought. We do not know the exact reasons for this drought resilience but one consideration may be the broader environment that the clump exists within. Recognizing the opportunistic nature of root growth, gaps adjacent to tree clumps may have provided greater resource availability to sustain large trees during drought periods.

An important concern, then, is the stem density of areas adjacent to the group. Historically, low-density areas or gaps surrounded clumps, and these openings may have increased resource availability for trees in the clump. With fire suppression, many of these areas are now filled with shade-tolerant trees, which may increase stress within the large tree clump. This suggests that, when emphasizing the large tree clump, thinning around clumps may be warranted, in place of the more traditional radial release thinning where much of the clump is thinned to increase the growth of one leave tree.

Stand Visualization Simulator Examples

Using the Stand Visualization Simulator, we constructed representative stands of common Sierra Nevada forest conditions. These images were then edited to demonstrate how treatments might increase heterogeneity in tree spacing and canopy layering, while reducing standwide fuel ladders.

A thinning following GTR 220 concepts might be based on producing different groups of trees and leave-tree densities. In most treated stands, the largest trees are left, regardless of their relative height in the overall stand, and suppressed trees, which may act as ladder fuels, are removed (e.g., left and right sides of fig. 9-1). However, in tree groups valued for potential wildlife habitat, understory trees (the intermediate and suppressed crown class) can be important clump components (e.g., central clump in fig. 9-1). While these suppressed trees provide understory cover in

Figure 9-1—Stand Visualization Simulator image of a hypothetical stand treated following U.S. Forest Service General Technical Report 220 concepts producing a high-density tree group, a gap, and lower density matrix (North et al. 2009).

tree groups with high habitat potential, they also increase the hazard of crown fire, as they can provide fuel ladders into the upper canopy. If the tree group is burned, fire may cause some level of overstory mortality, but gaps and low-density areas surrounding the tree group may reduce the risk of further crown fire spread. While potentially reducing the numbers of larger trees within the area, high postfire mortality in the tree group would contribute to large snag and down log recruitment. Over time, as other locations in the area develop into new groups, landscape-level conditions would be expected to compensate for the short-term loss of live large trees.

In fire-suppressed forests, current stand structure conditions may not significantly differ with slope position. After treatments designed to increase landscape heterogeneity have been completed, valley bottom, midslope and ridgetop stands would have different tree densities and resultant canopy cover levels (figs. 9-2 to 9-4). In general, upslope changes in slope position often correspond with reduced soil moisture availability and lower productivity. Parker (1982) developed the topographic relative moisture index (TRMI) to provide a relative measure of xeric (TRMI value of 0) to mesic (maximum value of 60) conditions that has been found to correspond with historical differences in stand structure (Taylor 2004, 2010). Historically, slope position also may have corresponded with increasing fire intensity that would have also affected stand density and canopy cover.

Figure 9-2—Valley bottom stand (A) before and (B) after treatment.

Figure 9-3—Mid-slope stand (A) before and (B) after treatment.

Figure 9-4—Ridgetop stand (A) before and (B) after treatment.

Forests lacking large trees, or that have uniform spatial distributions, may be the most difficult to mark when keying off of existing conditions.

Forests lacking large trees, or that have uniform spatial distributions, may be the most difficult to mark when keying off of existing conditions. Following GTR 220 concepts, microsite and landscape topography can be used to vary treatments. However many forests affected by early 1900s railroad logging and pre-1980s timber management plans have little topographic variation and few, if any, large legacy trees to anchor the location of tree groups (fig. 9-5). In most of these stands, however, there are differences in stem densities and sizes that can be used to increase the variability in tree distributions. Even in fairly homogeneous second growth, some trees are larger, and these may serve to identify leave-tree groups (fig. 9-5).

Younger planted forests with little crown class differentiation can be very difficult to shift toward higher levels of spatial heterogeneity because of relatively uniform distribution and tree size (fig. 9-6). In this case, thinning that enhances large tree development may take priority over creating spatial heterogeneity. Although the primary management objective might be tree density reduction to increase growth rates, even in plantations there are often opportunities to favor natural regeneration and to increase heterogeneity in both species composition and tree arrangements.

Figure 9-5—Second-growth stand with few older legacy structures (A) before and (B) after treatment.

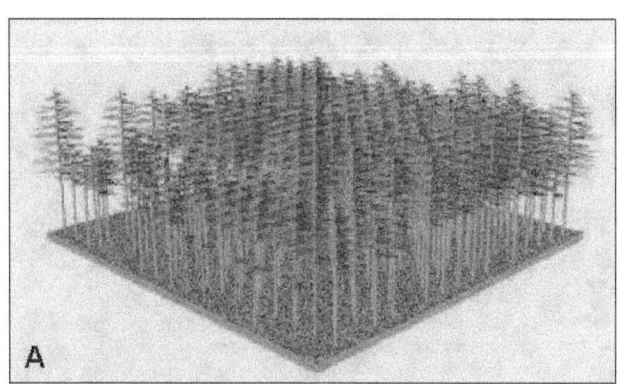 

Figure 9-6—Pine plantation (A) before and (B) after treatment.

Using FVS to Assess Heterogeneity

With a slight modification, both Common Stand Exam (CSE) data and the Forest Vegetation Simulator (FVS) can be used to assess whether treatments have increased forest heterogeneity. Here we present an approach that provides an effective estimation of the mean and variation in stand-level and within-stand forest attributes.

In practice, variable-radius sample plots are small. For example, using a 20-basal area factor (BAF) prism, sample area differs with target tree diameter, yet even for a 30-in (76-cm) diameter at breast height (d.b.h.) tree the sample area will be 0.24 ac (0.1 ha). This plot size falls within the range of tree group and gap sizes found in many reconstruction studies. This is important because statistical analyses can only detect patterns of variability at scales equal to or larger than the plot size.

The Field Sampled Vegetation (FSVeg), CSE, and FVS can be customized to annotate plots and assess different stand conditions such as high-density, low-density, and gap areas. For example with CSE-protocol stand exams, the Plot User field can be used to categorize the "type" of forest condition sampled such as high-density (HD tree cluster), low-density (LD matrix), and Gap.

After using FSVeg to create an FVS-ready Access database, an FVS_PlotInit table is available to simulate plots as stands. To enable this option, Suppose preferences must be set to "Process plots as stands" (fig. 9-7). Plots can then be grouped for simulation in the Select Stands process step. For example, if 15 plots are sampled in an analysis area, field technicians may have indicated that plots 1, 5, 12, and 14 are HD (tree cluster) plots in the Plot User field. These four plots are selected and "grown" or "treated" in the simulation together to provide information on HD tree group response. Several methods exist to summarize the results of this within-stand simulation approach. The use of the Average Summary Table post processor is one option (fig. 9-8). Continuing with our example, the same analysis can be completed for the LD, and Gap condition plots within the stand, and also completed for the entire set of plots to yield a stand-level average.

The creation of a table to compare variation between the entire sample and the posttreatment patches is simplified by using Suppose and Excel together. Within Suppose, specify an output database, in this case an Excel file, to capture the forest structural variable of interest. After each simulation, copy and paste the output for that variable into an Excel worksheet. Using Excel's statistical functions, the mean and coefficient of variation for stand- and patch-level attributes can be calculated using all plots and plots by patch type, respectively. By dividing a population's standard deviation by its mean, the coefficient of variation (CV) permits a comparison

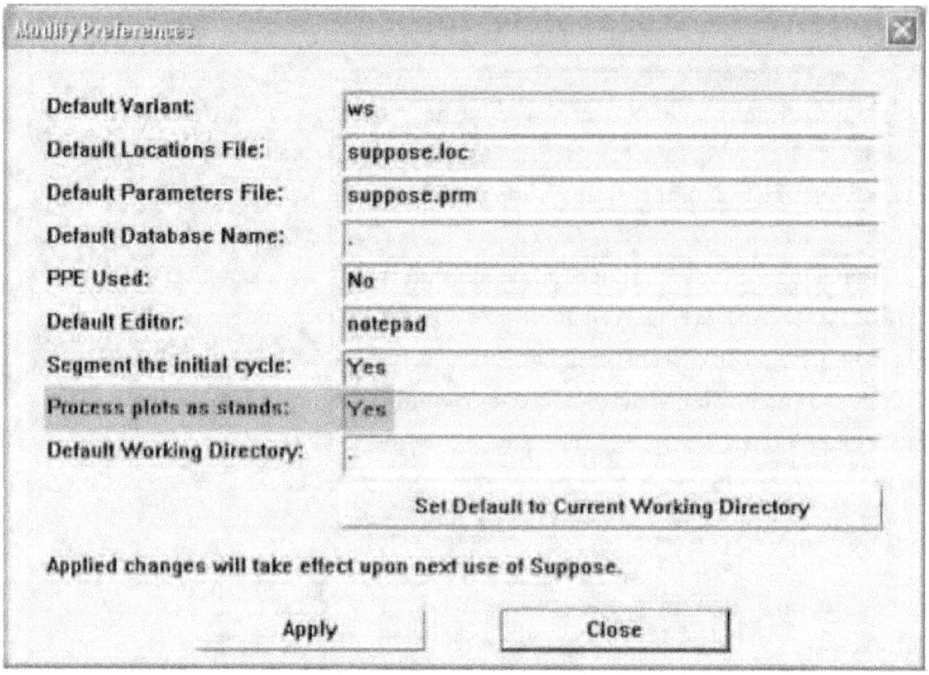

Figure 9-7—Screen capture image of the preferences menu in the Suppose module of the Forest Vegetation Simulator.

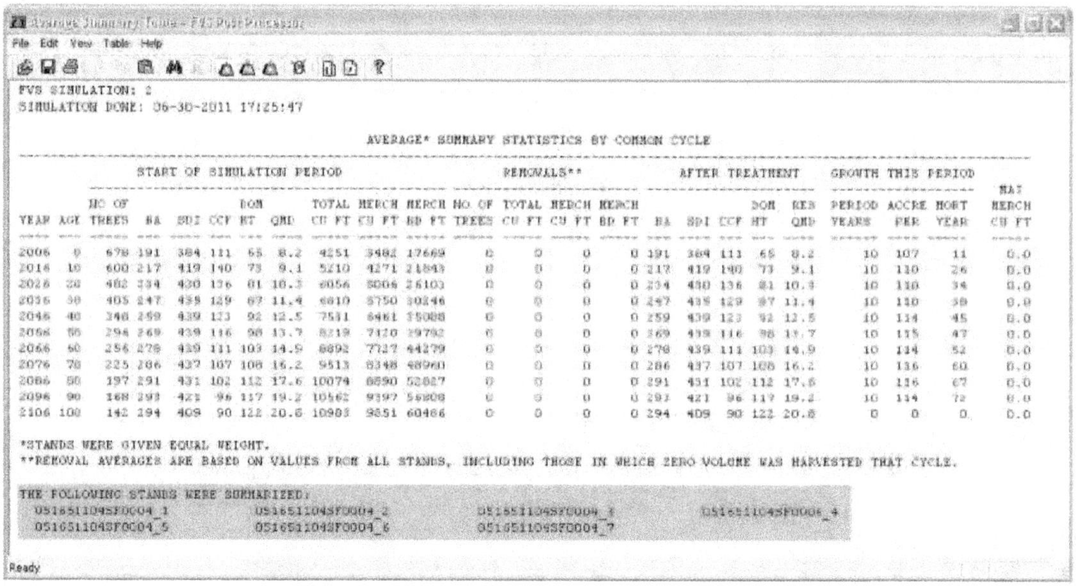

File Edit View Table Help

FVS SIMULATION: 2
SIMULATION DONE: 06-30-2011 17:25:47

AVERAGE* SUMMARY STATISTICS BY COMMON CYCLE

		START OF SIMULATION PERIOD									REMOVALS**				AFTER TREATMENT					GROWTH THIS PERIOD			
YEAR	AGE	NO OF TREES	BA	SDI	CCF	DOM HT	QMD	TOTAL CU FT	MERCH CU FT	MERCH BD FT	NO OF TREES	TOTAL CU FT	MERCH CU FT	MERCH BD FT	BA	SDI	CCF	DOM HT	RES QMD	PERIOD YEARS	ACCRE PER	MORT YEAR	MAI MERCH CU FT
2006	0	678	191	384	111	65	8.2	4251	3482	17669	0	0	0	0	191	384	111	65	8.2	10	107	11	0.0
2016	10	600	217	419	140	73	9.1	5210	4271	21843	0	0	0	0	217	419	140	73	9.1	10	110	26	0.0
2026	20	482	234	430	136	81	10.3	6056	5006	26103	0	0	0	0	234	430	136	81	10.3	10	110	34	0.0
2036	30	405	247	435	129	87	11.4	6810	5750	30246	0	0	0	0	247	435	129	87	11.4	10	110	38	0.0
2046	40	348	259	439	123	92	12.5	7531	6461	35088	0	0	0	0	259	439	123	92	12.5	10	114	45	0.0
2056	50	294	269	439	116	98	13.7	8219	7120	39792	0	0	0	0	269	439	116	98	13.7	10	115	47	0.0
2066	60	256	278	439	111	103	14.9	8892	7727	44279	0	0	0	0	278	439	111	103	14.9	10	114	52	0.0
2076	70	225	286	437	107	108	16.2	9513	8348	48960	0	0	0	0	286	437	107	108	16.2	10	116	60	0.0
2086	80	197	291	431	102	112	17.6	10074	8890	52827	0	0	0	0	291	431	102	112	17.6	10	116	67	0.0
2096	90	168	293	421	96	117	19.2	10562	9397	56808	0	0	0	0	293	421	96	117	19.2	10	114	72	0.0
2106	100	142	294	409	90	122	20.6	10983	9851	60486	0	0	0	0	294	409	90	122	20.6	0	0	0	0.0

*STANDS WERE GIVEN EQUAL WEIGHT.
**REMOVAL AVERAGES ARE BASED ON VALUES FROM ALL STANDS, INCLUDING THOSE IN WHICH ZERO VOLUME WAS HARVESTED THAT CYCLE.

THE FOLLOWING STANDS WERE SUMMARIZED:
0516511048F0004_1 0516511048F0004_2 0516511048F0004_3 0516511048F0004_4
0516511048F0004_5 0516511048F0004_6 0516511048F0004_7

Ready

Figure 9-8—Screen capture image of the Average Summary Table post processor in the Forest Vegetation Simulator.

of relative variability about different-sized means. In effect, CV, often expressed as a percentage, standardizes variability around the mean of the sample population.

In the example provided (fig. 9-9), basal area per acre was selected from each plot for a common year. After pasting the data into Excel, the program's statistical functions SDEV and AVERAGE are used. After these values are calculated, enter a user-defined formula for the CV (coefficient of variation = SDEV/AVERAGE).

A highly heterogeneous stand, after treatment, should have a large CV when all plots are pooled. This is because some plots will have sampled tree groups with high basal area, stand density index, and canopy cover, and other plots will sample gaps and the LD matrix, which will have much lower values. For each patch type, means should be significantly different from each other and be widely varied compared to the all-plots mean. The CVs for each patch type should be smaller than the CV for all plots combined. As a rule of thumb, higher stand-level CV and greater differences between the patch-type means will usually be associated with increased structural heterogeneity.

As a rule of thumb, higher stand-level CV [coefficient of variation] and greater differences between the patch-type means will usually be associated with increased structural heterogeneity.

Plot	Basal Area / Acre			
	All	HD	LD	Gap
1	310	310		
2	300	300		
3	280	280		
4	300	300		
5	280	280		
6	290	290		
7	170		170	
8	150		150	
9	120		120	
10	160		160	
11	170		170	
12	180		180	
13	180		180	
14	150		150	
15	180		180	
16	140		140	
17	150		150	
18	150		150	
19	150		150	
20	150		150	
21	140		140	
22	10			10
23	10			10
24	10			10
25	5			5
26	10			10
27	5			5
SDEV	98	12	17	3
AVERAGE	154	293	156	8
CV	64%	4%	11%	31%

Figure 9-9—Screen capture image of an Excel spreadsheet where the mean (average), standard deviation (SDEV) and coefficient of variation (CV) have been calculated for data pasted from the Forest Vegetation Simulator's Suppose module. HD = high density tree cluster; LD = low density matrix.

If sample plots are arranged on a systematic grid covering the treatment area, the percentage of plots in each patch type will also indicate the project's overall ratio of HD tree groups, gaps, and LD areas. Recording plot locations with a global positioning system receiver allows the data to be easily incorporated into geographic information system software and facilitates plot relocation for future repeated sampling. This type of analysis has the advantage of providing both mean and CV for the entire sample stand and the finer scale, patch type variability that creates within-stand structural heterogeneity.

References

Larson, A.J.; Churchill, D. 2012. Tree spatial patterns in fire-frequent forests of western North America, including mechanisms of pattern formation and implications for designing fuel reduction and restoration treatments. Forest Ecology and Management. 267: 74–92.

Ma, S.; Concilio, A.; Oakley, B.; North, M.; Chen, J. 2010. Spatial variability in microclimate in a mixed-conifer forest before and after thinning and burning treatments. Forest Ecology and Management. 259: 904–915.

North, M.; Chen, J. 2005. Introduction to the Teakettle Special Issue. Forest Science. 51: 185–186.

North, M.; Oakley, B.; Chen, J.; Erickson, H.; Gray, A.; Izzo, A.; Johnson, D.; Ma, S.; Marra, J.; Meyer, M.; Purcell, K.; Rambo, T.; Roath, B.; Rizzo, D.; Schowalter, T. 2002. Vegetation and ecological characteristics of mixed-conifer and red-fir forests at the Teakettle Experimental Forest. Gen. Tech. Rep. PSW-GTR-186. Albany, CA: U.S. Department of Agriculture, Forest Service, Pacific Southwest Research Station. 52 p.

North, M.; Stine, P.; O'Hara, K.; Zielinski, W.; Stephens, S. 2009. An ecosystem management strategy for Sierran mixed-conifer forests. Gen. Tech. Rep. PSW-GTR-220. 2nd printing with addendum. Albany, CA: U.S. Department of Agriculture, Forest Service, Pacific Southwest Research Station. 49 p.

Oliver, C.D.; Larson, B.C. 1996. Forest stand dynamics. Updated edition. New York, NY: John Wiley and Sons, Inc. 520 p.

Parker, A.J. 1982. The topographic relative moisture index: an approach to soil moisture assessment in mountain terrain. Physical Geography. 3: 160–168.

Sherlock, J.W. 2007. Integrating stand density management with fuel reduction. In: Powers, R.F., tech. ed. Restoring fire-adapted ecosystems: proceedings of the 2005 national silviculture workshop. Gen. Tech. Rep. PSW-GTR-203. Albany, CA: U.S. Department of Agriculture, Forest Service, Pacific Southwest Research Station: 55–66.

Taylor, A.H. 2004. Identifying forest reference conditions on early cut-over lands, Lake Tahoe Basin, USA. Ecological Applications. 14: 1903–1920.

Taylor, A.H. 2010. Fire disturbance and the structure and dynamics of an old-growth *P. ponderosa* forest in the southern Cascades, USA. Journal of Vegetation Science. 21: 561–572.

Wayman, R.; North, M. 2007. Initial response of a mixed-conifer understory plant community to burning and thinning restoration treatments. Forest Ecology and Management. 239: 32–44.

Zald, H.; Gray, A.; North, M.; Kern, R. 2008. Initial regeneration responses to fire and thinning treatments in a Sierra Nevada mixed-conifer forest, USA. Forest Ecology and Management. 256: 168–179.

Chapter 10: Geographic Information System Landscape Analysis Using GTR 220 Concepts

M. North,[1] R.M. Boynton,[2] P.A. Stine,[3] K.F. Shipley,[2] E.C. Underwood,[2] N.E. Roth,[2] J.H. Viers,[2] and J.F. Quinn[2]

Introduction

Forest Service General Technical Report "An Ecosystem Management Strategy for Sierran Mixed-Conifer Forests" (hereafter GTR 220) (North et al. 2009) emphasizes increasing forest heterogeneity throughout a range of spatial scales including within-stand microsites, individual stands, watersheds, and entire landscapes. For fuels reduction, various landscape strategies have been proposed and modeled, but there are few conceptual models for integrating forest restoration and wildlife habitat at larger scales. General Technical Report 220 proposes varying forest structure, composition, and fuels based on topographic characteristics, particularly slope position and aspect. The concept is an effort to emulate how frequent fire might have created landscape-scale forest heterogeneity and by inference increased forest resilience and habitat connectivity. In this chapter, we describe a raster-based geographic information system (GIS) tool developed to parse a landscape into basic topographic categories. The Landscape Management Unit (LMU) tool has two versions. An initial version closely follows the methods described in Underwood et al. (2010), binning the landscape into three slope positions crossed with three aspects (resulting in nine total categories). A second version addresses application considerations that managers have identified within the U.S. Forest Service. It condenses some of the topographic categories present in version 1 while adding a category based on mechanical operation limitations that usually occur around >30 percent slopes, resulting in six total categories. The second version also allows for more user modification. The user can change how topographic categories are defined, allowing managers to more closely parameterize the GIS tool for a project's particular topographic conditions.

[1] Research ecologist, U.S. Department of Agriculture, Forest Service, Pacific Southwest Research Station, 1731 Research Park Dr., Davis, CA 95618.

[2] Information Center for the Environment, Department of Environmental Science and Policy, One Shields Ave., University of California, Davis, Davis, CA 95616.

[3] National coordinator for experimental forests and ranges, U.S. Department of Agriculture, Forest Service, Pacific Northwest Research Station, The John Muir Institute, One Shields Ave., University of California, Davis, CA 95616.

Summary of Findings

1. **Two versions of a GIS tool have been developed for analyzing and binning a forested area into landscape management units (LMUs) based on topography using DEMs.**

2. **The first version divides an area into nine LMUs resulting from three slope positions (canyon bottom/drainage, midslope, ridge) and three slope aspects (Southwest, Northeast, and neutral) following earlier published work.**

3. **A second version divides an area into six LMUs (ridge, canyon bottom/drainage, Southwest mid-slope <30 percent, Southwest mid-slope >30 percent, Northeast mid-slope <30 percent, and Northeast mid-slope >30 percent) following feedback from forest managers.** This version also allows the user to modify three parameters: neighborhood size, minimum-elevation separation, and minimum area of the slope position units.

4. **The download site** for both versions 1 and 2: http://ice.ucdavis.edu/project/landscape_management_unit_lmu_tool/.

Foundations for the GIS Tool

Historically, frequent low-intensity fire was a strong influence on the structure, composition, and ecological functions of mid-elevation Sierra Nevada forests (Skinner and Chang 1996). Aspect, slope position, and slope steepness can influence fire frequency and severity, producing different forest structures and species compositions as changes in these topographic variables occur across a landscape (Hessburg et al. 2007, Taylor and Skinner 2004). These variables can also influence soil depth, microclimate conditions, and soil moisture availability (Ma et al. 2010, Meyer et al. 2007), affecting tree density, composition, forest productivity, and overall habitat characteristics (Parker 1982, Urban et al. 2000). Most reconstruction studies have suggested historical Sierra Nevada forests were highly heterogeneous, with forest conditions likely varying with fine- and landscape-scale changes in factors such as topography and soils.

Forest heterogeneity may be particularly important for providing a diverse array of wildlife habitats. While some species are associated with areas of high canopy cover and stem density (e.g., the Pacific fisher (*Martes pennanti*), northern goshawk

(*Accipiter gentilis*), and California spotted owl (*Strix occidentalis occidentalis*), preferred habitat for others (e.g., some songbirds and small mammals) may be more open, xeric forest conditions or shrub patches. Managing for the optimal spatial arrangement and connectivity of these different forest conditions is challenging because there are few species that have been studied in enough detail to provide guidance for management practices. In the absence of better information, a reasonable approach may be to mimic the pattern of forest conditions that might have been produced by topographic differences in fire regimes and forest productivity.

Forest managers are faced with developing project plans that must meet multiple objectives including fuels reduction, ecosystem restoration, increased forest resilience, and the provision of a variety of wildlife habitat, especially old-forest conditions, which may be at odds with, or are adversative to, fuels objectives. For landscape planning, this has sometimes resulted in different areas being managed for single objectives (e.g., fuels reduction near the wildland-urban interface, or no entry around known sensitive species use areas). There has not been a conceptual framework or spatially explicit method for integrating and balancing these different objectives across a landscape. The GIS tool described here is an initial attempt to analyze and spatially parse forest landscapes into topographic zones with different desired forest conditions. Managers may use the tool to develop plans for increasing forest heterogeneity while using the conceptual framework to communicate their intent to stakeholders and the public.

Managers may use the tool to develop plans for increasing forest heterogeneity while using the conceptual framework to communicate their intent to stakeholders and the public.

Background and Description of the GIS Tool

The first version of the GIS tool, developed by the Information Center for the Environment at the University of California, Davis can be downloaded from http://ice.ucdavis.edu/project/landscape_management_unit_lmu_tool.

It contains a series of scripts that work in Environmental Systems Research Institute ArcMap **version 10** (the scripts will not run in earlier versions). The essential inputs for the tool are the study area boundary and a digital elevation model (DEM) (ideally at 10 m (33 ft) resolution but it will also work on 30-m (98-ft) DEMs). The LMU tool contains three toolsets. The first is a preprocessing toolset that prepares the data sets, for example, by buffering the study area boundary and clipping the DEM by this extent. The main toolset parses the landscape into three classes of slope (ridgetop, midslope, canyon/drainage bottoms) and three classes of aspect (northerly, southerly, and a neutral class to reflect the amount of solar insolation received), and then recombines these into a total of nine LMUs (see table 10-1). Finally, the postprocessing toolset generates summary statistics for either each of the nine LMU groups or, alternatively, by the multiple individual units within each

Table 10-1—Classification of landscape management units

| | | Position on slope | | |
Description		Canyon/ drainage bottom	Slope	Ridge
	Code	1	2	3
Aspect class:				
Neutral (120° to 150° and 300° to 330°)	10	11 (neutral canyon)	12 (neutral slope)	13 (neutral ridge)
Northerly (centered at 45°)	20	21 (northerly canyon)	22 (northerly slope)	23 (northerly ridge)
Southerly (centered at 225°)	30	31 (southerly canyon)	32 (southerly slope)	33 (southerly ridge)

LMU type. The summary tables report elevation, slope (in degrees and percentage of rise), aspect, net mean aspect, aspect strength, and wetness index (i.e., the amount of water received from upslope in the watershed) (see Underwood et al. 2010 for details).

There are a number of options within the tool that can be selected by the user. For example, a spatial layer depicting streams or water bodies can be specified if the user wants to ensure these are all captured as canyons/drainage bottoms. Also, there is an option to simplify the size of the output units within each LMU to remove any that are less than 10 ac (4 ha) (see Underwood et al. 2010 for details). This size simplification may be useful when the GIS tool is used for planning, but users should communicate that prescriptions and marking in the field will differ on smaller scales (chapters 9 and 11 through 13).

Examples: Kings River and Sagehen

Terrain conditions differ widely across the Sierra Nevada with slope steepness tending to increase in the southern portion of the range. In the first version of the tool, thresholds used to determine slope position can be set for either moderate or steep slope conditions. We used different thresholds because slope classes are relative. A location's slope position is determined by comparing each cell in a DEM to its neighborhood. A slight difference in elevation of the target cell to its neighbors in a moderate-terrain landscape may distinguish it as a ridge, whereas the same difference in elevation in a steep-terrain landscape may not. In the steep terrain version, the minimum elevation difference between adjacent cells is 25 m (82 ft) for ridges and -20 m (-66 ft) for canyons/drainage bottoms. In the moderate terrain version, the minimum elevation difference between adjacent cells is 15 m (49 ft) for ridges and -14 m (46 ft) for canyons/drainage bottoms (table 10-2). These values were

Table 10-2—Thresholds used to determine slope position in "steep" and "moderate" terrain types

| Slope position | Variable | Units | Terrain type | |
			Steep	Moderate
Ridge	Neighborhood	Meters	500	500
	Minimum separation	Meters	25	15
	Minimum area	Square meters	20,000	20,000
Canyon/drainage bottom	Neighborhood	Meters	500	500
	Minimum separation	Meters	-20	-14
	Minimum area	Square meters	40,000	40,000
Slope	Any cells not identified as ridge or canyon/ drainage bottom			

developed iteratively with feedback from field personnel familiar with the two study areas presented here. The preprocessing tool will produce a table that gives summary statistics, most importantly mean and standard deviation, for the slope across the study area. The user can then use this to help determine whether the moderate or steep terrain version should be used in the main toolset analysis. For example, a region of steep terrain is the Kings River area in the Sierra National Forest with an average slope of 32.1 percent and a standard deviation of 19.6 percent (fig. 10-1). In contrast, an area of moderate terrain is the Sagehen Experimental Forest of the Tahoe National Forest with an average slope of 19.7 percent and a standard deviation of 14.3 percent (fig. 10-2).

User Input Version

The second version of the LMU tool has three adjustments to the basic tool that managers may find useful. These adjustments result in six final LMU classes rather than nine. This second version can also be downloaded from http://ice.ucdavis.edu/ project/landscape_management_unit_lmu_tool/.

The first adjustment is removal of the aspect categories for the ridge and canyon/drainage bottom slope position classes. The tool identifies canyons/drainage bottoms and ridges as locations where there is little elevation change between adjacent pixels. Forest managers suggested that, in general, aspect has less influence on forest conditions in these two slope position categories because slope steepness is minimal.

A second adjustment is modification of the midslope categories. First we removed the neutral category (120 to 150° and 300 to 330°) and adjusted the aspect classifications to either southwest (136 to 315°) or northeast (316 to 135°). Managers suggested that as a planning tool, the neutral classification was ambiguous and did

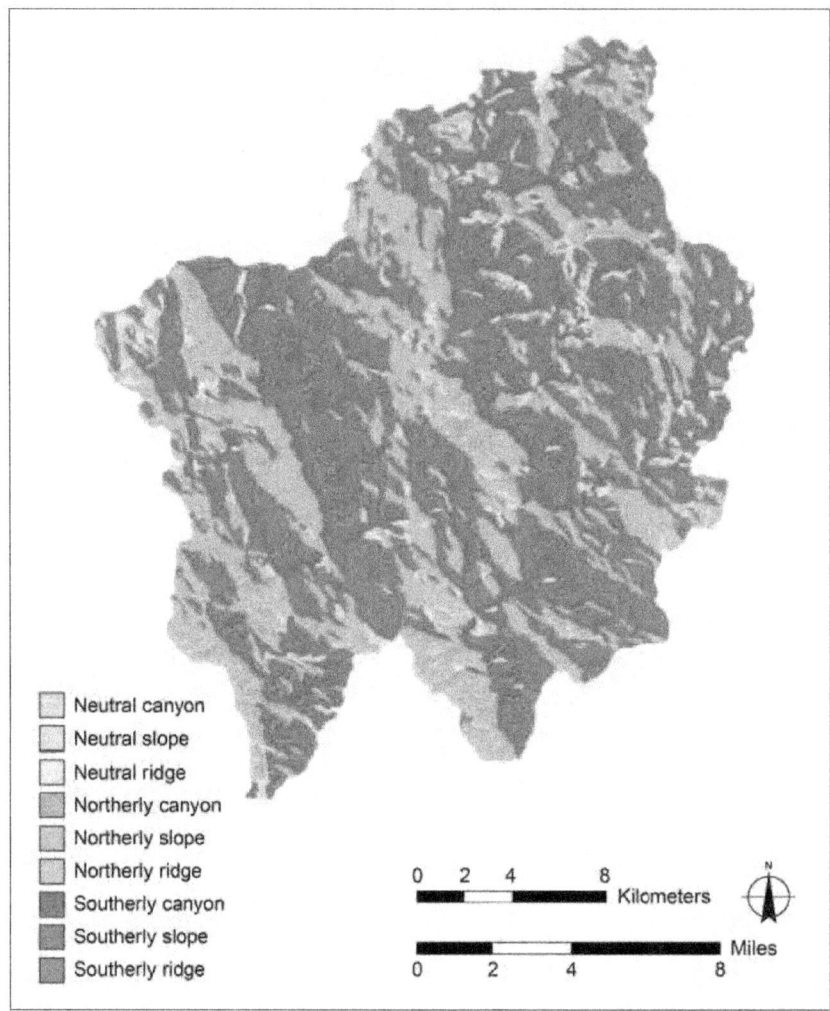

Figure 10-1—Landscape Management Units generated for the Kings River area in the Sierra National Forest, California.

not help identify management scenarios for those areas. In practice, on the ground assessments are often used to identify stand aspect and local conditions for these areas. We also split the midslope category into two classes, <30 percent and >30 percent steepness, for two reasons. Mechanical vehicles usually cannot be used on slopes steeper than 30 percent, necessitating hand thinning to reduce fuels. This limits the removal of cut material, leaving more activity fuel on site. In addition, steeper slopes can increase fire intensity particularly when high fuel loads are present, increasing potential tree mortality, and making suppression and containment more difficult (Safford et al. 2009). Planning treatments and managing these areas requires a different approach than more moderate slope conditions.

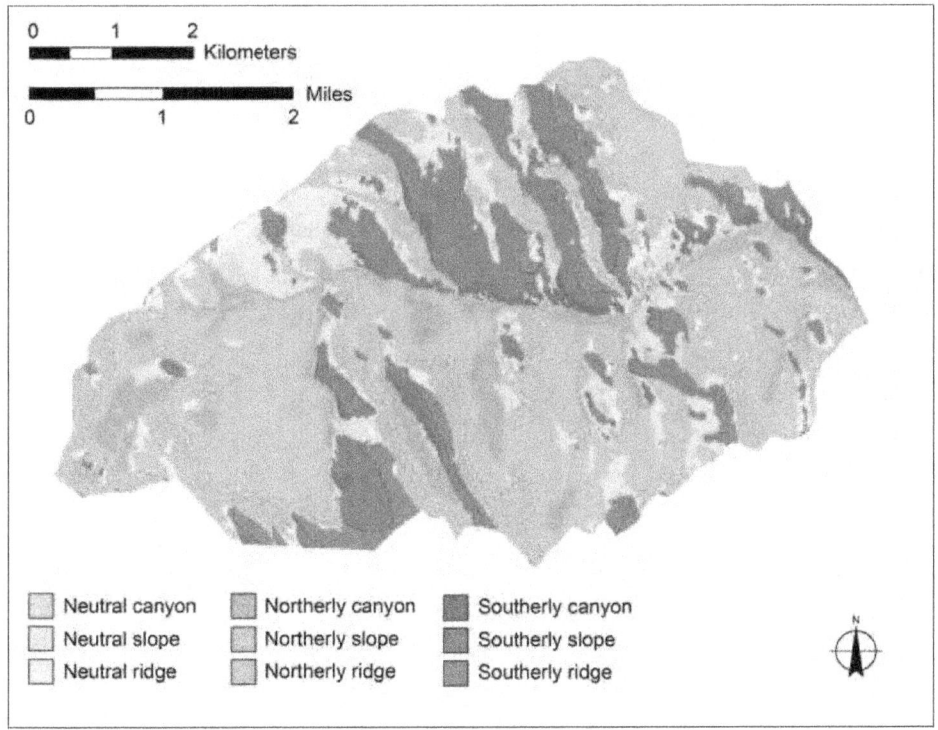

Figure 10-2—Landscape Management Units generated for the Sagehen area in the Tahoe National Forest, California.

Version 2 also has a third adjustment that lets the user modify three parameters: neighborhood size, minimum elevation separation, and the minimum area of the slope position units created. These adjustments only affect ridge and canyon/ drainage bottoms classification because slope areas are identified as any cells not classified as ridge or canyon/drainage bottoms. Neighborhood size determines the circular radius around each cell that is used to calculate average elevation and is compared to the target cell's elevation. This will allow users to adjust the grain size at which elevation is averaged. Adjusting the minimum elevation separation between the cell's elevation and that of its neighborhood will allow users to alter the slope position classifications for the area they are analyzing. Changing minimum area will allow users to reduce or increase canyon/drainage bottoms and ridge unit size for the scale of analysis that is practical for their planning applications. This flexibility may allow managers to adjust the classifications such that final output more closely agrees with expert knowledge from field personnel.

Chapter Summary

The GIS tool is designed to accommodate a range of forest types in the Western United States and can be applied to project areas of any size. It is also simple to implement requiring easily accessible, basic data inputs such as DEMs.

The GIS tool is designed to accommodate a range of forest types in the Western United States and can be applied to project areas of any size. It is also simple to implement requiring easily accessible, basic data inputs such as DEMs and consequently, the units generated are readily interpretable. These units can then provide a basis for storing data about each unit within a GIS framework. This foundation can be used for further spatial analyses such as calculating the solar radiation associated with each unit. It also may be a useful tool for communicating different management scenarios to stakeholders and the public.

All such tools progress through iterative stages of trial, learning, and adjustment. We expect that users of this tool will be able to offer important suggestions for improvement once they have had opportunities to test it with real world applications. Technical GIS experts within the agency are well positioned to work with managers, making adjustments as experience accumulates and needed improvements become apparent.

Forest Service managers have enormous challenges when contemplating a management strategy for any given landscape. They depend on sound science to form a foundation from which to build a management strategy. Part of this body of defensible scientific knowledge is a set of technical tools that can be used to evaluate ecological conditions and alternative strategies to manage a forested landscape toward a desired future condition. We hope the LMU tool is a helpful addition to their toolbox, adding analytical power for planning and evaluation of management alternatives.

Literature Cited

Hessburg, P.; Salter, R.; James, K. 2007. Re-examining fire severity relations in pre-management era mixed conifer forests: inferences from landscape patterns of forest structure. Landscape Ecology. 22: 5–24.

Ma, S.; Concilio, A.; Oakley, B.; North, M.; Chen, J. 2010. Spatial variability in microclimate in a mixed-conifer forest before and after thinning and burning treatments. Forest Ecology and Management. 259: 904–915.

Meyer, M.; North, M.; Gray, A.; Zald, H. 2007. Influence of soil thickness on stand characteristics in a Sierra Nevada mixed-conifer forest. Plant and Soil. 294: 113–123.

North, M.; Stine, P.; O'Hara, K.; Zielinski, W.; Stephens, S. 2009. An ecosystem management strategy for Sierran mixed-conifer forests. 2nd printing, with addendum. Gen. Tech. Rep. PSW-GTR-220. Albany, CA: U.S. Department of Agriculture, Forest Service, Pacific Southwest Research Station. 49 p.

Parker, A.J. 1982. The topographic relative moisture index: an approach to soil moisture assessment in mountain terrain. Physical Geography. 3: 160–168.

Safford, H.D.; Schmidt, D.A.; Carlson, C.H. 2009. Effects of fuel treatments on fire severity in an area of wildland-urban interface, Angora Fire, Lake Tahoe Basin, California. Forest Ecology and Management. 258: 773–787.

Skinner, C.N.; Chang, C.R. 1996. Fire regimes, past and present, in Sierra Nevada Ecosystem Project: final report to congress. Volume 2: Assessments and scientific basis for management options. Wildlands Resources Center Report No. 37. Davis, CA: University of California, Centers for Water and Wildland Resources: 1041–1070.

Taylor, A.H.; Skinner, C.N. 2004. Spatial patterns and controls on historical fire regimes and forest structure in the Klamath Mountains. Ecological Applications. 13: 704–719.

Urban, D.L.; Miller, C.; Halpin, P.N.; Stephenson. N.L. 2000. Forest gradient response in Sierran landscapes: the physical template. Landscape Ecology. 15: 603–620.

Underwood, E.C.; Viers, J.H.; Quinn, J.F.; North, M.P. 2010. Using topography to meet wildlife and fuels treatment objectives in fire-suppressed landscapes. Journal of Environmental Management. 46: 809–819.

Chapter 11: Dinkey North and South Project

M. North[1] and R. Rojas[2]

Introduction

Designing and implementing vegetation treatments that can move a forest landscape toward a desired future condition is often challenging. Faced with diverse stakeholder interests and the unknown effects of changing climate conditions, managers need to engage and build collaborative projects. One such effort is the Dinkey project designed to help restore a healthy, diverse, fire-resilient forest structure while maintaining and enhancing habitat for fisher (*Martes pennanti*) and California spotted owls (*Strix occidentalis occidentalis*). The project retained tree species and size classes that are the most drought tolerant; more resistant to insects, diseases, and air pollution; and have higher rates of postwildfire survival. Surface and ladder fuels were decreased to reduce the probabilities of crown fire ignition and fire severity. Large woody debris and

Summary of Findings

1. This project, the first to implement GTR 220 concepts, began with discussing and **agreeing upon a desired future condition for the project area**, which helped build consensus amongst diverse stakeholders.

2. At first, **prescription development and marking guidelines were difficult to write up, but became easier to communicate** after they were condensed into a series of decision steps.

3. **Field visits to test marks with the stakeholders allowed grounded discussion** of how GTR 220 concepts were being translated into practice and how and why marking decisions were made.

higher canopy closure were retained in some areas that may provide suitable habitat for sensitive species. Some torching and tree mortality were considered acceptable to support cavity nesting and denning structures, and a range of ecosystem functions over time. In areas where a reduction in potential fire intensity was essential, treatment included separating tree crowns to reduce the potential for crown-fire spread. Forest health and resilience were promoted by increasing the forest's capacity to withstand short-term impacts (e.g., drought) without causing long-term changes in the system's overall function. Mechanical, hand, and prescribed fire tools were used to meet these goals. The project was also designed to be conducted in an economically efficient manner with minimal outside funding.

---

[1] Research ecologist, U.S. Department of Agriculture, Forest Service, Pacific Southwest Research Station, 1731 Research Park Dr., Davis, CA 95618.

[2] District silviculturist, U.S. Department of Agriculture, Forest Service, Pacific Southwest Region, Sierra National Forest, High Sierra Ranger District, 29688 Auberry Rd., Auberry, CA 93651.

Context

The Dinkey North and South project (hereafter the Dinkey project) occurred on 3,000 ac (1214 ha) of Forest Service land ranging from 5,400 to 6,800 ft (1646 to 2073 m) in elevation about 30 mi (48 km) northeast of Fresno. Mixed-conifer constitutes most of the forest type (90 percent) with the remainder in ponderosa pine.

The project area supports known populations of fisher and California spotted owls. Monitoring and demographic studies have identified fisher rest sites and California spotted owls foraging areas within the project area (North et al. 2000, Purcell et al. 2009). Studies in the project area (Spencer et al. 2008) indicated that fisher habitat and populations are particularly vulnerable to severe fire. Habitat emphasis treatments recognize the importance of late-seral forest structures, home range conditions, large trees, and forest heterogeneity.

The project area has a history of fire exclusion that has led to a homogeneous landscape of dense conifer forest stands, with prolific establishment of 25- to 100-year-old, shade-tolerant white fir (*Abies concolor* (Gordon & Glend.) Lindley) and incense cedar (*Calocedrus decurrens* (Torrey) Florin). Ponderosa (*Pinus ponderosa* Laws.) and sugar (*Pinus lambertiana* Douglas) pine, and black oak (*Quercus kelloggii* Newberry) were notably underrepresented in the forest's current species composition. A fire history completed in the adjacent Teakettle Experimental Forest found an average fire-return interval of 12 to 17 years for 1700 to 1865, after which all fires stopped (North et al. 2005). In addition to fire suppression, past fires and mechanical harvest have created large areas dominated by shrubs and dense pockets of white fir and incense cedar. High tree density/biomass creates conditions that predispose about 50 percent of the landscape to high-severity fire, insect attack, and drought-induced mortality.

Information Used

Studies that had reconstructed forest conditions under an active fire regime were used to inform general objectives for posttreatment desired conditions. The area has lower annual precipitation (about 45 in/yr) (114 cm/yr) than more mesic west-side forests, so particular emphasis was given to studies that had been conducted in drier mixed-conifer areas such as the eastern side of the Lake Tahoe Basin (Taylor 2004) and the nearby Teakettle Experimental Forest (North et al. 2007). The stand density, basal area, and species compositions in these studies was used to set lower limits, which posttreatment conditions should not fall below. Upper bounds for posttreatment stand conditions were inferred from site capability, landscape zone, and stand density index values at which bark beetle mortality may increase (Oliver 1995).

The Dinkey project focused on implementing concepts found in U.S. Forest Service General Technical Report PSW-GTR-220, "An Ecosystem Management Strategy for Sierran Mixed-Conifer Forests" (hereafter GTR 220) (North et al. 2009). The project's collaborative group (see chapter 7) developed different prescriptions based on topographic design criteria including a slope position matrix (similar to table 10-1). In general, prescriptions were designed to promote heterogeneity by avoiding even spacing of residual trees (fig. 11-1) and protecting unique structures including wildlife trees, snags, large logs, clumps of large trees, understory vegetation (including shrubs), and hardwoods (especially black oaks).

A goal of the decision priorities (described below) was to balance the desire for a fire resilient, healthy forest with the fisher's association with areas of "maximum biomass" based upon habitat modeling work of the Conservation Biology Institute (Spencer et al. 2008). A priority was placed on retaining and promoting areas of large-tree-dominated forest sites with high canopy cover to benefit the fisher (i.e., 63 percent of its home range had > 60 percent canopy cover [Zielinski et al. 2004]) and other rare, old-forest associated species. These individual objectives were intended to provide ecological balance to marking crews as they implemented prescriptions while working within the overarching desire for a healthy, fire-resilient forest.

Figure 11-1—Variable density left in a white-fir-dominated stand after treatment in the Dinkey project.

Implementation

The mark was difficult to describe with a simplified written prescription; therefore, a series of sequential steps were followed.

The mark was difficult to describe with a simplified written prescription; therefore, a series of sequential steps were followed. The first step was to consider the overarching intent of GTR 220 before getting mired in prescription details and marking guidelines. A key aspect of GTR 220 is recognizing forest structure at a fine scale such as groups of trees and favorable regeneration microsites. While field crews have often been trained to recognize individual tree characteristics, they now needed to recognize characteristics of several trees in a group including fisher rest sites; groups of pine regeneration or potential sites for ponderosa pine regeneration; groups of older ponderosa pine; low-quality, even-aged groups of fir; oaks; and groups of younger pine. Markers were trained to recognize each microsite or group prior to implementing the mark.

In the second step, markers first focused on groups with high potential for being used as fisher rest sites. Visits to known fisher sites and conversations with researchers created an emphasis on looking for a particular group structure and not just a canopy cover goal. A dense group of trees did not necessarily mean it was good fisher habitat. The group also needed to have either large structures (live tree, snag, or log) or some "defect" condition. At high-quality fisher rest sites, the prescription was to have little, if any, manipulation. These sites were only about 3 percent of the total area, and therefore did not substantially compromise fuels reduction objectives. In moderate-quality fisher rest sites, ladder fuels were targeted for reduction but were not completely eliminated in the interest of maintaining some understory cover. The lowest quality fisher sites were selected for thinning to increase leave-tree size, so as to create better quality fisher habitat in the future.

Next, markers focused on areas of pine regeneration to obtain a working knowledge of local soil characteristics amenable to regeneration and the appropriate aspect and orientation of openings. The markers were shown examples of successful and unsuccessful shade-intolerant regeneration in small openings. Some collaborative partners were initially uncomfortable with creating holes in the canopy. Therefore the first places identified for regeneration were areas where openings could be expanded rather than created. Attention was paid to "feathering" the gap edge (i.e., reducing foliage density through thinning) and orienting the gap to maximize direct sunlight. It took some time to get markers to recognize what is an appropriate opening rather than just going to rocky or shallow soil locations.

In retrospect, it proved more efficient to identify potential regeneration areas prior to marking trees. This allowed markers to focus on a single task with unique criteria and skills. Depending on forest conditions and the tree markers' skills, other projects may find it easier to identify tree clumps prior to gaps.

To help markers recognize when to change their mark depending on forest conditions and stand location, they were trained to use a stepwise decision tree:

1. What is the emphasis: habitat/restoration or public safety?
2. What type of microsite or group are you in?
   a. Is it a high- or moderate-quality potential fisher rest site?
   b. If not, does the area provide an opportunity for a regeneration opening?
   c. Is tree structure grouped or better for the matrix of low-density large pine trees?
3. What landscape zone are you in?
4. What is the basal area retention in this microsite and landscape zone?

In step 1, the marker decided whether to emphasize ladder fuel reduction or canopy cover retention. Step 2 proved to be the most important step because the marker needed to identify whether to leave a tree group, create or expand a gap, or create more low-density pine-dominated matrix. Steps 3 and 4 required an awareness of aspect and slope position, and the overall basal area target, respectively.

Marking guidelines identified the choices relative to microsites and landscape zone in any particular stand. For example, there might be two landscape zones and four microsites (priorities) in a stand. Typically a marker would be given a residual basal area for pine groups, individual scattered pine, and fir groups. They were also told the likeliest location of high-quality fisher rest sites. Pine and fir group residual basal area would differ between landscape zones. Residual basal area would remain the same for the fisher rest site and lowered for scattered pines. Thus markers would use the five-step process in any stand to identify the appropriate residual basal area and tree characteristics for retention or removal. Marking guidelines were rarely more complex than this example.

Lessons Learned

Three main lessons were learned from the Dinkey project:

1. Move in a stepwise fashion to develop consensus on restoration treatments. The Dinkey project focused on a planning process that included the following steps:
   a. Clarify the overall strategy contained in GTR 220. Forum members needed to agree upon GTR 220 principles of restoration.
   b. Develop desired conditions consistent with GTR 220 and local forest processes. The Dinkey collaborative group sought to develop desired conditions consistent with the role of frequent fire. These desired conditions allowed collaborative members to identify forest structural components for retention or removal.

    c. Conduct field visits to identify key microsites and groups. Field visits with collaborative group members allowed retention priorities to be based upon observed rather than assumed stand conditions.

    d. Develop vegetation maps that capture within-stand heterogeneity. High-resolution mapping and subsequent modeling provided a context for decisions and end results.

    e. Develop decision priorities that are consistent with retaining key structures. Marking guidelines came only after looking at stand structures and discussing small-scale forest heterogeneity.

    f. Contract development that carries forward the previous steps. To that end, a stewardship contract was developed to implement the removal of commercial size trees, and precommercial size material as biomass, and treatment of existing and activity-created slash. The contract had to be modified to allow for the protection and identification of fisher rest sites and the small trees contained within them. The Dinkey project used flagging and a map of rest site locations to identify fisher rest sites. This proved tedious, underscoring the need for more efficient methods to differentiate high-quality fisher rest sites from the surrounding forest matrix. More work with contractors needs to be done to use global positioning system or less labor-intensive means of identifying contractually important field areas.

    g. Ongoing collaborative monitoring of the implementation and effectiveness of forest restoration treatments provided the opportunity for group learning, trust building, and adaptive management.

2. Use language and treatment descriptions consistent with the restoration objectives.

    a. The scale of restoration treatments required a set of terminology that described forest structural components consistently between forum members and marking crews. Clumps, groups, openings, gaps, aspect zones, rest sites, and microsites were terms used to convey the desired conditions both within stands and across the forest landscape.

    b. Retention of vertical within-stand heterogeneity within the context of tree density management is difficult to convey on paper. Field visits to sample marked areas or key structures proved most helpful. Photos or images of these same structures would be helpful in the future.

c. Focus restoration priorities on retaining forest structures not on eliminating structures. Language in marking guidelines and priorities that focused on tree retention proved most helpful in allowing markers and collaborative members to visualize end results. Leave tree marking proved less practical owing to the great number of trees being retained across the project area. Far fewer trees needed to be marked for removal than for retention. However, leave tree marking was conducted in sample marking areas to aid visualization.

d. Articulate how the removal or retention of any tree or group moves you closer to restoration goals. Collaborative group members were comfortable when removal of intermediate-size trees (20- to 30-in [51 to 76 cm] diameter at breast height) was based on meeting the desired conditions and ecological restoration objectives.

3. Train crews and keep them for more than one or two seasons. An investment in crew training and the ability of crews to apply marking guidelines at a group or gap scale proved essential in applying restoration treatments. The application of the restoration guidelines in the Dinkey area was possible because of the experience level and dedication of the marking crew.

What set the stage in the Dinkey project for building collaboration was first getting agreement on the desired future conditions. While the project began with a focus on fuels reduction, it transitioned to forest restoration, provision of wildlife habitat, and reducing potential wildfire severity. All participants immediately agreed that zones adjacent to homes should be prioritized for fuels reduction. Outside of those areas, however, the effort was to balance all three objectives by increasing forest heterogeneity. Any discussion that started to jump to specific locations in the forest or controversial issues (i.e., if, where, and when a larger tree might be thinned) was reined back until the collaborative group reached agreement on a desired future condition. Sometimes this was difficult, because participants were visualizing particular locations or wanted to discuss economic or revenue-related concerns.

The project design was based on the classification of topographic categories and establishment of treatment criteria in each category. This often started with suggesting initial prescriptions and working through the details with the collaborative group. After silvicultural and fuels management review, if the treatment did not appear to achieve the desired objective, the collaborative group was asked for further input. Although the forest staff might have ideas about the next logical step, giving the group room to see limitations and propose alternatives allowed for

Any discussion that started to jump to specific locations in the forest or controversial issues (i.e., if, where, and when a larger tree might be thinned) was reined back until the collaborative group reached agreement on a desired future condition.

more discovery, creativity, and consensus. For practical purposes, the silviculturist insisted that whatever treatment was decided upon, the group had to identify what target condition and retained basal area was desired.

At this point, there was enough consensus in the group to start working on specifics. We discussed where and when larger trees might be thinned and agreed that increasing structural heterogeneity, improving wildlife habitat or ecosystem restoration were reasonable criteria for selecting larger trees, rather than focusing on project economics. When the group visited stands where some larger trees were preliminarily marked for removal, the group often agreed with the mark. In places where there was disagreement, the silviculturist and marking crew explained the reasoning behind the mark and let the group discuss and revise the mark if desired. At this point, the collaborative group was matching the mark to the collective vision of the forest's desired future condition—a more diverse landscape that maintained or enhanced wildlife habitat, improved fire resiliency, and shifted structure and composition toward a pine-dominated, large-tree condition.

References

North, M.; Hurteau, M.; Fiegener, R.; Barbour, M. 2005. Influence of fire and El Niño on tree recruitment varies by species in Sierran mixed conifer. Forest Science. 51(3): 187–197.

North, M.; Innes, J.; Zald, H. 2007. Comparison of thinning and prescribed fire restoration treatments to Sierran mixed-conifer historic conditions. Canadian Journal of Forest Research. 37: 331–342.

North, M.P.; Steger, G.; Denton, R.; Eberlein, G.; Munton, T.; Johnson K. 2000. Association of weather and nest-site structure with reproductive success in California spotted owls. Journal of Wildlife Management. 64: 797–807.

North, M.; Stine, P.; O'Hara, K.; Zielinski, W.; Stephens, S. 2009. An ecosystem management strategy for Sierran mixed-conifer forests. 2nd printing, with addendum. Gen. Tech. Rep. PSW-GTR-220. Albany, CA: U.S. Department of Agriculture, Forest Service, Pacific Southwest Research Station. 49 p.

Oliver, W.W. 1995. Is self-thinning in ponderosa pine ruled by *Dendroctonus* bark beetles? In: Eskew, L.G., comp. Forest health through silviculture: proceedings of the 1995 national silviculture workshop. Gen. Tech. Rep. RM-GTR-267. Fort Collins, CO: U.S. Department of Agriculture, Forest Service, Rocky Mountain Research Station: 213–218.

Purcell, K.L.; Mazzoni, A.K.; Mori, S.; Boroski, B.B. 2009. Resting structures and resting habitat of fishers in the southern Sierra Nevada, CA. Forest Ecology and Management. 258: 2696–2706.

Spencer, W.D.; Rustigian, H.L.; Scheller, R.M.; Syphard, A.; Strittholt, J.; Ward, B. 2008. Baseline evaluation of fisher habitat and population status and effects of fires and fuels management on fishers in the southern Sierra Nevada. Unpublished report. http://consbio.org/products/reports/4/. (February 8, 2012).

Taylor, A.H. 2004. Identifying forest reference conditions on early cut-over lands, Lake Tahoe Basin, USA. Ecological Applications. 14: 1903–1920.

Zielinski, W.J.; Truex, R.L.; Schmidt, G.A.; Schlexer, F.V.; Schmidt, K.N.; Barrett, R.H. 2004. Resting habitat selection by fishers in California. Journal of Wildlife Management. 68: 475–492.

Chapter 12: The Variable-Density Thinning Study at Stanislaus-Tuolumne Experimental Forest

E. Knapp,[1] M. North,[2] M. Benech,[3] and B. Estes[4]

Introduction

Prior to historical logging and fire suppression, forests of the Sierra Nevada were extremely heterogeneous. Frequent low- to moderate-intensity fire was partly responsible for this heterogeneity, which in turn helped make forests resilient to high-severity stand-replacing events. Early observers of forests on the west slope of the Sierra Nevada noted the arrangement of large trees as grouped or clustered (Dunning 1923, Show and Kotok 1924) (fig. 12-1). Show and Kotok (1924) described the mixed-conifer forest as "uneven aged, or at best even-aged by small groups, and is patchy and broken; hence it is fairly immune from extensive devastating crown fire."

A major emphasis in forest management today is improving the resilience of stands to large-scale crown fires. To put forests on the path toward resilience after a long period of fire exclusion, stands are often first mechanically thinned, typically using some variation of thinning from below, which targets the smaller trees and retains the larger and more fire-resistant dominant and codominant individuals. With thinning from below, crowns of individual trees are typically separated from each other, which can lead to a relatively even forest structure. This evenness has sometimes been perceived to be in conflict with management of habitat for wildlife and other forest species. Thinning that produces a more

Figure 12-1—Mixed-conifer forest structure in 1929, within "methods-of-cutting" study units prior to cutting. These plots are located in what today is the Stanislaus-Tuolumne Experimental Forest within the Stanislaus National Forest. Note the relatively even age/size within groups but uneven age/size among groups, along with gaps containing robust understory vegetation.

[1] Research ecologist, U.S. Department of Agriculture, Forest Service, Pacific Southwest Research Station, 3644 Avtech Parkway, Redding, CA 96002.

[2] Research ecologist, U.S. Department of Agriculture, Pacific Southwest Research Station, 1731 Research Park Dr., Davis, CA 95618.

[3] Resource management program area leader, U.S. Department of Agriculture, Forest Service, Stanislaus National Forest, No. 1 Pinecrest Lake Rd., Pinecrest, CA 95364.

[4] Province ecologist, U.S. Department of Agriculture, Forest Service, Pacific Southwest Region, Eldorado National Forest, 100 Forni Rd., Placerville, CA 95667.

Summary of Findings

1. **The high-variability thinning treatment was designed to produce similar spatial heterogeneity** to what was noted on detailed maps of unlogged stands on the Stanislaus-Tuolumne Experimental Forest in 1929. These historical maps show trees arranged in distinct groups of varying density, intermixed with small gaps averaging about 0.25 ac (0.1 ha) in size (range: 0.1 to 0.5 ac) (0.04 to 0.2 ha).

2. **Marking prescriptions initially were difficult to write**, but crews in the field quickly adopted the approach of first identifying gaps and then tree groups using a combination of relative density, average tree size, and dominant species.

3. **The flexibility of the high-variability thinning treatment made it easier to respond to differing topography and forest conditions.** In addition, after some practice, the rate of marking crew progress began to approach the usual rate for more traditional prescriptions.

---

grouped arrangement of trees may be one means of creating heterogeneity at a scale beneficial for wildlife species that prefer different forest structures for nesting, roosting, and foraging, and understory plant species that thrive in different light environments, while simultaneously increasing resilience to wildfire.

The high-variability thinning prescription described in this chapter is part of a new variable-density thinning study on the Stanislaus-Tuolumne Experimental Forest (STEF) designed to investigate the ecological effects of structural variability retained during forest thinning operations (Stanislaus National Forest 2010). Three forest structure treatments (high variability, low variability, and an unthinned control), all with or without prescribed burning as a followup treatment, are being compared. The objective of the high-variability thinning treatment is to produce an arrangement of trees and degree of spatial complexity similar to what was once found in historical forests prior to logging and fire suppression. The study planning predates publication of U.S. Forest Service General Technical Report GTR 220 (North et al. 2009) and is therefore not among the projects designed specifically to implement principles therein. We include it here because the objective of the high-variability treatment is similar to a core concept in GTR 220 of increasing spatial heterogeneity and thus provides a useful illustration.

Context

The STEF is located near Pinecrest, California, at elevations ranging from 5,200 to 6,200 ft (1585 to 1890 m). Precipitation averages about 40 in (102 cm) per year with about half falling as snow. January minimum temperatures average 19 °F (-7.2 °C), and July maximum temperatures average 81 °F (27.2 °C). The vegetation is representative of much of the mid-elevation mixed-conifer forest on high-quality soils throughout the western slopes of the Sierra Nevada. Based on historical data and stem maps produced in 1929, dominant conifer species at that time were white fir (*Abies concolor* (Gordon & Glend.) Lindl. ex Hildebr.), sugar pine (*Pinus lambertiana* Douglas), incense cedar (*Calocedrus decurrens* Torr. Florin), ponderosa pine (*P. ponderosa* Laws), and Jeffrey pine (*Pinus jeffreyi* Balf.), in order of abundance. Some of the more important shrubs included bearclover (*Chamaebatia foliolosa* Benth), manzanita (*Arctostaphylos patula* Greene), and several species of Ceanothus (*C. cordulatus* Kellogg, *C. integerrimus* Hook & Arn, *C. parvifolius* (S. Watson) Trel.). A recently completed fire history study indicates that the historical fire-return interval was between 5 and 8 years, but that the last widespread fire occurred in 1889 (Skinner 2011). Therefore, about 15 to 22 cycles of fire have been missed.

The high-variability thinning prescription was applied to stands that were originally cut in the 1920s. At that time, most trees of merchantable size were removed. The forest that emerged in the years since logging and under a regime of fire exclusion contains a greater abundance of fir and incense cedar, and less pine than the historical forest (details below).

Information Used

Data about the historical forest structure that was used to develop the high-variability prescription were obtained from stand maps produced as part of a "methods-of-cutting" (MOC) study installed in 1929, under the direction of Duncan Dunning, an early U.S. Forest Service scientist. The study evaluated natural regeneration and growth of the residual stand after three different logging treatments that were representative of logging in the Sierra Nevada at the time. The MOC studies were established at other locations in the Western United States, including other sites in the Sierra Nevada, but only at STEF were data for ecological variables other than trees collected. In addition, the STEF MOC plots are the only ones known to remain intact and undisturbed from additional management activities.

For each of the three 10-ac (4 ha) plots, the well-known surveyor, E.A. Wieslander, drew extremely detailed stand maps based on data collected in 1929 (before and after logging). These maps show the location, species, and diameter of

Lack of light on the forest floor has resulted in shrubs declining from about 30 percent cover in 1929 to about 2 percent today.

all trees >3.6 in (9.1 cm), in addition to the spatial extent of shrubs by species and regeneration patches by species, snags, and downed logs. The maps were recently digitized and data associated with individual trees were discovered at the National Archives in San Bruno, California. All trees within plots were remapped in 2007 and 2008, using modern survey equipment (laser rangefinder with compass module mounted on a tripod and connected to a global positioning system unit). Preliminary analyses show that the number of trees >4 in (10.2 cm) in diameter at breast height (d.b.h.), which averaged 142 trees per acre (351 trees per hectare) in 1929 prior to logging (Hasel et al. 1934), has more than doubled today. The basal area in the MOC plots increased from 242 ft^2/ac (55.6 m^2/ha) in 1929 to 308 ft^2/ac (70.8 m^2/ha) today. Lack of light on the forest floor has resulted in shrubs declining from about 30 percent cover in 1929 to about 2 percent today. The proportion of basal area composed of pine species has declined while white fir and incense cedar have increased.

The 1929 prelogging data provide a model for forest structure that the high-variability thinning prescription is based on. These data show that trees were arranged in groups of varying density, basal area, and canopy cover, interspersed with gaps (fig. 12-2). Some groups consisted of widely spaced large trees, while others contained a much higher tree density with interlocking crowns. The historical data allowed us to describe some of the variability among tree groups, and also to quantify the spatial scale of the groups and gaps. Within these 10-ac (4-ha) plots, gaps averaged slightly less than a quarter of an acre (range 0.08 to 0.51 ac) (0.03 to 0.21 ha), with one gap occurring approximately every 2 acres (0.81 ha).

This gap size is similar to what has been reported in other forests in the Western United States with a history of frequent low- to moderate-intensity fire. Gaps in giant sequoia/mixed-conifer forest after numerous prescribed burns were found to average 0.25 ac (0.1 ha) (Demetry, unpublished data, cited in Stephenson [1999]), and a different survey of similar forests showed a large range of gap sizes between 0.16 and 2.89 ac (0.06 to 1.17 ha) (Demetry 1995). Most other studies have focused on the size of tree groups rather than gaps. Assuming groups of trees became established in gaps, group size should be less than the gap size (Stephenson 1999), because gaps have an edge effect with more light and other resources for tree growth in the center of the gap. Bonnickson and Stone (1981) found significant clustering of large living and dead trees (together approximating the historical stand) in mixed-conifer/giant sequoia forest in Kings Canyon National Park, and reported aggregations of trees ranging between 0.07 to 0.40 ac (0.03 to 0.16 ha).

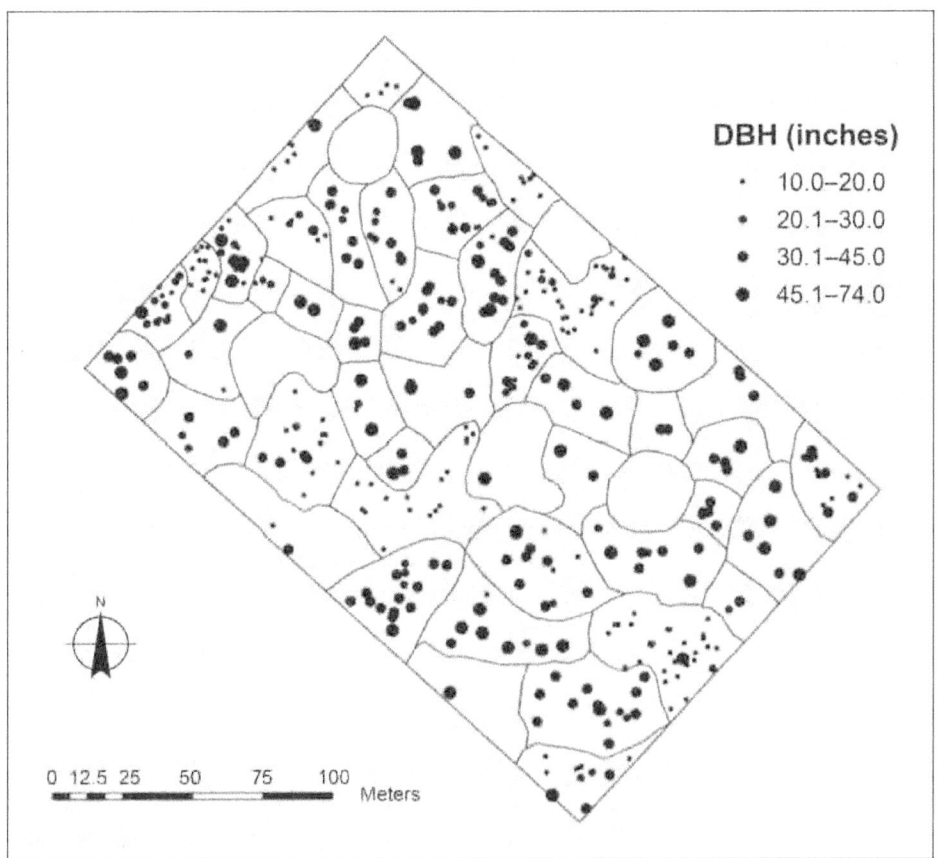

DBH (inches)

· 10.0–20.0

• 20.1–30.0

● 30.1–45.0

● 45.1–74.0

0 12.5 25   50   75   100
Meters

Figure 12-2—Stem map from 1929 showing trees >10 in (25.4 cm) diameter in an uncut stand, "methods-of-cutting" plot No.10, Stanislaus-Tuolumne Experimental Forest. Gaps and approximate groupings of trees of similar size, spatially separated from other groups, were drawn in for illustration. DBH = diameter at breast height.

Using a 1938 stand map from unlogged east-side ponderosa pine at Blacks Mountain (Lassen National Forest), Youngblood et al. (2004) found a random distribution of trees at smaller scales (<28 ft) (<8.5 m), but clustering at larger scales up to 79 ft (24.1 m). Assuming a circular shape, this would equate to tree group size of 0.11 ac (0.04 ha). In a stand reconstruction from old stumps and logs, North et al. (2007) determined clustering to occur at a scale up to 197 ft (60 m) [if circular, this would be a 0.69-ac area (0.28 ha)] in mixed-conifer forest. These patterns are not limited to forests in California. In ponderosa pine forests of Arizona, Cooper (Cooper 1960, 1961) reported that the size of tree groups ranged between 0.15 and 0.32 ac (0.06 and 0.13 ha), while White (1985) found a somewhat broader range of group sizes (0.05 to 0.72 ac) (0.02 to 0.29 ha), but a very similar average of 0.25 ac (0.1 ha). A reconstruction of a ponderosa pine forest in Washington indicated an average group size of 0.01 ac (0.004 ha) in more mesic plots to 0.49 ac (0.2 ha) in the driest plots

An analysis of all western North America studies of tree spatial patterns in fire-dependent forests found a common mosaic of three elements usually manifest at scales <1 ac (0.4 ha): openings, single trees, and clumps of trees with interlocking crowns.

(Harrod et al. 1999). Graham and Jain (2005) noted the existence of tree groups averaging 0.01 to 0.10 ac (0.004 to 0.04 ha) in ponderosa pine forests of southern Idaho. An analysis of all western North America studies of tree spatial patterns in fire-dependent forests found a common mosaic of three elements usually manifest at scales <1 ac (0.4 ha): openings, single trees, and clumps of trees with interlocking crowns (Larson and Churchill 2012).

Implementation

In developing the high-variability thinning prescription, we first examined existing published prescriptions designed to increase spatial variability. Graham and Jain (2005) introduced a silvicultural concept called "free selection" with the similar goal of increasing forest complexity. Free selection is described as a hybrid between even-age and uneven-age management, similar in concept to applying an even-age system in a fine-scale mosaic. One component of free selection is to include openings to regenerate early successional species. A prescription developed by Harrod et al. (1999) helps to define the scale of patchiness. Based on historical forest structure data, Harrod et al. (1999) visualized the forest as a series of approximately 98-ft diameter (0.17 ac) (0.07 ha) circles, each thinned to a varying extent—areas with smaller diameter trees thinned to 39 percent to 72 percent of maximum stand density index (SDI), depending on average tree diameter, to areas with larger trees thinned to 150 percent of maximum SDI. The Harrod et al. (1999) prescription also called for leaving the best trees, based on crown form, regardless of spacing. For the high-variability prescription at STEF, we used some of the same concepts and ideas outlined by Harrod et al. (1999) and Graham and Jain (2005), but refined our marking guidelines using data from the nearby 1929 MOC plots.

The first step in marking the stands was to walk through the entire unit and identify locations where gaps would be created. These gaps averaged one quarter of an acre (range 0.1 to 0.5 ac) (0.04 to 0.2 ha) and one was placed approximately every 2 ac (0.81 ha). Gaps varied in shape with dimensions taking into consideration shading from adjacent trees so that higher light conditions were produced. Priorities for gaps were areas currently lacking pine, and fir groups with evidence of root disease. Some gaps were designed to enlarge existing gaps (e.g., centered around remnant black oaks (*Quercus kelloggii* Newberry)), while others were located in more productive areas of the stand to ensure opportunities to grow groups of large trees, including pines, in the future. Gap edges were marked with flagging. Gaps occasionally included one large pine to provide a seed source. If a tree was left in the gap, preference was given to trees located near the northern edge of the opening where they would not interfere with the amount of light hitting the forest floor.

To better visualize the future stand, we used a leave-tree mark. This allowed us to also mark to retain patches of regeneration observed during this first walk through of the stand. We identified regeneration patches as saplings and young trees less than 10 in d.b.h. (25.4 cm), of good health (long crowns) or desired species composition (greater than 25 percent of the trees being pine). These regeneration patches would normally be removed during the biomass portion of the thinning operation. In some cases, the entire regeneration patch was marked for no entry. In other cases, just the most desirable young trees were retained at wider spacing. This latter situation may eventually lead to portions of the stand with a more open grown structure, which may provide important habitat for some wildlife species.

The second step was to view the portion of the stand not in gaps or regeneration patches as a series of continuous groups (similar to methods outlined in Harrod et al. 1999), each about a quarter acre, but varying from 0.1 to 0.5 ac (0.04 to 0.2 ha). The size and shape of groups depended on obvious breaks in composition or size of trees in the existing stand. Each group was then marked for thinning to either the median basal area target for treed areas (220 ft^2/ac; range 170 to 270 ft^2/ac) (50.5 m^2/ha; range 39.0 to 62.0 m^2/ha), or to low basal area (120 ft^2/ac; range 70 to 170 ft^2/ac) (27.5 m^2/ha; range 16.1 to 39.0 m^2/ha), or high basal area (320 ft^2/ac; range 270 to 370 ft^2/ac) (73.5 m^2/ha; range 62.0 to 85.0 m^2/ha). We chose basal area as our thinning metric, rather than the SDI proposed by Harrod et al. (1999), because we thought it would be easier for a marking crew to visualize. Because the historical data suggests that areas of the stand with a higher proportion of pine were generally of lower density, fir and cedar were thinned more heavily in groups where the largest trees were predominantly pine. In these cases, the existence of larger pines within the group determined the basal area category. For the high basal area groups, the existing stand was sometimes already at or near the basal area target, which resulted in no or few trees being marked for removal. In high basal area groups, care was taken in marking so that cut trees were ones that could be removed without damaging the residual trees. Each unit within the project ended up containing about the same number of each thinning level. However, some parts of the unit ended up with more high basal area groups and some parts more low basal area groups because the thinning target for each group was dictated by existing conditions in the stand rather than being systematically employed.

Within groups, the best trees (generally the largest trees and/or trees with the best crown form) were retained regardless of crown spacing. This led to cases where leave trees were in closer proximity or farther apart from each other than might otherwise occur under standard marking guidelines. Some trees with long (deep) crowns were also left to increase canopy cover for wildlife. Because of the current lack of pine compared with historical conditions, leave-tree priority among conifers was sugar pine > ponderosa/Jeffrey pine > incense cedar > white fir. An exception to selection based on size was sometimes made if the group contained smaller individuals of the favored pine species mixed with larger firs or cedars. No black oaks were cut, but all conifers within the drip line of black oaks were removed where damage to the oak could be avoided. Because leave-tree selection was based foremost on size and species and secondarily on crown form, some trees with relatively poor vigor (higher probability of mortality in the short term) and other characteristics important for wildlife were maintained. All snags larger than 15 in (38 cm) in diameter were retained whenever possible (i.e., when not a safety issue). From a starting studywide basal area of approximately 290 ft^2/ac (66.6 m^2/ha) (300 ft^2/ac (68.9 m^2/ha) in the high-variability units), the marking guidelines were designed to produce an average postthinning basal area of 200 ft^2/ac (45.9 m^2/ha) (range 150 to 250 ft^2/ac (34.4 to 57.4 m^2/ha)) over the unit (including gaps).

The environmental assessment (EA) for the project was completed by the Stanislaus National Forest with the interdisciplinary team consisting of district staff and U.S. Forest Service Pacific Southwest Research Station scientists. The decision notice was signed in August 2010. Two years of outreach, which became increasingly focused as the research plan and prescriptions evolved, preceded the writing of the EA and included tours of the study area by groups representing environmental as well as timber industry interests. Thinning commenced in July 2011 (fig. 12-3).

Figure 12-3—Portion of a unit within the "variable-density thinning" study on the Stanislaus-Tuolumne Experimental Forest thinned using the high-variability prescription. Photo was taken September 14, 2011, shortly after treatment.

Lessons Learned

Importance of Outreach

One of the challenges with writing a prescription to generate a high degree of structural variability is describing exactly what will be cut. As noted by Graham et al. (2007), complex forest structure defies easy description. Our objective with the high-variability prescription was to work with and accentuate residual structure that already exists within these second-growth stands. We were interested in what the stands will look like after thinning, not what will be removed. Having only stand exam data and lacking more detailed information such as complete stand maps, it was not possible to accurately describe what will be removed beforehand. We purposefully did not include diameter limits in the prescription because diameter limits can restrict opportunities for generating structural complexity. However, we were also aware of stakeholder concern about the lack of detail provided in metrics, such as diameter limits, that are typically stated in thinning prescriptions. Without diameter limits, it will be necessary to develop other descriptors that provide a sense of accountability to stakeholders.

Without diameter limits, it will be necessary to develop other descriptors that provide a sense of accountability to stakeholders.

We hope that experiments like this one, in which what is removed can be quantified after thinning, will provide stakeholders one example of the thinning effort required, given the starting conditions, to produce a highly variable structure approximating historical stands. Currently, examples are limited. Lacking such information, we used historical data and maps to define desired posttreatment stand conditions. Field visits with various stakeholder groups were also critical for developing an understanding of objectives and generating some amount of trust. Field visits often included walking into the nearby methods-of-cutting plots that were established in 1929. Seeing what the stem density, tree arrangement, and understory vegetation look like today compared with the 1929 maps provided a powerful visual guide. Field visits also included a walk into representative stands targeted for thinning, and discussion about what to cut at different places in the stand to produce the desired highly variable structure. On one field visit, tree-marking paint was given to participants and, after discussions about objectives, we collectively marked approximately 3 ac (1.2 ha) of a stand. Participants with widely varying backgrounds and perspectives came to surprisingly similar conclusions about what trees to leave and what trees to remove.

Training a Marking Crew to Visualize Tree Groups

In standard thinning-from-below prescriptions, marking crews typically make decisions about whether to leave or cut a tree by looking at the health of individual trees in relation to immediate neighboring trees. The high-variability prescription takes

This means few black and white decisions and no right or wrong answers, which was initially frustrating for some.

a broader view, requiring marking crews to consider a larger patch size (average of a quarter-acre group (0.1 ha)), and make decisions not only about how to mark the group, but how this group fits with other groups in the stand that are marked differently. This means few black and white decisions and no right or wrong answers, which was initially frustrating for some. We found that walking through the stand first and finding obvious structures that could be used as anchors helped. These included areas with thin soils, root disease pockets, remnant black oaks, and groups of larger legacy trees.

On the Stanislaus National Forest, we benefited by having discussions in the field and several iterations of sample marks with the district marking crew and other forest staff over the course of 3 years as the prescription evolved. In addition to members of existing marking crews, the marking crews for the variable-density thinning study included personnel with expertise in wildlife, botany, fuels, planning, and silviculture. We spent the first part of the initial days looking over illustrations of stand structure from the 1929 methods-of-cutting plots, which show the different types of stand conditions and tree arrangements that once existed. Walking through the stands together and discussing possible structures that could be created also helped. Finally, by following the lead of those with the most experience implementing this new prescription, those with less experience were able to develop a feel for what we were trying to accomplish. Many who helped noted that marking stands in this way was a challenge, requiring much more thought than the average prescription. However, frequently altering the mark to produce different postthinning structures also encouraged creativity, which was very satisfying to many of those involved.

Metrics for Describing Variability When Marking

We quickly realized that quantifying basal area within each tree group was tedious and impractical. In addition, basal area, while easier to visualize and mentally calibrate in the field than a percentage of maximum SDI (Harrod et al. 1999), was still an imperfect descriptor of the variability created with the prescription. For example, a low basal area group could consist of a medium to high density of small trees or very widely spaced large trees. In addition, a prism—the common field method for estimating basal area—does not cover a defined area and is thus not ideal for measurements within discrete tree groups. Therefore, we ended up marking more by "feel" rather than strictly adhering to the basal area targets/ranges for each group. We also began to describe groups using a combination of relative density (high/medium/low), average tree size (large, medium, small), and dominant species (pine, fir, incense cedar), rather than basal area. High-density areas were characterized by leave trees with interlocking or closely spaced crowns, while trees in low-density areas generally were relatively widely spaced (though not at a regular spacing, in most cases). Medium-density areas were intermediate, approximating densities used in standard thinning prescriptions for this forest type. (Note: while the tree densities within high, medium, and low groups generally also resulted in basal areas within the ranges listed in the prescription, some additional work still needs to be done to quantify these structural differences within the marked stands, using metrics most relevant to marking crews in the field.) For tree size, large was assumed to be leave trees averaging >24 in, (61 cm) medium = 14 to 24 in (36 to 61 cm), and small = <14 in (36 cm). These tree size categories can readily be tailored to the stand conditions at a site.

Spatial Scale

While we attempted to vary the mark in groups averaging about a quarter acre, the actual size of the groups ended up exceeding this value more often than not. Perhaps having a larger number of marking crew members working together caused the collective broader view. However, obvious boundaries within the stand such as changes in tree density, average tree size, or species composition also tend to occur at larger spatial scales today. Sometimes crews would continue to mark in one type of stand structure until a different type of stand structure was reached rather than breaking up areas that are relatively homogeneous today. To mark to produce discontinuities at the scale historical forests were structured may therefore require frequent recalibration of spatial-scale targets.

Time/Effort Required

One of the concerns voiced was the extra time, effort, and expertise marking such complex prescriptions might require if implemented on a broader scale. Several observations suggest that this may not be as big of an obstacle as initially feared. In our case, we were more rigid in implementing some aspects of the prescription (e.g., requiring five gaps in each 10-ac [4-ha] unit) than needs to be the case outside of research. While progress was initially slow until the marking crew became comfortable visualizing the forest in this new way, speed quickly increased throughout the 2-week marking period. By the time we finished, a marking crew of three (only two carrying paint, while the third produced a hand-drawn map recording what was done throughout the stand) was able to mark about 13 to 15 ac (5.3 to 6.1 ha) in a day. While still less than a seasoned marking crew can accomplish for simpler prescriptions, it is not unreasonable to expect that speed would continue to improve with additional experience. This prescription may not lend itself to the traditional format of a marking crew of five working in unison and each member taking an adjacent strip—a team of two working on a unit together may ultimately be the most efficient.

One of the concerns voiced was the extra time, effort, and expertise marking such complex prescriptions might require if implemented on a broader scale. Several observations suggest that this may not be as big of an obstacle as initially feared.

References

Bonnicksen, T.M.; Stone, E.C. 1981. The giant sequoia-mixed conifer forest community characterized through pattern analysis as a mosaic of aggregations. Forest Ecology and Management. 3: 307–328.

Cooper, C.F. 1960. Changes in vegetation, structure, and growth of southwestern pine forests since white settlement. Journal of Forestry. 92: 39–44.

Cooper, C.F. 1961. Pattern in ponderosa pine forests. Ecology. 42: 493–499.

Demetry, A. 1995. Regeneration patterns within canopy gaps in a giant sequoia-mixed conifer forest: implications for forest restoration. Flagstaff, AZ: Northern Arizona University. 266 p. M.S. thesis.

Dunning, D. 1923. Some results of cutting in the Sierra forests of California. Department Bulletin No. 1176. Washington, DC: U.S. Department of Agriculture. 27 p.

Graham, R.T.; Jain, T.B. 2005. Application of free selection in mixed forests of the inland northwestern U.S. Forest Ecology and Management. 209: 131–145.

Graham, R.T.; Jain, T.B.; Sandquist, J. 2007. Free selection: a silvicultural option. In: Powers, R.F., ed. 2005 national silviculture workshop: restoring fire-adapted ecosystems. Albany, CA: U.S. Department of Agriculture, Forest Service, Pacific Southwest Research Station: 121–156.

Harrod, R.J.; McRae, B.H.; Hartl, W.E. 1999. Historical stand reconstruction in ponderosa pine forests to guide silvicultural prescriptions. Forest Ecology and Management. 114: 433–446.

Hasel, A.A.; Wohletz, E.; Tallmon, W.B. 1934. Methods of cutting, California Forest and Range Experiment Station, Stanislaus Branch, Plots 9, 10, and 11, Progress report. On file with: U.S. Department of Agriculture, Forest Service, Pacific Southwest Research Station, 3644 Avtech Parkway, Redding, CA 96002.

Larson, A.J.; Churchill, D. 2012. Tree spatial patterns in fire-frequent forests of western North American, including mechanisms of pattern formation and implications for designing fuel reduction and restoration treatments. Forest Ecology and Management. 267: 74–92.

North, M.; Innes, J.; Zald, H. 2007. Comparison of thinning and prescribed fire restoration treatments to Sierran mixed-conifer historic conditions. Canadian Journal of Forest Research. 37: 331–342.

North, M.; Stine, P.; O'Hara, K.; Zielinski, W.; Stephens, S. 2009. An ecosystem management strategy for Sierran mixed-conifer forests. 2nd printing, with addendum. Gen. Tech. Rep. PSW-GTR-220. Albany, CA: U.S. Department of Agriculture, Forest Service, Pacific Southwest Research Station. 49 p.

Show, S.B.; Kotok, E.I. 1924. The role of fire in the California pine forests. Bulletin No. 1294. Washington, D.C.: U.S. Department of Agriculture. 80 pp.

Skinner, C. 2011. Personal communication. Geographer, U.S. Department of Agriculture, Forest Service, Pacific Southwest Research Station. 3644 Avtech Parkway, Redding, CA 96002.

Stanislaus National Forest. 2010. Experimental Forest Research (30298), Environmental Assessment. July 2010.

Stephenson, N.L. 1999. Reference conditions for giant sequoia forest restoration: structure, process, and precision. Ecological Applications. 9: 1253–1265.

White, A.S. 1985. Presettlement regeneration patterns in a southwestern ponderosa pine stand. Ecology. 66: 589–594.

Youngblood, A.Y.; Max, T.; Coe, K. 2004. Stand structure in eastside old-growth ponderosa pine forests of Oregon and northern California. Forest Ecology and Management. 199: 191–217.

Chapter 13: Applying GTR 220 Concepts on the Sagehen Experimental Forest

P. Stine[1] and S. Conway[2]

Introduction

Applying science to the practice of forest management is a difficult process. Scientific results tend to be expressed in terms such as variances, confidence intervals, and probability distributions. Rarely does science provide unequivocal information, yet land managers must make definitive decisions on the ground. The General Technical Report "An Ecosystem Management Strategy for Sierran Mixed-Conifer Forests," published by the U.S. Forest Service (hereafter GTR 220) (North et al. 2009) presented some important concepts for land managers to consider; however, implementation of these principles into detailed, site-specific application requires some novel approaches.

Summary of Findings

1. With GIS, **the Sagehen fuels reduction project was partitioned into subunits based on topographic categories, and each subunit was designated with an emphasis** that established a priority for providing habitat, reducing fuels, or restoring forest resilience.

2. **Emphasis areas allow reconciliation of conflicting demands by providing due attention to all of the chosen priorities.** Different prescriptions were developed for each of the different emphases, allowing silviculture to be tailored to each area's priorities.

3. **Field trips and test plots helped ground discussions** so participants could visualize how new prescriptions would alter forest conditions.

Context

The "Sagehen Fuels Reduction Project" began almost 10 years ago with the goal of reducing the risk of a high-severity fire. Over this period, several plans were developed. Early in 2010, the Truckee Ranger District, the Pacific Southwest Research Station, the University of California at Berkeley, and copartners in managing the experimental forest, agreed to take a step back from the internal planning that had been completed to date. In its place, they initiated a collaborative planning process to engage all interested public and private parties to thoroughly examine the issues pertaining to fuels reduction management. Strong encouragement was offered for this idea from Sierra Forest Legacy, a prominent consortium of environmental groups concerned with forest management in the Sierra Nevada. A grant was obtained from the Sierra Nevada Conservancy to support an independent facilitator,

[1] National coordinator for experimental forests and ranges, U.S. Department of Agriculture, Forest Service, Pacific Northwest Research Station, The John Muir Institute, One Shields Ave., University of California, Davis, CA 95616.

[2] Vegetation management office, U.S. Department of Agriculture, Forest Service, Tahoe National Forest, Truckee Ranger District, 10811 Stockrest Springs Rd., Truckee, CA 96161.

and the effort was launched in May 2010. One constraint on this effort was to limit planning to the areas covered by previous planning efforts where a suite of survey activities had already been completed. These required surveys (e.g., of archeological sites) are expensive and time consuming. Opening up the planning process to the entire basin would have added significant costs and time to the project. Thus the collaborative planning team (the team) agreed to view this project as a first step toward a longer term set of objectives that could be developed and implemented over time in the Sagehen basin.

Sagehen presented an ideal test bed for developing innovative ideas for forest management for a number of reasons. Perhaps foremost, almost the entire basin was designated as an experimental forest in 2005. There are 80 experimental forests and ranges throughout the United States, designated specifically to provide an environment where research can examine new forest management methods. The Sagehen basin has also been the home of the Sagehen Creek Field Station of the University of California at Berkeley for over 60 years. A wealth of research information and monitoring data has been collected in this area. In addition, when Truckee Ranger District staff first contemplated some fuels reduction treatments, scientists from the University of California developed a research approach to examine the effects of Strategically Placed Area Treatments (SPLATs), the principle landscape fuels reduction strategy employed by the Forest Service throughout the Sierra Nevada (Finney 2001). Research has a prominent role at Sagehen and offers some important advantages for trying new management ideas.

The Sagehen basin is a 9,000-ac (3642-ha) watershed at the upper reaches of Sagehen Creek, a tributary of the Truckee River just on the east side of the Sierra Nevada range, about 10 mi (16 km) north of Truckee, California. The west end of the basin begins at the crest of the Sierra Nevada at just over 9,000 ft (2743 m) elevation and extends east, ultimately flowing into Stampede Reservoir. Five major vegetation cover types can be found in the basin: herbaceous (fen, wet montane meadow, and dry montane meadow), montane shrub, mixed conifer, true fir, and conifer plantation. The majority of the basin is in mixed conifer (Jeffrey pine [*Pinus jeffreyi* Balf.], incense cedar [*Calocedrus decurrens* Torr. Florin], white fir [*Abies concolor* (Gordon & Glend.) Lindl. ex Hildebr.]) or a true fir (red fir [*Abies magnifica* A. Murray bis] and white fir) at higher elevations. The basin has a Mediterranean type climate with cold, wet winters and warm, dry summers. Monthly average maximum temperature ranges from 39 °F (3.9 °C) in December to 79 °F (26.1 °C) in July; monthly average minimum temperature ranges from 14 °F (-10 °C) in January to 37 °F (2.8 °C) in July. Annual precipitation is about 33 in (83 cm); snowfall accounts for greater than 80 percent of the annual precipitation and averages over 200 in (508 cm).

The basin is almost entirely national forest land within the Truckee Ranger District of the Tahoe National Forest. Portions of the basin have been subject to high-severity fire in the past, most notably the Donner Fire that occurred in the fall of 1960. Staff on the Truckee Ranger District recognize the risk of another high-severity fire and several fuel reduction plans have been in development.

Information Used

To our advantage, we had a fairly rich foundation of data with which to work. Key data sources included vegetation maps (both recent and from ca. 1980), detailed forest stand plot data and stand exam data, American marten (*Martes americana*) survey data (Moriarty et al. 2011), and published research findings and recommendations from several different time periods. Perhaps most important was the planning and execution of two test field plots to demonstrate the ideas of spatial heterogeneity. These test plots provided both visual examples and quantitative data for what dense cover areas and small openings looked like and what the resulting stand composition and structure would be after treatment (fig. 13-1). We even included a prescribed burn for one of the two test plots. This proved very effective in communicating the anticipated outcomes of treatments to the collaboration team.

Figure 13-1—Test plot mechanically thinned and prescribe burned at the Sagehen Experimental Forest to produce a group and gap structure.

Not all localities have this level of information, but, by the same token, every location has limitations in data availability. Even in this situation, as on many national forests, we wanted more data. An important feature of this effort was the presence of a facilitator. Among many tasks, our facilitator particularly helped present a neutral position, kept meetings progressing and the project on pace, and organized efforts to gather and assimilate feedback. We also had a technical working group, particularly the professionals on the district staff, who brought a positive, problemsolving attitude. We encountered many instances in which we had to adjust expectations and address problems, but we always worked within the principle that a solution could be found.

Perhaps the biggest challenge was incorporating the concept of landscape heterogeneity at multiple spatial scales into silvicultural prescriptions.

Implementation

Perhaps the biggest challenge was incorporating the concept of landscape heterogeneity at multiple spatial scales into silvicultural prescriptions. As the team developed approaches to incorporate heterogeneity at different spatial scales (e.g., retention of small patches of dense cover areas embedded within certain emphasis areas), we realized that it would be difficult to translate into a prescription and to write direction for a marking crew. Implementing these ideas using standard silvicultural practices that are grounded in defining and managing toward average conditions of a stand will be difficult. Promoting forest heterogeneity, particularly at multiple spatial scales, is antithetical to some standard forest management practices (e.g., equally spacing between leave trees to maximize growth and resistance to crown fire [fig. 6-2]). At present, there are no simple silvicultural tools available to operationalize this approach. Yet there are considerable benefits (accompanied inevitably with growing pains) to emulating the landscape complexity created by an active fire regime.

Lessons Learned

The innovations that made this project unique and intriguing include some applications that are easily transferable and others that will still need development. The lessons learned offer a starting point for other land managers. New tools have been developed to assess within-stand heterogeneity (chapter 9) and to divide a forested landscape in different topographic categories (chapter 10). Other localities in the Sierra Nevada are exploring ways to implement GTR 220 concepts, but there are still challenges that need to be addressed.

The process was intended to prepare the Truckee Ranger District to move forward with National Environmental Policy Act (NEPA) procedures while providing ample advanced opportunity for satisfying the concerns of all involved parties.

The expectation was to apply the concepts of GTR 220 to accomplish an array of objectives for a single landscape. By discussing and exploring issues in advance of any official NEPA action, the team could collectively reveal and deal with many issues prior to crafting and putting forth a proposed action. The key advantages and discoveries of this process we implemented and that may be transferable to similar forest management planning efforts include:

1. Identify and categorize all potential issues, no matter how small, in advance.

2. Focus attention on the most complex and compelling issues:
   a. Habitat protection and enhancement for a key species of concern, American marten (designated as a sensitive species in Forest Service Pacific Southwest Region).
   b. Ecological restoration to create more resilient forest stands, capable of being sustained through a warming climate, future droughts, and fire.
   c. Restoration of fire resiliency; enabling the forest (throughout the basin) to be better able to withstand wildfire.

3. Craft objectives to address each of the issues that would be used to direct management actions to be taken. The intent was to develop management objectives that were achievable, given the current conditions within the basin, with an understanding that this was the first of perhaps several treatments that could happen over time. While not achieving everything we might strive for, these first treatments would be able to redirect the trajectory of forest structure and composition.

4. Partition the landscape into subunits using topographic variables (aspect, elevation) (chapter 10), one of the key principles in GTR 220, as a determining factor in defining appropriate forest composition and structure, as well as other key sources of spatially explicit information, such as the locations of high-value marten habitat. Not all areas have equal value (as habitat) or have equal ecological potential (for one kind of forest stand or another) or generate equal concern (for fire behavior). Partitioning the landscape enabled us to explicitly address and provide for the landscape heterogeneity that is inherent in this, and most other, project areas.

5. Formulate "emphasis areas" that dictate which objectives would be given priority in a given location (fig. 13-2). Emphasis areas are an important innovation that enabled a purposeful differentiation of the landscape to promote and manage for the notion of landscape heterogeneity.

Formulate "emphasis areas" that dictate which objectives would be given priority in a given location.

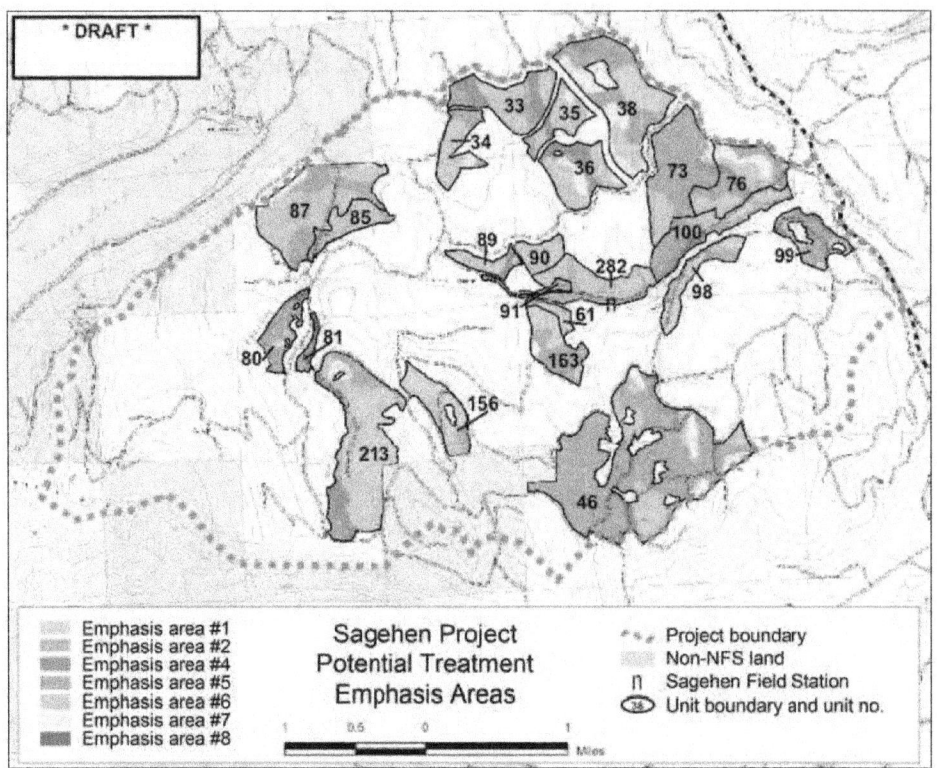

Figure 13-2—Sagehen Experimental Forest with treatment areas classified by emphasis area. Emphasis areas are (1) high-value marten habitat on north-facing slopes, on ridges, and on higher elevation south-facing slopes (above 6,725 ft) (2050 m); (2) drainage bottoms with high-value marten habitat; (3) high-value marten habitat on lower elevation (below 6,725 ft) (2050 m) south-facing slopes; (4) drainage bottoms that do not currently support marten habitat; (5) north-facing slopes that are not currently marten habitat; (6) vegetation types not identified as marten habitat on south-facing slopes; (7) vegetation types not identified as marten habitat on ridges; and (8) aspen stands targeted for ecological restoration. NFS = National Forest System.

6. Partition the landscape into emphasis areas to better reconcile conflicts and provide due attention to all of the chosen priorities. Emphasis areas allowed us to apply sound rationale and understand the collective implications of these choices at a watershed scale.

7. Based on these objectives, craft different silvicultural strategies to meet the needs of each of the emphasis areas. Some of these silvicultural prescriptions employed relatively conventional approaches, whereas others required innovations to achieve the intended outcomes.

A number of details are unresolved, most notably the translation of the written objectives and prescriptions to crews who will mark stands for treatment. This step is always a delicate link in the process; more so with the novel strategies imbedded in this approach. Plans for handling this process include members of the collaborative planning team joining district staff in the exploratory field efforts and subsequent training sessions for the crews. However, experiences from the test plots suggest a fairly quick learning process for understanding the intentions of variable thinning and the other features of this approach. Overall, we see the efforts accomplished to date as a good example of how the principles of GTR 220, combined with an open process with ample opportunity for input from all interested parties, can lead to well-founded forest management strategies.

References

Finney, M.A. 2001. Design of regular landscape fuel treatment patterns for modifying fire growth and behavior. Forest Science. 47: 219–228.

Moriarty, K.M.; Zielinski, W.J.; Forsman, E. 2011. Decline in American marten occupancy rates at Sagehen Experimental Forest, California. Journal of Wildlife Management. 75: 1774–1787.

North, M.; Stine, P.; O'Hara, K.; Zielinski, W.; Stephens, S. 2009. An ecosystem management strategy for Sierran mixed-conifer forests. Gen. Tech. Rep. PSW-GTR-220. 2nd printing, with addendum. Albany, CA: U.S. Department of Agriculture, Forest Service, Pacific Southwest Research Station. 49 p.

Chapter 14: Clarifying Concepts

M. North[1] and P. Stine[2]

Introduction

There are some topics that continue to be raised by managers that were not sufficiently addressed in the first and second edition of U.S. Forest Service General Technical Report GTR 220 "An Ecosystem Management Strategy for Sierran Mixed-Conifer Forests." All of them concern issues about where and when GTR 220 concepts apply and how these concepts relate to current management practices. The first section discusses the appropriate ecological conditions where GTR 220 concepts might be applied. The second section attempts to clarify the types and potential wildlife uses of defect trees in an effort to make them more recognizable in the field. The third section defines and distinguishes canopy cover and closure, an important distinction because some current management practices are focused on canopy cover targets. Some aspects of GTR 220 conditions, particularly localized wildlife habitat, may be better assessed with canopy closure. The final section examines the link between heterogeneity and ecosystem resilience, a core concept behind GTR 220's emphasis on increasing variability in managed forests. General Technical Report 220 is a conceptual framework for managing forests and intentionally lacks the specificity that practitioners might sometimes want. We hope that clarifying the following concepts may help elucidate the GTR's intent without constraining management options.

Summary of Findings

1. **GTR 220 concepts could be applied to forest types that historically had low-intensity, frequent fire regimes in locations with topographic relief.**

2. **"Defect" structures used by wildlife are often large live or dead trees with decay, irregular bole or crown shapes, broken tops, broomed foliage or hollows created by torn branches** (examples in appendix).

3. **Canopy closure, the percentage of the sky hemisphere obscured by vegetation over a point, should be distinguished from canopy cover, a measure of canopy porosity averaged over a stand.** For some wildlife, including several sensitive species, high variability in canopy closure may be as important as stand average canopy cover.

4. **Heterogeneity in vegetation structure and composition has been strongly linked to ecosystem resilience, but direct empirical evidence is sparse.** Increasing research suggests microclimate variability and refugia from temperature extremes may be one mechanism linking site and vegetation heterogeneity with ecosystem resilience.

[1] Research ecologist, U.S. Department of Agriculture, Forest Service, Pacific Southwest Research Station, 1731 Research Park Dr., Davis, CA 95618.

[2] National coordinator for experimental forests and ranges, U.S. Department of Agriculture, Forest Service, Pacific Northwest Research Station, The John Muir Institute, One Shields Ave., University of California, Davis, CA 95616.

Forest Types and Landscapes Where GTR 220 Concepts Apply

In a broad sense, the GTR 220 strategy could be applied to any low-intensity, frequent-fire forest community within the Western United States. These forests generally are the highest priority for fuels reduction and forest restoration treatments because of their potential to burn at uncharacteristically high severity in the event of a wildfire after decades of fire suppression (Brown et al. 2004). The management concepts hinge on mimicking the variable forest conditions that would have been created by the effect of topography on fire behavior (North et al. 2009; however, see Scholl and Taylor 2010). Areas with no topographic relief may still have experienced variable fire intensities that create a patchy landscape. That variability was probably influenced by weather conditions during the burn or small-scale differences in fuels, making the pattern of the resulting forest conditions difficult to predict. The topographic "roughness" necessary to start directly influencing fire intensity has not been studied in the Sierra Nevada. Working with large, widely distributed fire scar data, research in eastern Washington mixed-conifer forests has started to examine interactions between topography and the scale of fire events (Kellogg et al. 2008, Kennedy and McKenzie 2010). These studies suggest modern fires are larger than historical burns, overriding topographic features that often constrained past wildfires. Contrasts between flatter and more rugged "firesheds" suggest that historically, topography did have a bottom-up influence on fire size, but the "roughness" at which this occurs has yet to be quantified (Kennedy and McKenzie 2010).

In Sierra Nevada landscapes with some topographic relief, forest types with a historically frequent, low-intensity fire regime include mixed conifer, ponderosa pine (*Pinus ponderosa* Lawson and C. Lawson), Jeffrey pine (*P. jeffreyi* Balf.), Douglas-fir (*Pseudotsuga menziesii* Mirbel Franco), giant sequoia (*Sequoiadendron giganteum* (Lindl.) J. Buchholz), and combinations of white fir (*Abies concolor* (Gordon & Glend.) Lindl. ex Hildebr), incense cedar (*Calocedrus decurrens* Torr. Florin), California black oak (*Quercus kelloggii* Newberry), and sugar pine (*P. lambertiana*, Douglas) (Sugihara et al. 2006). Many forests, however, at higher elevation or with more mesic conditions such as red fir (*A. magnifica* A. Murray bis), lodgepole pine (*P. contorta* Douglas ex Lounden var. *Murryana* (Balf.) Engelm), and western white pine (*P. monticola* Douglas ex D. Don) have different fire regimes (i.e., more infrequent and mixed or high severity), and forest conditions may not have been as strongly influenced by topography. The GTR 220 strategy also is probably not appropriate for some forests in northern California with a high hardwood composition (e.g., >30 percent of basal area) that can occur in forests with

> **In a broad sense, the GTR 220 strategy could be applied to any low-intensity, frequent-fire forest community within the Western United States.**

an abundance of tanoak (*Lithocarpus densiflorus* (Hook. & Arn.) Rehder), madrone (*Arbutus menziesii* Pursh), or interior live oak (*Q. wislizeni* A. DC.) mixed with Douglas-fir and ponderosa pine sometimes referred to as mixed evergreen. The low densities and gap conditions suggested by GTR 220 for drier conditions might favor a transition of treated areas to hardwood dominance unless the area was repeatedly treated with mechanical thinning or prescribed fire (Stuart et al. 1993).

Defect Trees

What characteristics make a "defect" tree valuable habitat for wildlife? Although this topic is frequently raised, preferred tree structural conditions for many wildlife species have not yet been specifically defined in the literature for most species. Most of the available research has focused on a few sensitive species such as the fisher (*Martes pennanti*) or spotted owl, or general groups such as bats, small mammals, and cavity-nesting songbirds. Furthermore, the number of studies that occurred in the Sierra Nevada is limited. There is evidence, however, of the preferred use patterns for some well-studied individual and groups of species in western coniferous forests.

Several studies have examined the role of legacy trees; large, old individuals left in a matrix of younger second growth following a past timber harvest or other disturbance. In commercially managed coastal redwoods (*Sequoia sempervirens* (Lamb. ex D. Don) Endl.), Mazurek and Zielinski (2004) found significantly higher diversity and richness of the wildlife they were surveying (bats, small mammals, and birds) in forests that contained some old legacy trees and snags. They suggested the higher diversity might result from the structural complexity offered by legacy trees, particularly the basal hollows produced by fire scarring. Other animals using legacy or old-growth residual trees include northern (*Strix occidentalis caurina*) (Moen and Gutierrez 1997, North et al. 1999) and California spotted owls (*S. o. occidentalis*) (Irwin et al. 2000, North et al. 2000), fisher (Zielinski et al. 2004), southern red-backed voles (*Clethrionomys gapperi*) (Sullivan and Sullivan 2001), northern flying squirrels (*Glaucomys sabrinus*) (Carey 2000), and bats (Pierson et al. 2006). Although most of these studies do not quantify the characteristics of these legacy trees, they note that the trees were often left during earlier timber harvest because of some structural "defect." The exact habitat value of these trees is unknown, but they probably offer some kind of special substrate that can provide cover and protection from inclement weather and predators.

Trees and snags selected by primary cavity nesters, woodpeckers and nut-hatches, may be particularly important because once vacated, the cavities are used by other birds and mammals (Bull et al. 1997). Several studies have found cavity availability can limit the abundance of some of these species in managed forests (Carey et al. 1997, 2002; Cockle et al. 2011; Wiebe 2011). A meta-analysis of the global distribution of tree cavities found that forest management tends to reduce the fungal heart-rots most associated with cavity abundance, thereby increasing reliance on primary cavity-nesters for creating suitable cavities (Remm and Lõhmus 2011).

A summary of forest structures favored by wildlife in interior forests of the Pacific Northwest focused on five conditions: living trees with decay, hollow trees, broomed trees, dead trees, and logs (Bull et al. 1997). The first three conditions might have been considered "defects" in past silviculture practices focused on stand improvement, and systematically removed. Certainly in some highly managed Sierra Nevada forests, these structures may be more rare than large, old trees as a result of stand improvement management. Bull et al. (1997) suggested identifying these structures by looking for dead and broken tops, large dead branches, wounds, fungal fruiting bodies, cavities, bole bends (where a new leader formed after top breakage), brooms caused by mistletoe, rust fungi, and Elytroderma disease. Bull et al. (1997) also suggested retaining large-diameter, relatively intact (decay classes 1 to 3) snags, and large (>15 in [38 cm] in diameter), long, and if available, hollow downed logs. Example pictures of some of these conditions are presented in the appendix.

The general pattern across these studies is that wildlife use is associated with larger trees that have structural characteristics, which can facilitate a cavity or a platform, enabling nesting, denning, roosting, or resting. Examples of these structures include irregular bole (e.g., hollows, forks, etc.) and crown (multiple or broken tops, platforms, concentrations of dense foliage) shapes. Care will be needed to identify and maintain these structures during mechanical thinning and prescribed fire operations. In some cases where these structures are rare, creating a no-mechanical-entry zone or encircling an area with fire line might be warranted. In some areas, management practices, such as prescribed fire, should be encouraged for their role in actively recruiting these structures.

Canopy Cover and Closure

Canopy cover is often cited as an important habitat feature for a number of sensitive species associated with old-forest conditions in the Sierra Nevada (Hunsaker et al. 2002). The standards and guides in the 2004 Sierra Nevada Framework (SNFPA 2004) have specific minimum canopy cover targets designed to provide suitable habitat for sensitive species such as the California spotted owl. Some managers concerned that canopy cover would fall below levels in the standards and guides have been hesitant to create gaps in treated stands. Creating a gap will lower canopy closure (a point measure) over the opening, but may not significantly lower canopy

[Look] for dead and broken tops, large dead branches, wounds, fungal fruiting bodies, cavities, bole bends, brooms caused by mistletoe, rust fungi, and Elytroderma disease... [as well as] large-diameter, relatively intact snags, and large, long, and if available, hollow downed logs.

cover (a stand-level average). Canopy closure should be distinguished from canopy cover to accurately assess forest canopy conditions and characteristics that matter to key wildlife species. This distinction is particularly important because, following GTR 220 concepts, treatments are intended to produce tree groups, gaps, and areas with a low density of large trees.

Forest canopies are typically measured at two different scales (i.e., point and stand), with different instruments, to distinguish between two different qualities of canopy structure that create different wildlife habitat features. Jennings et al. (1999) distinguish these two structural qualities by referring to the point measure as canopy closure and the stand-level measure as canopy cover (fig. 14-1).

Canopy closure is a measurement of the percentage "of the **sky hemisphere** obscured by vegetation when **viewed from a single point**" (Jennings et al. 1999) (emphasis added). Closure measures the canopy hemisphere within an angle of view (i.e., a cone) over the sample point. Closure provides valuable information about the understory light, microclimate, and microhabitat environment at a specific location (Nuttle 1997). It is probably most useful for understanding how available light may influence plant composition and growth, and the potential climate conditions and vegetative cover over a specific microhabitat site (e.g., nest site cover to discourage predation). Traditionally, canopy closure has been assessed with a spherical densiometer, "moosehorn," or hemispherical photograph. Different methods of measurement affect the canopy closure estimation (Paletto and Tosi 2009). As the viewing angle (i.e., the width of the observation cone) increases, closure estimates increase and within-stand variability between point estimates decreases (Fiala et al. 2006). Spherical densiometers use a reflective mirror held in front of the observer, which produces a large viewing angle and hence high canopy closure estimates. Spherical densiometers have large measurement errors at the mid-range of canopy closure owing to this large viewing angle (Cook et al. 1995). The moosehorn and hemispherical photograph reduce this problem because the image is taken straight up and the measurement of canopy closure is typically restricted to 45 to 60° off of vertical. Hemispherical photographs have a benefit over other closure estimates in that computer programs (e.g., the freeware Gap Light Analyzer) can easily and precisely calculate the total direct and diffuse light reaching the point on the forest floor over the course of a year. These light levels are highly correlated with surface microclimate conditions (Bigelow et al. 2011, Ma et al. 2010).

In contrast, canopy cover is the percentage "of forest floor covered by the vertical projection of the tree crowns" (Jennings et al. 1999). Cover is always measured vertically with a very narrow angle of view that approaches a point. It is **a stand-level measure of canopy porosity** (e.g., how much rain falls directly

> **Canopy closure should be distinguished from canopy cover to accurately assess forest canopy conditions and characteristics that matter to key wildlife species.**

153

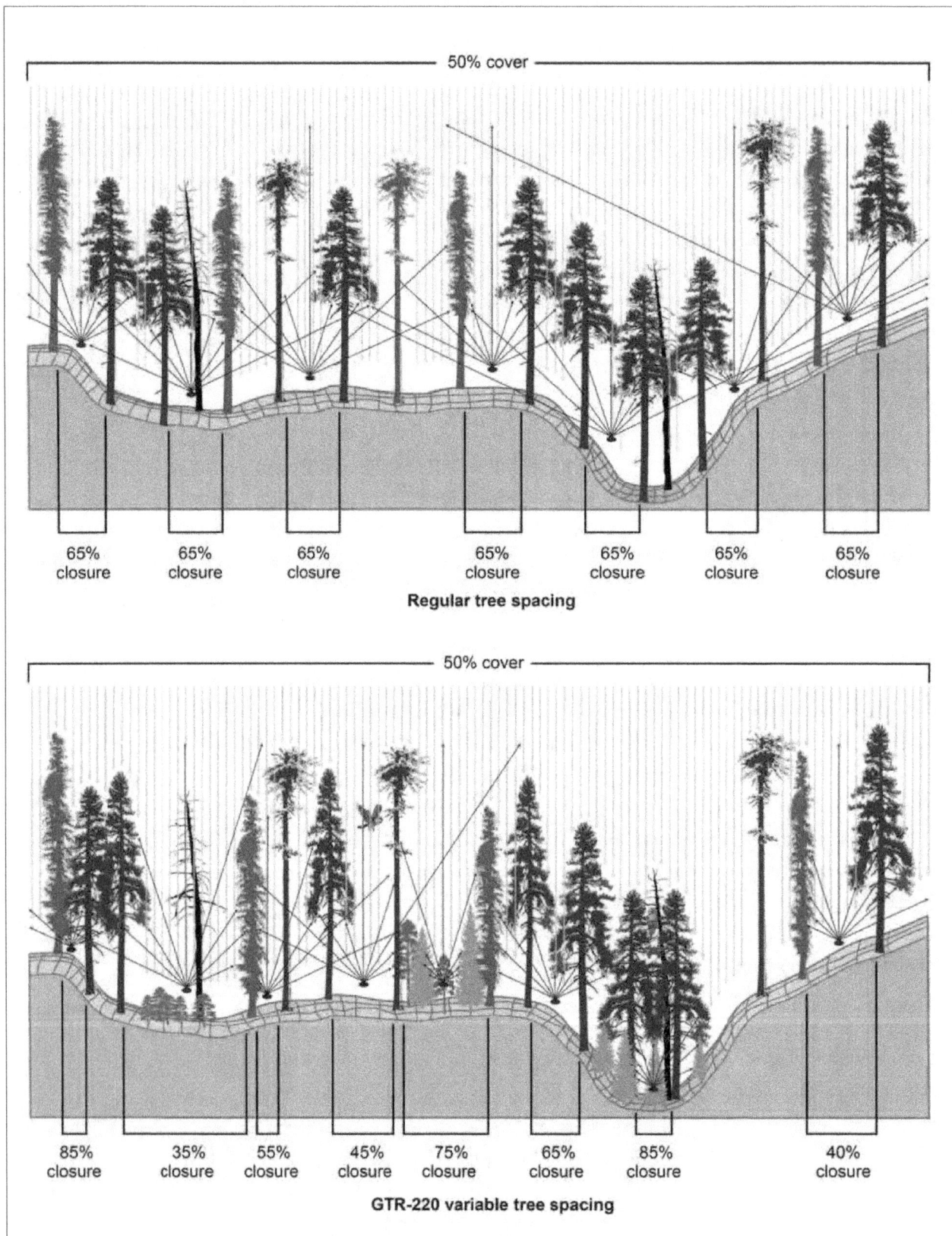

Figure 14-1—The difference between canopy closure and canopy cover in forests treated to produce regular and variable tree spacing. Illustration by Steve Oerding.

on the forest floor) that indicates how much of the forest floor is vertically overtopped with canopy. Canopy cover is usually either directly measured with a densitometer (sighting tube) or indirectly estimated from plot data using the Forest Vegetation Simulator (FVS).[3] Typically, direct densitometer measurements are taken at 100 or more points, sampled along a walked grid, in which the observer records the percentage of points where the sky directly overhead is obscured. Densitometer measurements provide a relatively unbiased estimate of canopy cover for the particular area (i.e., the walked grid) assuming that the stand is well sampled (Korhonen et al. 2006).

Indirect estimates of canopy cover are often made by FVS based on stand exam and plot data. As an indirect estimate, however, FVS assumes a certain amount of crown overlap (Crookston and Stage 1999), but it does not account for spatial variability in tree locations (Christopher and Goodburn 2008). Two stands having the same number, species, and size of trees will have the same FVS calculated canopy cover even if one has regular spacing and the other is mostly open with the trees concentrated in high-density clumps. The FVS will tend to underestimate a stand's actual canopy cover if trees are regularly spaced (i.e., less overlap than the model would predict). The FVS will overestimate a stand's actual canopy cover if trees are clumped (i.e., greater overlap than the model assumes). The FVS estimates should be viewed with caution because the program is unlikely to accurately estimate stand-level canopy cover in stands with a high degree of spatial variability or those with complex canopy structure such as those resulting from application of GTR 220 concepts.

The FVS estimates of stand-level canopy cover do not provide information on whether a stand has points of high canopy closure habitat associated with some sensitive species. For example, Purcell et al. (2009) compared FVS estimates of canopy cover and measures of canopy closure made with a spherical densiometer and a moosehorn in five studies of fisher resting sites. They found substantial differences in the estimates between the three methods. In another comparison, Ganey et al. (2008) evaluated model estimates of canopy cover developed from stand exam data with those derived from in-field densitometer (sighting tube) data at sites used by Mexican spotted owls (*Strix occidentalis lucida*). The model estimates ranged from 50 to 200 percent of field-based measurements, particularly in mesic mixed-conifer forest with multilayered canopies (Ganey et al. 2008).

FVS estimates should be viewed with caution because the program is unlikely to accurately estimate stand-level canopy cover in stands with a high degree of spatial variability.

---

[3] Two other remotely sensed methods of estimating canopy cover are not addressed in this discussion; they include using grid overlaps on aerial photographs and light detection and ranging (LiDAR).

Canopy cover measurements alone may not capture aspects of canopy structure important to some sensitive species because it is a stand-level average. Historical forests can provide some inference about canopy conditions that were suitable habitat for these species. A recent study using FVS to derive current and historical canopy cover estimated an average cover of only 22 percent in 1911 compared to current (2005–2007) cover estimates of 28, 42, and 53 percent for the same area in moderate, low, and no fire-severity classes, respectively (Collins et al. 2011). In general, FVS estimates of stand-level average canopy cover would likely be very low if applied to the consistently low tree densities found in reconstruction studies, historical data sets, or photographic records. However, almost all of these sources indicate that trees were grouped in clusters, suggesting that active-fire regime forests had high-canopy closure at many points.

Assessing point-level canopy closure within treated stands may improve assessment of habitat conditions. Using hemispherical photographs, a moosehorn, or a spherical densiometer, closure measurements could be collected with a stratified sampling of gap, low-density, and tree cluster conditions (see suggestions in chapter 9 section "Using FVS to Assess Heterogeneity"). With GTR 220's goal of producing variable forest structure across a treated area, point-level canopy closure values will be low in gaps and areas with a low density of large trees, and high in tree groups. Canopy closure, and its coefficient of variation, can provide an assessment of canopy heterogeneity within a stand among microhabitat locations. In contrast, canopy cover can provide a mean assessment of stand-level conditions. Canopy cover is best assessed with a densiometer in which at least 100 observations are collected in a systematic sample (i.e., a grid) within an area representative of the stand's variability. Distinguishing between cover and closure, and the canopy characteristic that each measures and the technique used for canopy estimation, may improve assessments of canopy conditions for wildlife species.

Heterogeneity and Resilience

The Forest Service definition of ecological restoration focuses on reestablishing the resilience or adaptive capacity of ecosystems. This approach is consistent with a recent review of catastrophic shifts in many different ecosystems that suggested maintaining resilience was the best strategy for sustainable management (Scheffer et al. 2001). How then might heterogeneity increase a forest's resilience? Although it is intuitive that spatial heterogeneity, species diversity, and ecosystem resilience are linked, the connection has been difficult to rigorously test. One study examining the species-rich littoral forests of Madagascar, did find that forest spatial heterogeneity was associated with the resilience and maintenance of high species diversity

Although it is intuitive that spatial heterogeneity, species diversity, and ecosystem resilience are linked, the connection has been difficult to rigorously test.

over the last 6,000 years of climatic perturbations (Virah-Sawmy et al. 2009). The foundation of the concept, however, is probably more theoretical, based on the synthesis of decades of ecosystem research.

Holling (1973) was among the first to define ecological resilience as "the capacity of an ecosystem to return to the precondition state following a perturbation, including maintaining its essential characteristics, taxonomic composition, structures, ecosystem functions, and process rates." Definitions of resilience, however, evolved as many ecologists moved away from Clements' ideas that ecosystems inherently have a climax or stable state (Clements 1916). A more recent definition by Walker et al. (2004) is "the capacity of a system to absorb disturbance and reorganize while undergoing change so as to still retain essentially the same function, structure, identity, and feedbacks." In a review of factors associated with loss of resilience and regime shifts in ecosystems, altered disturbance regimes was cited as a common driver (Folke et al. 2004). Recently, Holling (2010) has suggested that there are two aspects to resilience: "the more traditional [engineering] definition concentrates on stability near an equilibrium steady state, where resistance to disturbance and speed of return to the equilibrium are used to measure" resilience. The more ecological definition emphasizes conditions far from any equilibrium, "where instabilities can flip a system into another regime of behavior" and "resilience is the magnitude of disturbance that can be absorbed before the system changes its structure by changing the variables and processes that control behavior." Ultimately Holling (2010) suggests that ecological resilience hinges on "designing interrelations between people and resources that are sustainable in the face of surprises and the unexpected."

Beyond its theoretical foundation, empirical plant research has focused on identifying how variable microclimate conditions, driven by topographic heterogeneity, are associated with species resilience to changing climate. Some studies, examining how plant species persisted during past droughts and glacial advances, have identified variability in microenvironments as important in mediating climate change and enhancing species persistence (Suggitt et al. 2011). Microrefugia that support lower minimum temperatures may be particularly important for retaining both cold-adapted and mesophilous taxa (Dobrowski 2011, Scherrer and Körner 2011). The local climate, or topoclimate (Thornthwaite 1953) experienced by individuals is affected by regional advection and local terrain. Several studies have found good estimates of the lowest minimum temperature in a landscape can be made using terrain variables that characterize surface water accumulation (Chung et al. 2002, Daly et al. 2010, Dobrowski et al. 2009, Lookingbill and Urban 2003). Slope, aspect,

Variable microclimate conditions, driven by topographic heterogeneity, are associated with species resilience to changing climate.

and slope shape are strong influences on local microclimate affecting water balance (Dobrowski 2011). These studies support the GTR 220 concept that varying forest conditions in response to topography may be consistent with increasing fine-scale contrasts in microclimate. Such a strategy may compliment one of the mechanisms by which species persist in landscapes as climate conditions change.

In Sierra Nevada forests, resilience, in part, will hinge on the ability of trees to persist under future conditions that may include greater or more frequent drought stress. A consistent pattern associated with the onset of tree mortality is a drop off in annual increment growth. Some studies (Das et al. 2007, 2008; Franklin et al. 1987) have suggested that these decreases eventually cross a threshold after which survival is unlikely. Many studies have documented reductions in tree growth as stem density increases. Drought also decreases annual radial increment growth, and can increase susceptibility to bark beetle attack. Competition from other trees, particularly from high stand density conditions, interact with climate stressors increasing the risk of mortality (Hurteau et al. 2007, Linares et al. 2010). Collectively these studies suggest that stand density reduction and variable forest structure that provides greater microclimate heterogeneity can make trees more resilient to mortality-induced stress. There are still many unknowns in the appropriate scale and mechanisms by which heterogeneity may increase ecosystem resilience.

Measuring Resilience

Moving from metaphors to measurement of ecological resilience requires clearly defining indicators of stress resilience that can be adapted to the context-specific conditions of different ecosystems.

Ecological resilience is an attractive concept, but often lacks measureable indicators. Quantifying resilience will be critical for identifying thresholds of probable concern when adaptively managing forests in the face of climate change (Scheffer et al. 2001). Unfortunately, resilience and adaptive capacity are often described as theoretical constructs rather than measurable indicators of system response to stress or disturbance (Carpenter et al. 2001). Moving from metaphors to measurement of ecological resilience requires clearly defining indicators of stress resilience that can be adapted to the context-specific conditions of different ecosystems.

If resilience is described in a manner similar to engineering resilience (sensu Holling 1973, Gunderson 2000), then (1) resistance can be defined as either no reduction or a smaller reduction in ecosystem response to a stress event; (2) recovery is the ability to resume a state relative to the damage experienced during an event; and (3) resilience is the capacity to reach pre-event ecosystem condition. A recent paper presented a quantitative method for assessing resistance, recovery, and resilience (fig. 14-2), in the context of tree radial growth response (Lloret et al. 2011). This approach may have much wider application for measuring and assessing response and resilience of many different ecosystem components (i.e., sensitive

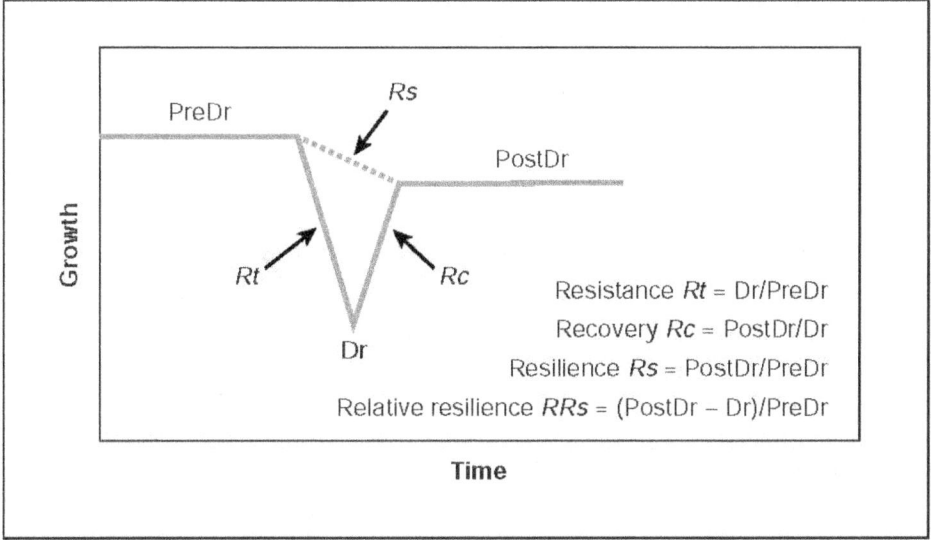

Figure 14-2—Conceptual diagram of resilience components for tree growth response to a drought event (Dr), modified from Lloret et al. (2011). Resistance (*Rt*), recovery (*Rc*), resilience (*Rs*), and relative resilience (*RRs*) are calculated based on tree growth prior to (PreDr), during (Dr), and after (PostDr) a drought event.

species reproduction, understory plant diversity, tree mortality rates, etc.). Managers might consider using this approach when monitoring and measuring ecosystem response to new forest practices and changing climate conditions.

References

Bigelow, S.; North, M.; Salk, C. 2011. Using light to predict fuels-reduction and group-selection effects on succession in Sierran mixed-conifer forest. Canadian Journal of Forest Research. 41: 2051–2063.

Brown, R.T.; Agee, J.K.; Franklin, J.F. 2004. Forest restoration and fire: principles in the context of place. Conservation Biology. 18: 903–912.

Bull, E.L.; Parks, C.G.; Torgersen, T.R. 1997. Trees and logs important to wildlife in the interior Columbia River basin. Gen. Tech. Rep. PNW-GTR-391. Portland; OR: U.S. Department of Agriculture, Forest Service, Pacific Northwest Research Station. 55 p.

Carey, A.B. 2000. Effects of new forest management strategies on squirrel populations. Ecological Applications. 10: 248–257.

Carey, A.B. 2002. Response of northern flying squirrels to supplementary dens. Wildlife Society Bulletin. 30: 547–556.

Carey, A.B.; Wilson, T.M.; Maguire, C.C.; Biswell, B.L. 1997. Dens of northern flying squirrels in the Pacific Northwest. Journal of Wildlife Management. 61: 684–699.

Carpenter, S.; Walker, B.; Anderies, J.M.; Abel, N. 2001. From metaphor to measurement: Resilience of what to what? Ecosystems. 4: 765–781.

Christopher, T.A.; Goodburn, J.M. 2008. The effects of spatial patterns on the accuracy of Forest Vegetation Simulator (FVS) estimates of forest canopy cover. Western Journal of Applied Forestry. 23: 5–11.

Chung, U.; Seo, H.H.; Hwang, K.H.; Hwang, B.S.; Yun, J.I. 2002. Minimum temperature mapping in complex terrain based on calculation of cold air accumulation. Korean Journal of Agriculture and Forest Meteorology. 4: 133–140.

Clements, F.E. 1916. Plant succession: an analysis of the development of vegetation. Washington, DC: Carnegie Institution of Washington. 512 p.

Cockle, K.L.; Martin, K.; Wesolowski, T. 2011. Woodpeckers, decay, and the future of cavity-nesting vertebrate communities worldwide. Frontiers in Ecology and the Environment. 9: 377–382.

Collins, B.M.; Everett, R.G.; Stephens, S.L. 2011. Impacts of fire exclusion and recent managed fire on forest structure in old growth Sierra Nevada mixed-conifer forests. Ecosphere 2: Article 51.

Cook; J.G.; Stutzman, T.W.; Bowers, C.W.; Brenner, K.A.; Irwin, L.L. 1995. Spherical densiometers produce biased estimators of forest canopy cover. Wildlife Society Bulletin. 23: 711–727.

Crookston, N.L.; Stage, A.R. 1999. Percent canopy cover and stand structure statistics from the Forest Vegetation Simulator. Gen. Tech. Rep. RMRS-GTR-24. Ogden, UT: U.S. Department of Agriculture, Forest Service, Rocky Mountain Research Station. 11 p.

Daly, C.; Conklin, D.R.; Unsworth, M.H. 2010. Local atmospheric decoupling in complex topography alters climate change impacts. International Journal of Climatology. 30: 1857–1864.

Das, A; Battles, J.J.; Stephenson, N.L.; van Mantgem, P.J. 2007. The relationship between tree growth patterns and likelihood of mortality: a study of two tree species in the Sierra Nevada. Canadian Journal of Forest Research. 37: 580–597.

Das, A; Battles, J.J.; van Mantgem, P.J.; Stephenson, N.L. 2008. Spatial elements of mortality risk in old-growth forests. Ecology. 89: 1744–1756.

Dobrowski, S.Z. 2011. A climatic basis for microrefugia: the influence of terrain on climate. Global Change Biology. 17: 1022–1035.

Dobrowski, S.Z.; Abatzoglou, J.; Greenberg, J.A.; Schladow, G. 2009. How much influence does landscape-scale physiography have on air temperature in a mountain environment? Agricultural and Forest Meteorology. 149: 1751–1758.

Fiala, A.C.S.; Garman, S.L.; Gray, A.N. 2006. Comparison of five canopy cover estimation techniques in the western Oregon Cascades. Forest Ecology and Management. 231: 188–197.

Folke, C.; Carpenter, S.; Walker, B.; Scheffer, M.; Elmquvist, T.; Gunderson, L.; Holling, C.S. 2004. Regime shifts; resilience; and biodiversity in ecosystem management. Annual Review of Ecology and Evolution. 35: 557–581.

Franklin, J.F.; Shugart, H.H.; Harmon, M.E. 1987. Tree death as an ecological process. BioScience. 37: 550–556.

Ganey, J L.; Cassidy, R.H.; Block, W.M. 2008. Estimating canopy cover in forest stands used by Mexican spotted owls: Do stand-exam routines provide estimates comparable to field-based techniques? Res. Pap. RMRS-RP-72WWW. Fort Collins, CO: U.S. Department of Agriculture, Forest Service, Rocky Mountain Research Station. 8 p.

Gunderson, L.H. 2000. Ecological resilience—in theory and application. Annual Review of Ecology and Systematics. 31: 425–439.

Holling, C.S. 1973. Resilience and stability of ecosystems. Annual Review of Ecological Systems. 4: 1–23.

Holling, C.S. 2010. Engineering resilience versus ecological resilience. In: Gunderson, L.H.; Allen, C.R.; Holling, C.S. eds. Foundations of ecological resilience. Washington; DC: Island Press. 51–66.

Hunsaker, C.T.; Boroski, B.B.; Steger, G.N. 2002. Relations between canopy cover and the occurrence and productivity of California spotted owls. In: Scott, J.M.; Heglund, P.J.; Morrison, M.L. eds. Predicting species occurrences: issues of accuracy and scale. Covelo, CA: Island Press: 687–700.

Hurteau, M.; Zald, H.; North, M. 2007. Species-specific response to climate reconstruction in upper-elevation mixed-conifer forests of the western Sierra Nevada, California. Canadian Journal of Forest Research. 37: 1681–1691.

Irwin, L.L.; Rock, D.F.; Miller, G.P. 2000. Stand structures used by northern spotted owls in managed forests. Journal of Raptor Research. 34: 175–186.

Jennings, S.B.; Brown, N.D.; Sheil, D. 1999. Assessing forest canopies and understorey illumination: canopy closure; canopy cover and other measures. Forestry. 72: 59–73.

Kellogg, L.K.B.; McKenzie, D.; Peterson, D.L.; Hessl, A.E. 2008. Spatial models for inferring topographic controls on historical low-severity fire in the eastern Cascade Range of Washington, USA. Landscape Ecology. 23: 227–240.

Kennedy, M.C.; McKenzie, D. 2010. Using a stochastic model and cross-scale analysis to evaluate controls on historical low-severity fire regimes. Landscape Ecology. 25: 1561–1573.

Korhonen, L.; Korhonen, K.T.; Rautiainen, M.; Stenberg, P. 2006. Estimation of forest canopy cover: a comparison of field measurement techniques. Silva Fennica. 40: 577–588.

Linares, J.C.; Camarero, J.J.; Carreira, J.A. 2010. Competition modulates the adaptation capacity of forests to climatic stress: insights from recent growth decline and death in relict stands of the Mediterranean fir *Abies pinsapo*. Journal of Ecology. 98: 592–603.

Lloret, F.; Keeling, E.G.; Sala, A. 2011. Components of tree resilience: effects of successive low-growth episodes in old ponderosa pine forests. Oikos. 120: 1909–1920.

Lookingbill, T.R.; Urban, D.L. 2003. Spatial estimation of air temperature differences for landscape scale studies in montane environments. Agricultural and Forest Meteorology. 114: 141–151.

Ma, S.; Concilio, A.; Oakley, B.; North, M.; Chen, J. 2010. Spatial variability in microclimate in a mixed-conifer forest before and after thinning and burning treatments. Forest Ecology and Management. 259: 904–915.

Mazurek, M.J.; Zielinski, W.J. 2004. Individual legacy trees influence vertebrate wildlife diversity in commercial forests. Forest Ecology and Management. 193: 321–334.

Moen, C.A.; Gutiérrez, R.J. 1997. California spotted owl habitat selection in the central Sierra Nevada. Journal of Wildlife Management. 61: 1281–1287.

North, M.; Franklin, J.; Carey, A.; Forsman, E.; Hamer, T. 1999. Forest structure of the northern spotted owl's foraging habitat. Forest Science. 45: 520–527.

North, M.; Stine, P.; O'Hara, K.; Zielinski, W.; Stephens, S. 2009. An ecosystem management strategy for Sierran mixed-conifer forests. 2nd printing, with addendum. Gen. Tech. Rep. PSW-GTR-220. Albany, CA: U.S. Department of Agriculture, Forest Service, Pacific Southwest Research Station. 49 p.

North, M.P.; Steger, G.; Denton, R.; Eberlein, G.; Munton, T.; Johnson, K. 2000. Association of weather and nest-site structure with reproductive success in California spotted owls. Journal of Wildlife Management. 64: 797–807.

Nuttle, T. 1997. Densiometer bias? Are we measuring the forest or the trees? Wildlife Society Bulletin. 25: 610–611.

Paletto, A.; Tosi, V. 2009. Forest canopy cover and canopy closure: comparison of assessment techniques. European Journal of Forest Research. 128: 265–272.

Pierson, E.D.; Rainey, W.E.; Chow, L.S. 2006. Bat use of the giant sequoia groves in Yosemite National Park: a report to Save-the-Redwoods League. 152 p. Unpublished report. http://www.savetheredwoods.org/media/pdf_pierson.pdf. (February 8, 2012.)

Purcell, K.L.; Mazzoni, A.K.; Mori, S.R.; Boroski, B.B. 2009. Resting structures and resting habitat of fishers in the southern Sierra Nevada, California. Forest Ecology and Management. 258: 2696–2706.

Remm, J.; Lõhmus, A. 2011. Tree cavities in forests—the broad distribution pattern of a keystone structure for biodiversity. Forest Ecology and Management. 262: 579–585.

Scheffer, M.; Carpenter, S.; Foley, J.A.; Fole, C.; Walker, B. 2001. Catastrophic shifts in ecosystems. Nature. 413: 591–596.

Scherrer, D.; Körner, C. 2011. Topographically controlled thermal-habitat differentiation buffers alpine plant diversity against climate warming. Journal of Biogeography. 38: 406–416.

Scholl, A.E.; Taylor, A.H. 2010. Fire regimes; forest change; and self-organization in an old-growth mixed-conifer forest; Yosemite National Park, USA. Ecological Applications. 20: 362–280.

Sierra Nevada Forest Plan Amendment [SNFPA]. 2004. Sierra Nevada Forest Plan Amendment: final supplemental environmental impact statement. R5-MB-046. Washington, DC: U.S. Department of Agriculture, Forest Service, Pacific Southwest Region. 492 p.

Stuart, J.D.; Grifantini, M.C.; Fox, L., III. 1993. Early successional pathways following wildfire and subsequent silvicultural treatment in Douglas-fir/hardwood forests; NW California. Forest Sciences. 39: 561–572.

Suggitt, A.J.; Gillingham, P.K.; Hill, J.K.; Huntley, B.; Kunin, W.E.; Roy, D.B.; Thomas, C.D. 2011. Habitat microclimates drive fine-scale variation in extreme temperatures. Oikos. 120: 1–8.

Sugihara, N.G.; van Wagtendonk, J.W.; Shaffer, K.E.; Fites-Kaufman, J.; Thode, A.E, eds. 2006. Fire in California's ecosystems. Berkeley, CA: University of California Press. 596 p.

Sullivan, T.P.; Sullivan, D.S. 2001. Influence of variable retention harvests on forest ecosystems. II. Diversity and population dynamics of small mammals. Journal of Applied Ecology. 38: 1234–1252.

Thornthwaite, C.W. 1953. A charter for climatology. World Meteorological Organization Bulletin. 2: 40–46.

Virah-Sawmy, M.; Gillson, L.; Willis, K.J. 2009. How does spatial heterogeneity influence resilience to climatic changes? Ecological dynamics in southeast Madagascar. Ecological Monographs. 70: 557–574.

Walker, B.; Holling, C.S.; Carpenter, S.R.; Kinzig, A. 2004. Resilience; adaptability and transformability in social–ecological systems. Ecology and Society. 9: 5.

Wiebe, K.L. 2011. Nest sites as limiting resources for cavity-nesting birds in mature forest ecosystems: a review of the evidence. Journal of Field Ornithology. 82: 239–248.

Zielinski, W.J.; Truex, R.L.; Schmidt, G.A.; Schlexer, F.V.; Schmidt, K.N.; Barrett, R.H. 2004. Resting habitat selection by fishers in California. Journal of Wildlife Management. 68: 475–492.

Chapter 15: A Desired Future Condition for Sierra Nevada Forests

M. North

Introduction

An unexpected outcome of U.S. Forest Service General Technical Report PSW-GTR 220, "An Ecosystem Management Strategy for Sierran Mixed-Conifer Forests" (North et al. 2009), was how it generated discussion about a desired future condition for Sierra Nevada forests. The paper did not convey leading-edge research results or provide an exhaustive literature review. Rather it was an effort to take findings generally accepted amongst scientists, and synthesize them into a conceptual model for how Sierra Nevada forests might be managed. When the GTR has been used in implementing projects, the conceptual model often generates discussion about a desired endpoint toward which management and treatments could move a forest. Initially that discussion can seem removed from the project at hand, but agreement on a desired future condition is a foundation for building collaboration.

Yet in discussions of desired future conditions for Sierra Nevada forests there remain some challenges that are more fundamental than clarifying GTR 220 concepts or providing more detailed science summaries. During field visits to project sites, discussions with managers and through dialogue with stakeholders, three areas keep being brought up. Collectively they are issues that may require basic changes in how Sierra Nevada forests are managed: changes in the way forests are perceived and measured, the scale and economics of how forests are managed, and an institutional change in management that internalizes science and course correction.

Summary of Findings

1. **Silviculture should consider broadening the measures and scales by which forests are assessed** beyond the current focus on averages and stands.

2. For practical, ecological, and economic reasons, **forest projects should be scaled up to treat an entire fireshed, and then, where safety allows, convert the fireshed's future management to maintenance through managed wildfire and prescribed fire.** Rough calculations suggest fuels should be reduced on 437,000 ac of Forest Service land each year to mimic historical fire regimes.

3. **Question-driven, science-based monitoring should be integrated into management** to address uncertainties arising from climate change and new forest practices.

The Limitations of Stand-Level Averages

Silviculture remains the heart of forest management because it has provided powerful and useful tools for understanding how forest growth responds to manipulation and disturbance. An essential tool in current silviculture applications is the Forest Vegetation Simulator (FVS), a model based on hundreds of studies in many

---

[1] Research ecologist, U.S. Department of Agriculture, Forest Service, Pacific Southwest Research Station, 1731 Research Park Dr., Davis, CA 95618.

different forest types, which has proved invaluable for forest planning and scenario testing for different management practices. Yet silviculture and models of forest dynamics are strongly imprinted with treating forests as a collection of stands, "a spatially continuous group of trees and associated vegetation having similar structures and growing under similar soil and climatic conditions" (Oliver and Larson 1996). The concept of the stand can be traced back to European management efforts to parse forests into relatively homogenous units that could be efficiently managed for more predictable commodity production (Puettmann et al. 2009). The stand concept tends to set a scale at which most forest attributes are then evaluated. Some attributes such as bark beetle damage are well correlated with stand-level measures such as the Stand Density Index (SDI) (chapter 2). However, clearly some of the processes that strongly shape forest ecosystems such as fire, climate, and edaphic conditions, to name only a few, operate across multiple scales. When those processes shape habitat, microclimate, or ecosystem functions at scales other than the stand, managing and measuring forests as a collection of stands is unlikely to be congruent with those processes or accurately assessed with stand-level metrics (fig. 15-1). Just within the topics raised in this collection of papers, authors have suggested that stand-level assessments may not accurately capture how forests respond to fire and climate change, what forest conditions provide habitat for marten, fisher and California spotted owl, or how we measure canopy structure and its influence on microclimate and fine-scale wildlife habitat.

Figure 15-1—A mixed-conifer forest with complex structure created by frequent fire in the Illilouette Basin, Yosemite National Park. Identifying "stands" and describing them with averages would probably not accurately represent the forest's variability across different scales.

Management focused at the stand level can lead toward an emphasis on averages.

A second problem with management focused at the stand level is that it can lead toward an emphasis on averages. The stand concept is an effort to express forest landscape variability by differences between units (i.e., stands) that have been delineated as areas with relatively homogenous conditions. Quantifying the average of the forest conditions best captures attributes of each unit, because within the stand, those conditions should be similar. Heterogeneity is then expressed as the variability between stands within a landscape. In practice, silviculturists often create fine-scale variability within stands by responding to existing forests conditions and accordingly adjusting their treatment. However, with metrics and descriptions of seral development and ecological response that are scaled to the stand, it has been difficult to communicate to stakeholders how that finer-scale variability is sometimes created. This has hindered support for some management practices by suggesting greater uniformity than may actually be present in treated forests. Field visits can help overcome this problem but do not change the fact that currently the language and metrics of silviculture often fall short of capturing the heterogeneity and complexity of forest ecosystems.

A recent critique of silviculture suggested it inherently promotes uniformity and discourages variability (Puettmann et al. 2009). Silviculture, however, has been tremendously adaptable, as public priorities for a forest's ecosystem services have changed over time. Its tools can be modified (chapter 9) and new avenues of research can adapt silviculture practices to a broader range of spatial and temporal scales. This could include developing tools and metrics that measure heterogeneity at scales relevant to ecological processes of interest.

Economics and Treatment Scale

General Technical Report 220 did not address economics, yet costs often determine whether a project is even viable. It's difficult to synthesize information about the potential economic impacts of revising forest management practices. The costs of any particular forest project are highly idiosyncratic depending on many factors such as current wood market prices, diesel costs, hauling distances, and processing infrastructure. However, current trends in economic conditions are not favorable. Many projects require service contracts to remove the noncommercial, small-diameter trees, and available revenue for these costs are decreasing as Forest Service budgets shrink. Out of necessity many national forests in the Sierra Nevada limit projects to areas where the economics are favorable or locations where funds for service contracts can be secured. There are good reasons for rethinking this approach through changing the scale of projects and specifically planning for and linking together areas that can generate revenue with restricted or sensitive areas requiring minimal treatment and revenue support.

How much Sierra Nevada forest would the Forest Service need to treat each year to mimic historical patterns of fuel reduction when there was an active (pre-1850) fire regime? Acreage that may have historically burned each year was estimated using a Geographic Approach to Planning (GAP) analysis that identified the

With metrics and descriptions of seral development and ecological response that are scaled to the stand, it has been difficult to communicate to stakeholders how finer-scale variability is sometimes created. This has hindered support for some management practices by suggesting greater uniformity than may actually be present in treated forests.

The Forest Service's current pace and scale of treatments in the Sierra Nevada is an order of magnitude less than what is needed to keep up with accumulating fuels from forest growth.

acreage and agency ownership of different forest types in the Sierra Nevada (Davis and Stoms 1996) and sources summarizing historical fire regime studies (Stephens et al. 2007, Van de Water and Safford 2011, FEIS 2011). Of the Forest Service's 4.8 million forested acres (1.9 million ha) (Plumas National Forest south through Sequoia National Forest, including Inyo National Forest), approximately 488,000 ac (197 000 ha) may have burned each year before the arrival of Europeans. From 1986 to 2010, on average 51,000 ac/yr (20 600 ha/yr) are burned by wildfire (with great annual variability) (Bilyea 2011), leaving 437,000 ac/yr (177 000 ha/yr) that would need to be treated to mimic historical fuel reduction levels. Over the last 8 years, the Forest Service has averaged 28,600 ac/yr (11 600 ha/yr) of mechanical fuels reduction and 8,300 ac/yr (3360 ha/yr) of prescribed burning (Sherlock 2011) for a total of 36,900 ac/yr (14 930 ha/yr) treated or about 8.4 percent of the 437,000 ac. Despite the best efforts of managers, the current rate of treatment will leave most of the forest in high density, high fuel load conditions susceptible to an altered disturbance regime. Even if projects are not slowed by legal or administrative challenges, the Forest Service's current pace and scale of treatments in the Sierra Nevada is an order of magnitude less than what is needed to keep up with accumulating fuels from forest growth.

Another problem with current fuels treatment practices is that most sensitive areas with special value such as threatened and endangered species habitat or riparian conservation areas (Van de Water and North 2010, 2011) are excluded from projects or have minimal treatment. These areas often have high stem densities, moisture stress, and heavy fuels accumulations, decreasing their resilience to wildfire and drought. Yet these areas often are the last to be treated because of increased risk of litigation and high cost, because lighter treatments usually do not include removing trees with commercial value. Without some change in current practices, many of the areas with greatest ecological and habitat value will be prone to high overstory mortality and loss of large live trees.

[Scale] up the size of treatments with an objective, where possible, of treating entire firesheds and then converting their future management to maintenance through managed wildfire and prescribed fire.

An additional economic consideration is that in many forests the only potential for generating revenue will be in the first management entry, when some intermediate-size trees with commercial value may be thinned. Future treatments for maintenance of fuels reduction will probably have expenses that exceed any revenue. At current budget levels, it seems unlikely that such extensive and expensive treatment can be accomplished for second and future fuels reduction entries.

One possible approach to revising management practices within these economic constraints is to consider scaling up the size of treatments with an objective, where possible, of treating entire firesheds and then converting their future management to maintenance through managed wildfire and prescribed fire. This approach would increase the scale of treatments and provide an opportunity to bundle revenue-generating areas with lightly treated areas that are revenue sinks. For example, across a fireshed, revenue from heavier thinning on upper slopes designed to restore low-density large pine conditions, might be used to support hand thinning or pre-scribed burning that maintains high canopy cover in the parallel track of forest that's in the drainage bottom. Once treatments are completed, the burnshed could largely be maintained by allowing it to burn under wildfire or prescribed fire conditions determined by local managers. This approach probably cannot be used in areas with high home density because of liability from escaped fire. It would, however, restore fire and its ecological benefits (Stephens et al., in press) to many forests currently degraded by fire exclusion and reduce future maintenance costs. The larger scale of treatments and the practical need to spread them out over several years would make for a steady, more predictable flow of wood for local mills and potential biomass plants. Biomass use of small-diameter fuels holds promise for improving the economics of fuels treatments. The lack of consistent biomass supply can limit development of processing infrastructure; however, large-scale, long-term treat-ment planning can overcome some of these limitations (Hampton et al. 2011). Even with some firesheds being turned over to maintenance by fire, there would still be a substantial need for thinning other firesheds ensuring a continuing supply of wood for local communities.

This approach may be criticized as impractical, but at least it could stimulate discussions between stakeholders and forest managers about current and future economic constraints on management options. Without proactively addressing some of these conditions, the status quo will relegate many ecologically important areas to continued degradation from fire exclusion.

Monitoring

Science should become an integral part of forest management, and monitoring may be the best means of achieving this inclusion. Monitoring is an important course cor-rection tool particularly as new silvicultural practices are implemented. It is essential not only for understanding management impacts on focal wildlife species but also for assessing ecosystem response under changing climatic conditions. It is likely that some new management practices will not achieve their objectives and will need adjustment. Furthermore, we have limited information about how best to increase forest resilience under warming conditions, and some trial and error is inevitable. Monitoring is a candid admission that all forest management is experimental and needs to adapt to uncertain outcomes, changing conditions, and new information.

Monitoring is a candid admission that all forest management is experimental and needs to adapt to uncertain outcomes, changing conditions, and new information.

Monitoring Policy

There is now a window of opportunity, prompted by the Washington office of the Forest Service, to make meaningful improvements in monitoring. The interest in establishing an integrated Inventory Monitoring and Assessment Strategy and Implementation Plan is driven by several agency initiatives, including the new planning rule, the climate change scorecard, the watershed condition framework, the ecological integrity index, and a focus on ecosystem restoration. Integrating the inventory, monitoring, and assessment components of these ongoing activities will improve the consistency and scalability of information and analyses, and hopefully enable the Forest Service to capture cost efficiencies.

Monitoring Implementation

What should be monitored and how will managers know how effective their restoration efforts are? The type of monitoring can determine how informative the data are. Passive and mandated monitoring often produces trend observations, whereas question-driven monitoring guided by a conceptual model can test à priori predictions (Lindenmayer and Likens 2010). The Society for Ecological Restoration has suggested restoration should be assessed in three general areas: species diversity, ecological processes, and vegetation structure (Ruiz-Jaen and Aide 2005a, 2005b). Monitoring changes in vegetation is fairly common, but assessing changes in species diversity and ecological processes is often viewed as difficult and expensive. One approach for species is to target taxa that are more likely to be affected by management practices and examine how generalist and specialist species respond (Clavel et al. 2011 [e.g., Meyer et al. 2007a, 2007b]). Some ecological processes are not difficult to assess using changes in vegetation growth (e.g., tree mortality and growth response assessed with increment core samples). National forest system ecologists familiar with research methods could help design protocol and have study designs peer reviewed.

Monitoring at the landscape level may not be as daunting as it seems if testable hypotheses are well defined. A large-scale restoration project in northern Arizona used regularly spaced permanent plots to assess where forest structure and coarse woody debris approximated presettlement conditions (Roccaforte et al. 2010). One suggestion (DeLuca et al. 2010) has been that monitoring might occur even on limited federal budgets through using a combination of collaborative partnerships, volunteers, prioritized sampling designs (e.g., statistical sampling strategies that focus on a limited number of intensively monitored sites), and emerging remote sensing technologies. It is important to develop a well-structured monitoring approach that is founded on the most basic and crucial questions. Initial efforts should probably be modest and build success and trust towards a more thorough program over time.

Monitoring only has value if its information is incorporated using an adaptive management approach (Nichols and Williams 2006). Yet adaptive management has often become an agency mantra without a well-defined set of implementation measures (Allen et al. 2011; Williams 2011a, 2011b). The feedback between learning and decisionmaking needs to be incorporated into management procedures so that learning and adjustment actually occurs. Bormann et al. (2007) suggest that "adaptive management is less about current decisions than about mutual learning that might lead to better future decisions. Mutual learning calls for managers to consider learning as a core business and for the science community to improve their performance in civic science and their delivery of integrated, science-based evidence and tools."

Uncertainty, Collaboration and Monitoring

Uncertainty about the effects of climate change could bring about a fundamental shift toward adaptive management and active monitoring that has long been proposed; yet rarely implemented. This uncertainty could be viewed as license for unending litigation since no environmental assessment will be able to adequately present all outcomes. Uncertainty, however, can also be an opportunity for a different approach, one where management practices are tried, evaluated, and modified iteratively. Such an approach will require candid acknowledgment of unknowns, public participation, and transparent collaborative planning.

Studies of sustainable resource stewardship suggest that several social, administrative, and economic conditions are needed, with effective management often requiring long-term collaboration that builds trust (Dietz et al. 2003, Ostrom 2009). In forestry, good management hinges on flexible practices that can respond to different onsite conditions. Forest practices restricted with set prescriptions do not allow this flexibility, producing predictable treatments often poorly adapted to different ecosystem conditions. Deliberative collaboration, discussed in chapters 7 and 8, is one means of moving beyond restrictive prescriptions. The pace and cost of these efforts may frustrate some, but under the right conditions they can eventually allow managers greater flexibility.

Monitoring can provide the institutional glue for long-term collaboration.

Monitoring can provide the institutional glue for long-term collaboration. Often, however, monitoring has not had a clear scientific objective and initial efforts fade as funding dwindles. Yet with uncertain forest outcomes, new management practices need longitudinal data and an institutional mechanism for incorporating that information into adaptive course correction. Science-based, objective monitoring can build trust. The adage applied to U.S.-Soviet arms treaties, "trust but verify," may be equally apropos to new forest management strategies.

Chapter Summary

"If we open a quarrel between past and present, we shall find that we have lost the future." (Winston Churchill)

Forestry is an art as well as a science, a creative response to existing forest conditions based on the best silviculture, ecology, and wildlife biology. The challenge has always been how to best provide a forest's multiple ecosystem services with imperfect knowledge of management's effects. Conflicts over the priority of those ecosystem services (e.g., timber, fuels reduction, wildlife habitat) on public forest lands has often resulted in management by restrictive prescription. Yet the best forestry has always required flexibility, innovation, and the latitude to respond to ecological context. How can forest management in the Sierra Nevada regain its art?

Ironically, the uncertainty of global climate change could be a catalyst for restoring flexible management if agencies consider some changes. No one can predict exactly how changing climatic conditions may affect forests. All forest projects will be experimental, requiring assessment at multiple scales and including patterns of variation. Acknowledging this uncertainty, committing to monitoring forest response, then adapting management practices as information accumulates, would institutionalize flexibility. It would also require managers and stakeholders explicitly discuss and develop a desired future condition against which to measure forest conditions. The hope of GTR 220 and this collection of papers is that it can provide a starting point for that discussion.

References

Allen, C.R.; Fontaine, J.J.; Pope, K.L.; Garmestani, A.S. 2011. Adaptive management for a turbulent future. Journal of Environmental Management. 92: 1339–1345.

Bilyeu, A. 2011. Personal communication. Natural resource planning specialist, U.S. Department of Agriculture, Forest Service, Pacific Southwest Region, Fire, Fuels and Aviation Management. 3237 Peacekeeper Way, Suite 101, McClellan, CA 95652.

Bormann, B.T.; Hanes, R.W.; Martin, J.R. 2007. Adaptive management of forest ecosystems: Did some rubber hit the road? BioScience. 57: 186–191.

The adage applied to U.S.-Soviet arms treaties, "trust but verify," may be equally apropos to new forest management strategies.

Clavel, J.; Julliard, R.; Devictor, V. 2011. Worldwide decline of special species: toward a global functional homogenization? Frontiers in Ecology and the Environment. 9: 222–228.

Clements 1916. Plant succession: an analysis of the development of vegetation. Washington, DC: Carnegie Institution of Washington. 654 p.

Davis, F.W.; Stoms, D.M. 1996. Sierran vegetation: a gap analysis. In: Sierra Nevada Ecosystem Project: final report to Congress. Vol. II. Assessments and scientific basis for management options. Wildland Resources Center Report No. 37. Davis, CA: University of California, Centers for Water and Wildlands Resources: 671–690.

DeLuca, T.H.; Aplet, G.H.; Wilmer, B.; Burchfield, J. 2010. The unknown trajectory of forest restoration: a call for ecosystem monitoring. Journal of Forestry. 108: 288–295.

Dietz, T.; Ostrom, E.; Stern, P.C. 2003. The struggle to govern the commons. Science. 302: 1907–1912.

Fire Effects Information System [FEIS]. 2011. U.S. Department of Agriculture, Forest Service, Rocky Mountain Research Station, Fire Sciences Laboratory (Producer). Available: http://www.fs.fed.us/database/feis. (December 15, 2011).

Hampton, H.M.; Sesnie, S.E.; Bailey, J.D.; Snider, G.B. 2011. Estimating regional wood supply based on stakeholder consensus for forest restoration in northern Arizona. Journal of Forestry. 109: 15–26.

Lindenmayer, D.B.; Likens, G.E. 2010. Effective ecological monitoring. Collingwood, Australia: CSIRO Publishing. 184 p.

Meyer; M.; Kelt, D.; North, M. 2007a. Effects of burning and thinning on lodgepole chipmunks (*Neotamias speciosus*) in the Sierra Nevada, California. Northwestern Naturalist. 88: 61–72.

Meyer, M.; Kelt, D.; North, M. 2007b. Microhabitat associations of northern flying squirrels in burned and thinned stands of the Sierra Nevada. American Midland Naturalist. 157: 202–211.

Nichols, J.D.; Williams, B.K. 2006. Monitoring for conservation. Trends in Ecology and Evolution. 21: 668–673.

North, M.; Stine, P.; O'Hara, K.; Zielinski, W.; Stephens, S. 2009. An ecosystem management strategy for Sierran mixed-conifer forests. 2nd printing, with addendum. Gen. Tech. Rep. PSW-GTR-220. Albany, CA: U.S. Department of Agriculture, Forest Service, Pacific Southwest Research Station. 49 p.

Oliver, D.D.; Larson, B.C. 1996. Forest stand dynamics. New York City, NY: John Wiley and Sons, Inc. 520 p.

Ostrom, E. 2009. A general framework for analyzing sustainability of social-ecological systems. Science. 325: 419–422.

Puettmann, K.J.; Coastes, K.D.; Messier, C. 2009. A critique of silviculture: managing for complexity. Washington, DC: Island Press. 189 p.

Roccaforte, J.P.; Fulé, P.Z.; Covington, W.W. 2010. Monitoring landscape-scale ponderosa pine restoration treatment implementation and effectiveness. Restoration Ecology. 18: 820–833.

Ruiz-Jaen, M.C.; Aide, T.M. 2005a. Restoration success: How is it being measured? Restoration Ecology. 13: 569–577.

Ruiz-Jaen, M.C.; Aide, T.M. 2005b. Vegetation structure; species diversity; and ecosystem processes as measures of restoration success. Forest Ecology and Management. 218: 159–173.

Sherlock, J. 2011. Personal communication. Regional silviculturist, U.S. Department of Agriculture, Forest Service, Pacific Southwest Region, 1323 Club Drive, Vallejo, CA 94592.

Sierra Nevada Forest Plan Amendment [SNFPA]. 2004. Sierra Nevada Forest Plan Amendment: final supplemental environmental impact statement. R5-MB-046. Washington DC: U.S. Department of Agriculture, Forest Service, Pacific Southwest Region. 492 p.

Stephens, S.L.; Martin, R.E.; Clinton, N.E. 2007. Prehistoric fire area and emissions from California's forests, woodlands, shrublands, and grasslands. Forest Ecology and Management. 251: 205–216.

Stephens, S.L.; McIver, J.D.; Boerner, R.E.J.; Fettig, C.J.; Fontaine, J.B.; Hartsough, B.R.; Kennedy, P.; Schwilk, D.W. [In press]. Effects of forest fuel reduction treatments in the United States. BioScience.

Van de Water, K.; North, M. 2010. Fire history of coniferous riparian forests in the Sierra Nevada. Forest Ecology and Management. 260: 384–395.

Van de Water, K.; North, M. 2011. Stand structure, fuel loads, and fire behavior in riparian and upland forests, Sierra Nevada Mountains, USA; a comparison of current and reconstructed conditions. Forest Ecology and Management. 262: 215–228.

Van de Water, K.M.; Safford, H.D. 2011. A summary of fire frequency estimates for California vegetation before Euro-American settlement. Fire Ecology. 7: 26–58.

Williams, B.K. 2011a. Adaptive management of natural resources—framework and issues. Journal of Environmental Management. 92: 1346–1353.

Williams, B.K. 2011b. Passive and active adaptive management: approaches and an example. Journal of Environmental Management. 92: 1371–1378.

Metric Equivalents

When you know:	Multiply by:	To get:
Inches (in)	25.4	Millimeters
Inches (in)	2.54	Centimeters
Feet (ft)	.3048	Meters
Acres (ac)	.405	Hectares
Miles (mi)	1.609	Kilometers
Square feet per acre (ft^2/ac)	.229	Square meters per hectare
Square miles (mi^2)	2.59	Square kilometers
Degrees Fahrenheit	0.556 (°F – 32)	Degrees Celsius

Acknowledgments

We thank the seven reviewers who provided thoughtful and constructive reviews of all or part of this collection of papers and Haiganoush Preisler for managing the review process. We thank Carolyn Wilson for editing the manuscript, and Jamie Shields and Esther Cole for help incorporating edits and revisions into the manuscript. We are indebted to Harold Zald for discussing and sharing some of his ideas on resilience. We also thank Steve Oerding of IET Academic Technology Service at the University of California, Davis for the canopy closure and cover graphic. We are particularly grateful to dozens of Forest Service managers and technicians who have shared their knowledge of Sierra Nevada forests.

Appendix: Examples of Forest Structures That May Provide Wildlife Habitat

D. Walsh[1] and M. North[2]

The photos in this appendix may help identify some of the unique branching formations or bole characteristics in trees that can make a tree particularly valuable for wildlife, either for nesting, roosting, and use as hunting perches, or other uses. We have organized these following Bull et al.'s (1997)[3] focus on five conditions: live trees with decay, hollows or brooms, snags, and logs. We've also included in these photos examples of understory areas with vertical diversity and hiding cover created by the retention of understory saplings, intermediate-sized trees, hardwoods, and brush.

---

[1] Forester, U.S. Department of Agriculture, Forest Service, Pacific Southwest Region, Eldorado National Forest, Georgetown ranger district, 7600 Wentworth Spring Rd., Georgetown, CA 95634.

[2] Research ecologist, U.S. Department of Agriculture, Forest Service, Pacific Southwest Research Station, 1731 Research Park Dr., Davis, CA 95618.

[3] Bull, E.L.; Parks, C.G.; Torgersen, T.R. 1997. Trees and logs important to wildlife in the interior Columbia River basin. Gen. Tech. Rep. GTR-PNW-391. Portland, OR: U.S. Department of Agriculture, Forest Service, Pacific Northwest Research Station. 55 p.

Figure A-1—Live tree with hollow structure. The tree has an old dead top with cavity nests and a new healthy top leader grown up along side, providing some shelter. The tree is healthy overall with a high live crown ratio and no ladder fuel concern.

Figure A-2—Live tree with decay. The tree has a potential platform nest site that is somewhat protected by adjacent trees. This site could be used for nesting, or could break and provide a platform for nests or for roosting.

Figure A-3—Live tree with broom structure. The arrow is pointing at a potential nesting site formed by an unusual branching pattern most likely associated with an old break in the bole of the Douglas-fir (*Pseudotsuga menziesii* (Mirbel) Franco).

Figure A-4— Live tree with broom structure. A relatively young Douglas-fir has a nest associated with its forked top.

Figure A-5— Live tree with broom structure. The tree's unique forking pattern could easily serve as a nest site for a larger bird. In some stands, these types of trees are extremely prevalent, in which case it may not be necessary to leave all trees with this characteristic.

Figure A-6—Live tree with broom structure. A medium-size tree with a snag top that may provide nesting opportunities, especially when protected by surrounding trees.

Figure A-7a—Living tree with decay. Older snag-topped trees may provide good nesting opportunities or perching locations, and a source of wood-boring insects that provide ready food sources for woodpeckers or opportunities for cavity-nesting species.

Figure A-7b—Closer view of the snag in the previous photo.

Jaime Shields

Figure A-8—Live tree with hollow. Bayonet top trees, such as the sugar pine (*Pinus lambertiana* Douglas) in the center, can provide roosting and nesting opportunities in the dead top and the "inner platform" of the arm.

Figure A-9—Live tree with hollow. The broken-off large limb on this black oak can provide wildlife habitat.

Figure A-10—Live tree with decay, hollow, and broom structure. Crown reiteration can occur with some broken tops providing unique habitat features.

Figure A-11—A snag with extensive cavities, probably created by pileated woodpeckers (*Dryocopus pileatus*), which may provide habitat for secondary cavity users.

Figure A-12—Large logs, even when fairly well decayed, can still provide hiding and resting cover for some wildlife. A northern flying squirrel was tracked with radio telemetry to this location.

Don Errington

Figure A-13—Example of retaining understory trees to provide wildlife hiding cover and vertical diversity. This retained pocket of natural regeneration is on the Sun Dawg Fuels Project, Georgetown Ranger District, Eldorado National Forest.

Don Errington

Figure A-14—An example of retaining intermediate-size conifers and protecting hardwoods. Around a group of overstory trees, understory mixed hardwoods and intermediate-sized conifers were retained to keep an area of diversity within an otherwise relatively uniform stand treatment. The trees that have both blue and orange paint are being retained from a size class that would typically have been removed. The orange paint indicates "retention trees" so that the sale administrator understands that these trees were intentionally retained. The blue paint under it is from the original mark. The Quintette Fuel Reduction Project is on the Georgetown Ranger District, Eldorado National Forest.